St. George Jackson Mivart

Dogs, Jackals, Wolves, and Foxes

A monograph of the Canidae

St. George Jackson Mivart

Dogs, Jackals, Wolves, and Foxes
A monograph of the Canidae

ISBN/EAN: 9783337295189

Printed in Europe, USA, Canada, Australia, Japan

Cover: Foto ©Andreas Hilbeck / pixelio.de

More available books at **www.hansebooks.com**

DOGS, JACKALS, WOLVES, AND FOXES:

A

MONOGRAPH

OF

THE CANIDÆ.

BY

ST. GEORGE MIVART, F.R.S.

WITH WOODCUTS, AND 45 COLOURED PLATES
DRAWN FROM NATURE BY J. G. KEULEMANS AND HAND-COLOURED.

LONDON:
R. H. PORTER, 18 PRINCES STREET, CAVENDISH SQUARE, W.,
AND
DULAU & CO., 37 SOHO SQUARE, W.
1890.

ALERE FLAMMAM.

PRINTED BY TAYLOR AND FRANCIS,
RED LION COURT, FLEET STREET.

PREFACE.

MANY years have now elapsed since any general work was published on the subject to which this volume is dedicated. Its object is to make known and describe the species and leading varieties of existing wild *Canidæ*.

For this purpose the rich and unrivalled stores of Canine animals accumulated in the British Museum of Natural History have been most liberally and kindly placed at the disposal of the author by the authorities of that Institution. The writer cannot hope to have in all cases rightly determined the vexed questions as to the limits of species and varieties and those of synonymy. He trusts, however, by means of his studies, by full references to the literature concerning each species, and by carefully drawn figures from nature, and sometimes from life, to have at least provided a fresh starting point whence new explorations into the Natural History of the group may fruit-

PREFACE.

fully take place. To facilitate this, he has been careful to have drawn, when possible, the actual types of original descriptions, and no less than fourteen representations of such types have been here figured.

The author desires to express his warm thanks for the kind aid given him by his scientific friends; especially by Professor Flower, C.B., F.R.S., Dr. Günther, F.R.S., Dr. P. L. Sclater, F.R.S., Mr. Blanford, F.R.S., Mr. Oldfield Thomas, F.Z.S., and Mr. R. Lydekker, F.G.S.

He also desires to record his grateful sense of the zeal, patience, and skill with which his Plates have been executed by Mr. J. G. Keulemans.

Hurstcote, Chilworth,
April 29th, 1890.

TABLE OF CONTENTS.

PREFACE.
TABLE OF CONTENTS.
LIST OF PLATES.
  ,,   WOODCUTS.
ERRATA.

	Page
INTRODUCTION	i
CHARACTERS OF THE FAMILY CANIDÆ	1
,, GENUS CANIS	2
CANIS LUPUS	3
,, SIMENSIS	18
,, JUBATUS	21
,, ANTARCTICUS	26
,, LATRANS	30
,, AUREUS	35
,, ANTHUS	41
,, MESOMELAS	45
,, ADUSTUS	49
,, MAGELLANICUS	52
,, CANCRIVORUS	57
,, MICROTIS	62
,, AZARÆ	66
,, PARVIDENS	76

TABLE OF CONTENTS.

	Page
CANIS UROSTICTUS	81
,, VIRGINIANUS	85
,, VULPES	92
,, VELOX	104
,, LAGOPUS	108
,, CORSAC	117
,, FERRILATUS	121
,, LEUCOPUS	123
,, BENGALENSIS	127
,, CANUS	132
,, PROCYONOIDES	134
,, CHAMA	140
,, PALLIDUS	142
,, FAMELICUS	144
,, ZERDA	147
,, DINGO	153
,, FAMILIARIS	161
CHARACTERS OF THE GENUS CYON	177
CYON JAVANICUS	179
,, ALPINUS	186
CHARACTERS OF THE GENUS ICTICYON	189
ICTICYON VENATICUS	190
CHARACTERS OF THE GENUS LYCAON	195
LYCAON PICTUS	196
CHARACTERS OF THE GENUS OTOCYON	201
OTOCYON MEGALOTIS	202
INDEX	209

LIST OF PLATES.

PLATE
I. The Common Wolf. *Canis lupus.*
II. ,, ,, Variety *niger.* (**Type.**)
III. ,, ,, Variety *chanco.* (**Type.**)
IV. ,, ,, Indian variety *pallipes.*
V. ,, ,, American variety *occidentalis.*
VI. The Abyssinian Wolf. *C. simensis.* (**Type.**)
VII. The Maned Wolf. *C. jubatus.*
VIII. The Antarctic Wolf. *C. antarcticus.*
IX. The Prairie-Wolf. *C. latrans.*
X. The Indian Jackal. *C. aureus.*
XI. The North-African Jackal. *C. anthus.*
XII. The Black-backed Jackal. *C. mesomelas.*
XIII. The Side-striped Jackal. *C. adustus.*
XIV. The Colpeo. *C. magellanicus.* (**Type.**)
XV. The Carasissi. *C. cancrivorus.*
XVI. The Small-eared Dog. *C. microtis.* (**Type.**)
XVII. Azara's Dog. *C. azaræ.* (**Type.**)
XVIII. The Small-toothed Dog. *C. parvidens.* (**Type.**)
XIX. The Striped-tailed Dog. *C. urostictus.* (**Type.**)
XX. The Colishé. *C. virginianus.*
XXI. The Common Fox. *C. vulpes.*
XXII. ,, ,, Variety *montanus.* (**Type.**)
XXIII. ,, ,, ,, *flavescens.* (**Type.**)
XXIV. ,, ,, ,, *argentatus.*

LIST OF PLATES.

PLATE
XXV. The Kit Fox. *C. velox.*
XXVI. The Arctic Fox. *C. lagopus.*
XXVII. The Corsac Fox. *C. corsac.*
XXVIII. The Thibet Fox. *C. ferrilatus.* (**Type.**)
XXIX. The Desert-Fox. *C. leucopus.*
XXX. The Indian Fox. *C. bengalensis.*
XXXI. The Hoary Fox. *C. canus.* (**Type.**)
XXXII. The Raccoon-like Dog. *C. procyonoides.*
XXXIII. The Asse Fox. *C. chama.* (**Type.**)
XXXIV. The Pale Fox. *C. pallidus.*
XXXV. Rüppell's Fennec. *C. famelicus.*
XXXVI. The True Fennec. *C. zerda.*
XXXVII. The Dingo. *C. dingo.*
XXXVIII. The Esquimaux Dog. *C. familiaris.*
XXXIX. The Mexican Lap-Dog. *C. familiaris.*
XL. The Southern Dhole. *Cyon javanicus.*
XLI. ,, ,, Variety *dukhunensis.* (**Type.**)
XLII. The Northern Dhole. *Cy. alpinus.*
XLIII. The Bush-Dog. *Icticyon venaticus.*
XLIV. The Hyæna Dog. *Lycaon pictus.*
XLV. The Large-eared Cape Dog. *Otocyon megalotis.*

LIST OF WOODCUTS.

Figure		Page
1.	Under surface of fore foot of *Icticyon venaticus*	xv
2.	,, hind ,, ,,	xv
3.	Cervical vertebræ of Dingo	xvi
4.	Skull of Wolf: side view	xvii
5.	,, dorsal view	xvii
6.	,, ventral aspect	xvii
7.	Details of *basis cranii* of Wolf	xviii
8.	Section of auditory bulla of Dog	xix
9.	Skeleton of fore paw of Dingo	xx
10.	,, hind paw ,,	xx
11.	Abnormal teeth of *Canis cancrivorus*	xxiv
12.	Teeth of Wolf	xxv
13.	Cæcum of Dog	xxviii
14.	,, *Icticyon venaticus*	xxviii
15.	Brain of *Icticyon venaticus*, dorsal view	xxx
16.	,, ,, lateral view	xxx
17.	*Canis hodophylax* (facsimile of Japanese drawing)	14
18.	Skull of *C. simensis*	19
19.	,, *C. jubatus*	24
20.	,, *C. anthus*	43
21.	,, *C. magellanicus*	55
22.	,, *C. microtis*	63
23.	Upper molars of *C. microtis*	63
24.	Lower ,, ,,	63
25.	Skull of *C. azaræ* (var. *fulvipes*)	70
26.	Upper molars of *C. azaræ*	70
27.	Lower ,, ,,	70

LIST OF WOODCUTS.

Figure		Page
28.	Skull of *C. parvidens*	78
29.	Upper molars of *C. parvidens*	78
30.	Lower ,, ,,	78
31.	Skull of *C. urostictus*	82
32.	Upper molars of *C. urostictus*	82
33.	Lower ,, ,,	82
34.	Skull of *C. virginianus* (dorsal view)	89
35.	Side view of lower jaw of *C. virginianus*	89
36.	Skull of *C. lagopus*	115
37.	,, *C. leucopus*	125
38.	,, *C. bengalensis*	130
39.	,, *C. procyonoides*	137
40.	,, *C. zerda* (side view)	150
41.	,, ,, (basis cranii)	150
42.	,, Bull-dog	164
43.	,, Japanese Pug: side view	166
44.	Foramen magnum of Japanese Pug	166
45.	Fontanelle of Japanese Pug	166
46.	Front view of skull of Japanese Pug	166
47.	Skull of *Cyon javanicus*	182
48.	Upper molars of *Cyon javanicus*	182
49.	Lower ,, ,,	182
50.	Upper molars of *Cy. alpinus*	187
51.	Lower ,, ,,	187
52.	Skull of *Icticyon venaticus*	192
53.	Upper molars of *Icticyon venaticus*	192
54.	Lower ,, ,,	192
55.	Skull of *Lycaon pictus*	198
56.	,, *Otocyon megalotis* (dorsal view)	204
57.	,, ,, (side view)	205
58.	Upper molars of *Otocyon megalotis*	205
59.	Lower ,, ,,	205

ERRATA.

Page xii, line 5 from bottom, *for* javanicus *read* venaticus.
On pages 47, 51, and 83, *instead of* " Ovalion to sphenoideum,"
read " Basion to sphenoideum."

INTRODUCTION.

(The whole group of animals to the Natural History of which this volume is devoted, may possess an interest for many readers who are not zoologists, as well as for men of science.) There is no animal which has been from such ancient times so closely associated with man as the Dog, or one which now holds so high a place in his affection and esteem. The habits and modes of life of various wild Canine species present interesting analogies with those of our domestic breeds, instinctively associating as they do in packs, and jointly pursuing a prey which would escape or defy them if pursued singly. Curious abnormalities of structure have also been occasionally observed which seem to throw light on the origin of very exceptional characters possessed by certain domestic breeds. Such facts may also suggest a hope of our discovering what was the first origin of the Domestic Dog, but as yet that problem seems to us insoluble. Yet, however insoluble it may be, one thing is certain: either, in a very brief period (geologically speaking) descendants of the same stock have become extraordinarily diversified in form and habit, or the blended offspring of species originally distinct have commingled to form one universally prolific race. Each of these alternatives is full of interest and highly suggestive. But to the zoologist the group of the Dogs is especially interesting, both on account of the remarkable divergence of its members from all those other animals to which they are most nearly allied, and also because of their close structural agreement one with another.

All the various kinds and varieties of Dogs, Jackals, Wolves, and Foxes which now exist are considered by naturalists to form one natural "family" of Beasts, the family *Canidæ*. This family is one of several others which together make up the "Order" of "Beasts of Prey" or *Carnivora*, which, with some fifteen other orders, constitute the "Class" of "Animals which suckle their young," the Class *Mammalia*.

The other families which comprise the order Carnivora are: the family of Bears (*Ursidæ*), the family of Weasels and Otters (*Mustelidæ*), the family of the Raccoon and its allies (*Procyonidæ*), the family of the Civets (*Viverridæ*), and the family of the Cats (*Felidæ*), in which last family the character of a "Beast of Prey" appears to find its highest and most developed expression*.

From all these other families, the existing *Canidæ*, as already said, widely diverge, while amongst themselves they agree in structure to a very remarkable extent, apart from the modifications which occur amongst Domestic Dogs.

Attempts have been made to divide the different species of the family amongst upwards of a dozen genera, but we have found it impossible

---

* It was on this account that, in a previous publication, we selected the Cat as our type. The work referred to was designed to supply a want of which we had for a long time felt the need,—the want of a work, in one volume, designed to impart a sufficient knowledge of the anatomy, physiology, classification, development, and geographical and geological relations of some animal of the highest class, to fit its readers for the fruitful study of any group of animals. In this work ('The Cat:' John Murray, London; and C. Scribner and Sons, New York) there will be found (p. 440) a statement of the principles of zoological classification, and of the values of the terms employed therein. At p. 392, zoological nomenclature is explained; while at its commencement (pp. 8-12) the different ways in which a living organism may be regarded are set out, and the various sciences enumerated which are included within, or are subsidiary to, the science of Living things, or Biology, for the study of which the work was intended to serve as an introduction. The dermal structures, skeleton, muscles, alimentary, circulating, and respiratory organs, the nervous system, the process of development, and relations of the chosen type with the living and inorganic worlds, past and present, are described in successive chapters. Obviously in a work such as our 'Monograph of the *Canidæ*,' space cannot be devoted to making known matters of the kind to readers as yet unacquainted with them. It will therefore be convenient, as the occasion arises, to refer such readers to the pages of our preceding work, wherein will be found the explanations they may require.

to divide them amongst more than five, and for even those five genera only small distinctive characters can be assigned.

The whole of the *Canidæ* are either much like the Common Wolf or the Common Fox, though with much divergence as to size. The legs may be somewhat longer or shorter, and the tail may be shorter than the Wolf's, though it is never longer than is the Fox's "brush." The ears are occasionally very large, though always erect in undomesticated forms. The coloration generally varies from grey to yellowish or reddish brown. The back, the upper surface of the head, and some parts of the limbs are mostly darker than the flanks. The underparts are almost always paler or even white, and the tips and inner margins of the ears are also often white, while the external aspect of the ears is sometimes characteristically coloured. Frequently a dark mark occurs between the eye and the tip of the nose, and on the dorsum of the tail not far from its root; while the end of the tail is often either white or black. But stripes or patches of dark or light colour are mostly rather ill-defined, though they may be distinctly marked. With the single exception, however, of the Hyæna Dog (*Lycaon pictus*) no canine species presents varied markings comparable with those found amongst the Cats (*Felidæ*) or Civets (*Viverridæ*).

The coloration of each species is subject to much individual variation, even apart from those seasonal changes which seem to commonly occur. The hairy coat is longer and more abundant in the winter, and in individuals which inhabit cold mountain-heights. It is also generally paler in winter than in summer, and in one species, the Arctic Fox (*C. lagopus*), habitually turns white during the coldest part of the year. Occasionally other species (the Wolf and the Fox) have been found quite white; while an opposite tendency to blackness ("melanism") affects various individuals, and black wolves have been found in both hemispheres.

Inconstancy of hue is favoured by the varied coloration of the individual hairs which make up the coat, and which differ in different parts of the body and in different seasons of the year. There may or may not also be a soft woolly underfur beneath and amongst the long hairs which make up the externally visible coat.

INTRODUCTION.

Thus sometimes one and the same species may be greyish or reddish or yellowish, or light, or dark; and not only colour, but absolute size may vary, individuals from Northern or Southern regions often differing in this respect no less than in colour.

The members of the family present also a very remarkable uniformity in their internal structure as well as in their external conformation. If we except the four species which form the three genera *Cyon*, *Icticyon*, and *Otocyon*, an almost complete uniformity exists in the dentition, although certain teeth may present differences in relative size and in the details of their conformation.

Dental characters are amongst the most constant which can be found in the *Canidæ*; nevertheless even these vary somewhat from individual to individual, so that such minute characters, taken by themselves absolutely, can rarely, if ever, afford a satisfactory basis for the distinction and definition of a species.

The general uniformity which exists in the external and internal conformation of all the species of the family is the more noteworthy, on account of the exceedingly wide geographical distribution of the group; for some or other species of the Dog-family are to be found over the greater part of the habitable globe, in addition to those which have been disseminated by the civilized races of mankind.

Although the existing *Canidæ* differ so much from the other Carnivora which now inhabit the world, they show, as we shall see later, some very curious resemblances to creatures of a very different kind—belonging to a most distinct order. These resemblances suggest various questions as to the origin and affinities of the family: questions as to which we have but little to say, but that little must be deferred to the end of this introductory chapter.

As already remarked, different naturalists have tried to divide the *Canidæ* into a variety of genera, and they have also enumerated many species distinguished by small differences of colour or size. Till within the last thirty years very little attention was paid to variation, and there was a general disposition to accept any single exceptionally coloured skin as sufficient evidence of the existence of a new and distinct species. Until a considerable number of skins and skulls of one and the same species could be compared together, the amount of variability to which one species may be liable could not be properly appreciated.

We have arrived at the conclusion that only five genera can be distinguished. Of these *Icticyon*, *Lycaon*, and *Otocyon* each contain but one species, while *Cyon* may be taken as consisting of two. All the rest of the *Canidæ* we place in the typical genus *Canis*. Such animals as the Common Fox and the Fennec would seem at first sight to be without any doubt generically distinct from the Jackal and the Wolf. Nevertheless, when all the series of intermediate forms are examined, the difficulty of drawing any valid generic distinction will, we think, be found insuperable. The shape which the pupil of the eye may assume is a character which is practically of little use, since, with regard to various species, we have no evidence on the subject. Moreover the character itself, if it could always be ascertained, appears to be a rather trivial one, since amongst the Cats, which undoubtedly form one genus, it may be either linear or oblong, or round, according to the species *.

As the result of our studies, we offer the following list (p. vi) of what we deem probable species; although, as in some cases, we have been able to examine only a few specimens of one kind, it may well happen that some forms we have treated as species may ultimately prove to be but well-marked varieties.

Indeed, so great is the variability of many of these animals that in some instances whether a form is to be reckoned as a species or a variety can only be matter of individual opinion. Our own tendency is rather to unite doubtful forms than to separate them as distinct kinds. Nevertheless we willingly adopt, provisionally, even a mere difference of hue, if there appears to be any good reason for thinking it may be a constant difference. We shall also rank as distinct, any two forms which exhibit definite and peculiar markings of diverse kinds, even though there may be individuals in which the markings are so indistinct that they can only doubtfully be referred to either. Such may not be truly " transitional forms," but only individuals with the characters of their kind very imperfectly developed. We do not ourselves doubt that

---

* See the Proceedings of the Zoological Society for 1882, pp. 141 and 517.

true species exist, but from the existence of species it by no means follows that we must always be able to define them. We place, then, in the genus *Canis* the Wolves, Jackals, South-American Wild Dogs, Foxes of all kinds, and Fennecs, as well as the Dingo of Australia and the truly Domestic Dog.

In the following list we have not given names to forms which we regard as being most probably mere varieties:—

(1) *Canis lupus.*
(2) *C. simensis.*
(3) *C. jubatus.*
(4) *C. antarcticus.*
(5) *C. latrans.*
(6) *C. aureus.*
(7) *C. anthus.*
(8) *C. mesomelas.*
(9) *C. adustus.*
(10) *C. magellanicus.*
(11) *C. cancrivorus.*
(12) *C. microtis.*
(13) *C. azaræ.*
(14) *C. parvidens.*
(15) *C. urostictus.*
(16) *C. virginianus.*
(17) *C. vulpes.*
(18) *C. velox.*
(19) *C. lagopus.*
(20) *C. corsac.*
(21) *C. ferrilatus.*
(22) *C. leucopus.*
(23) *C. bengalensis.*
(24) *C. canus.*
(25) *C. procyonoides.*
(26) *C. chama.*
(27) *C. pallidus.*
(28) *C. famelicus.*
(29) *C. zerda.*
(30) *C. dingo.*
(31) *Cyon javanicus.*
(32) *Cy. alpinus.*
(33) *Icticyon venaticus.*
(34) *Lycaon pictus.*
(35) *Otocyon megalotis.*

All the species of the family feed naturally, by preference, on animal substances, in common with most species of the order *Carnivora.*

Various species, including, as every one knows, the Wolf, hunt their living prey in packs, and some will thus destroy and devour both cattle and men. But not all the largest species are thus ferocious, for the South-American Wolf (*C. jubatus*) is by no means dangerous—living, as it does, a solitary life, and only attacking small game. Some kinds, like the Jackals, live largely on carrion, and full-grown or young birds and eggs are generally welcome; while many species will devour lizards, mice, snails, and insects, including white-ants and moths. Species which frequent the margins of rivers or the sea-shore will eat various forms of Crustacea and Mollusca, and may be, like the Arctic Fox (*C. lagopus*), devourers of fish. Various species will also eat vegetable substances and greedily devour fruits of various kinds.

All the *Canidæ*, so far as we know, pursue their prey largely by scent, though some do so more than others. In all, the olfactory organs are largely developed, though the senses of sight and hearing are also acute. Almost all, if not all, are active during, at least, part of the night, though many are abroad also during some portion of the day. Though none possess modifications of structure fitting them for an arboreal life, yet some manage to ascend trees, the branches of which are conveniently disposed, by a succession of dexterous jumps. Some domestic breeds take readily to the water, but beyond a slight degree of web-footedness no structure fitting them for an aquatic life is found amongst the Dog-family.

The *Canidæ* generally give out cries which may be called "howls," but some wild kinds emit a yelping bark. Wild species which do not naturally bark at all, will soon learn to do so when confined in the vicinity of barking dogs, which they will spontaneously imitate.

Not only the Wolf and the Jackal, but various other species, may be perfectly tamed, even wild kinds from the Brazilian forests, such as *C. cancrivorus*. There is, however, much individual difference between members of the same species, as regards their susceptibility to domesticating influences.

The odour which various species diffuse is exceedingly offensive to most persons in civilized countries, but this scent varies greatly from species to species. Thus, though all varieties of the Common Fox possess a rank odour, the Arctic Fox is altogether free from it, nor does the Bengal Fox possess it.

The wide distribution of the family over the earth's surface proves that the constitution of the group is naturally susceptible of enduring great differences of climate, and this faculty must have greatly facilitated the domestication of wild species during any migrations which may have taken place amongst the earliest races of mankind.

All the *Canidæ*, the habits of which are known, either make use of burrows which they themselves excavate, the deserted burrows of other animals, caves or cavities amidst rocks, or hollow trees. The burrows may be quite solitary, or so associated as to form a sort of underground canine village.

A litter generally consists of from three to a dozen young, which, so far as known, are brought forth blind, as in the Domestic Dog. The period of gestation is supposed to vary within narrow limits—from about sixty-two to sixty-eight days.

The mammary glands are from six to ten in number, but the variation which is found in the Domestic Dog as regards this character may lead us to anticipate that it may not be a constant one in wild species.

There is no doubt that species universally ranked as distinct—such as the Wolf and the Jackal—can produce hybrids; but we have no evidence of the fertility of such hybrids *inter se*. Hybrids between the Dog and the Wolf on the one hand, and the Dog and the Jackal on the other, have, however, been proved to be thus fertile, though for no long period.

GEOGRAPHICAL DISTRIBUTION.

As we have said, the wild *Canidæ* are distributed over the greater part of the habitable globe. In the Old World they are found from Spitzbergen and Siberia to the Cape of Good Hope and Java.

In the New World they are to be met with from the shores of the Arctic Ocean to Tierra del Fuego and the Falkland Islands. The far greater number of kinds—twenty of our list of species—are found in the Northern Hemisphere, while only twelve are peculiar to regions south of the equator, three at the least being common to both.

Certain regions of the world are conspicuous from the circumstance that none of the *Canidæ* inhabit them except the Dingo, which has probably been introduced by man. We have included it in our list, because we treat of existing *Canidæ*, and it is now certainly to be reckoned a wild form; but if we exclude it, then in the whole continent of Australia, the vast island of New Guinea, with Tasmania, New

INTRODUCTION.   ix

Zealand, Celebes, the Philippine Islands, and Ceylon, no members of the family are naturally indigenous.

When we recollect how very peculiar the fauna of Madagascar is, and how distinct are its animal inhabitants from those of Africa, it may seem at first to be in no way surprising that none of the *Canidæ* inhabit it. But when we further reflect that there are wild Canines in South America as well as in South Africa, then the fact does become noteworthy, seeing that so many Madagascar animals of different kinds closely resemble others which inhabit the southern section of the New World.

No wild Dogs are to be found in the West Indies, but that is not remarkable since so very many animals of the American Continent are wanting in those islands. Such is the case, for example, with the Monkeys—Trinidad not being really a West-Indian island, but a detached portion of the South-American continent.

If our views as to the specific identity of the various forms of the Wolf on the one hand, and of the Fox on the other, be correct, then *C. lupus*, *C. vulpes*, and *C. lagopus* are species which are common to both the Old and the New Worlds. Of the remaining thirty-two species, twenty belong to the former, while only twelve are peculiar to the latter.

Of the three species common to both worlds, *C. lagopus* has but a very restricted range southwards from the Arctic regions; while both the Wolf and the Fox extend far southwards in both Asia and North America, though the Wolf is absent from Africa.

Including these three species, thirteen are found in Europe or in Asia north or north-west of the Himalaya, or in Africa north of the Sahara and west of Egypt,—that is, in what is called the Palæarctic Region. Only six are found in the Indian Region, whereof two also enter the Palæarctic area. Africa south of the Sahara, with Egypt and the Nile Valley, is known as the Ethiopian Region, and three Palæ-arctic African forms (*C. anthus*, *C. vulpes*, and *C. zerda*) extend into it, while there are eight other African forms, whereof one may extend into South-western Asia.

South and Central America, with the West Indies, are commonly

c

INTRODUCTION.

spoken of as the Neotropical Region, and the rest of America as the Nearctic, but it will be more convenient for us to divide America into North and South by the Isthmus of Panama.

Apart from the three forms common to both worlds, three species are thus North-American, and nine are South-American. Only one, the Dingo, is Australian.

Thus the species may be arranged in lists as follows, those with an asterisk being found in two or more categories:—

NORTHERN HEMISPHERE.	SOUTHERN HEMISPHERE.
Canis lupus.	Canis jubatus.
C. simensis.	C. magellanicus.
C. latrans.	C. cancrivorus.
C. aureus.	C. microtis.
C. anthus.	C. azaræ.
C. mesomelas *.	C. mesomelas *.
C. adustus *.	C. adustus *.
C. virginianus.	C. parvidens.
C. vulpes.	C. urostictus.
C. velox.	C. chama.
C. lagopus.	C. dingo.
C. corsac.	
C. ferrilatus.	
C. leucopus.	
C. bengalensis.	
C. canus.	
C. procyonoides.	
C. pallidus.	
C. famelicus.	
C. zerda.	
Cyon javanicus *.	Cyon javanicus *.
Cy. alpinus.	Icticyon venaticus.
Lycaon pictus *.	Lycaon pictus *.
	Otocyon megalotis.

OLD WORLD.	NEW WORLD.
Canis lupus *.	Canis lupus *.
C. simensis.	C. jubatus.
C. aureus.	C. antarcticus.
C. anthus.	C. latrans.

INTRODUCTION.

OLD WORLD.	NEW WORLD.
C. mesomelas.	C. magellanicus.
C. adustus.	C. cancrivorus.
C. vulpes*.	C. microtis.
C. lagopus*.	C. azaræ.
C. corsac.	C. parvidens.
C. ferrilatus.	C. urostictus.
C. leucopus.	C. virginianus.
C. bengalensis.	C. vulpes*.
C. canus.	C. velox.
C. procyonoides.	C. lagopus*.
C. chama.	
C. pallidus.	
C. famelicus.	
C. zerda.	
C. dingo.	
Cyon javanicus.	
Cy. alpinus.	Icticyon venaticus.
Lycaon pictus.	
Otocyon megalotis.	

PALÆARCTIC FORMS.

Common to Europe, Asia, and Africa.

C. vulpes.

Common to Europe and Palæarctic Asia.

C. lupus, C. aureus, C. lagopus, C. corsac.

Peculiar to Asia.

C. ferrilatus, C. leucopus, C. bengalensis, C. canus.
C. procyonoides, Cy. alpinus.

Common to Palæarctic Africa and Europe.

C. vulpes.

Common to Palæarctic Africa and Asia.

C. vulpes, C. famelicus.

Peculiar to Africa.

C. anthus, C. zerda.

Ethiopic African Forms.

Canis simensis, C. anthus, C. mesomelas, C. adustus, C. vulpes, C. chama, C. pallidus, C. famelicus, C. zerda, Lycaon pictus, and Otocyon megalotis.

Ethiopic African forms also found in the Palæarctic Region.
C. anthus, C. vulpes, C. famelicus, C. zerda.

Forms of the Indian Region
(*i. e.* in Hindostan and South-eastern Asia).

C. lupus, C. aureus, C. vulpes, C. bengalensis, C. canus, Cyon javanicus.

Australian Region.
C. dingo.

North America.
C. lupus, C. latrans, C. virginianus, C. vulpes, C. velox, C. lagopus.

South America.
C. jubatus, C. antarcticus, C. magellanicus, C. cancrivorus, C. microtis, C. azaræ, C. parvidens, C. urostictus, Icticyon javanicus.

Form common to Europe, N. America, Palæarctic Asia and Africa, and to the Indian Region.
C. vulpes.

These facts may be expressed in a tabular form, as follows :—

INTRODUCTION.   xiii

	Europe with Spitzbergen.	Northern and North-western Asia.	Hindustan and South-eastern Asia.	Palæarctic Africa.	Ethiopic Africa.	N. America.	S. America.	Australia.
Canis lupus......	*	*	*	..	..	*		
C. simensis	..	..	..	..	*			
C. jubatus	..	..	..	..	..		*	
C. antarcticus....	..	..	..	..	..	..	*	
C. latrans	..	..	..	..	..	*		
C. aureus	*	*	*					
C. anthus	..	..	..	*	*			
C. mesomelas....	..	..	..	..	*			
C. adustus	..	..	..	..	*			
C. magellanicus ..	..	..	..	..	..	..	*	
C. cancrivorus ..	..	..	..	..	..	..	*	
C. microtis	..	..	..	..	..	..	*	
C. azaræ	..	..	..	..	..	..	*	
C. parvidens ...	..	..	..	..	..	..	*	
C. urostictus	;.	..	..	..	..	..	*	
C. virginianus....	..	..	..	..	..	*		
C. vulpes........	*	*	*	*	*	*		
C. velox	..	..	..	..	..	*		
C. lagopus	*	*	..	..	..	*		
C. corsac........	*	*						
C. ferrilatus	..	*						
C. leucopus	..	*						
C. bengalensis....	..	..	*					
C. canus	..	*	*					
C. procyonoides ..	..	*						
C. chama	..	..	..	..	*			
C. pallidus	..	..	..	..	*			
C. famelicus	..	*	..	..	*			
C. zerda	..	..	..	*	*			
C. dingo	..	..	..	..	..	..	..	*
Cyon javanicus ..	..	..	*					
Cy. alpinus......	..	*						
Icticyon	..	..	..	..	..		*	
Lycaon	..	..	..	..	*			
Otocyon	..	..	..	..	*			

ANATOMY OF THE CANIDÆ.

In their external anatomy all the wild *Canidæ* are similar to the Common Wolf, save as regards size and greater or less relative length of ears, tail, and muzzle. Only in *Icticyon venaticus* is the tail really short, and only in *C. zerda* and *Otocyon megalotis* are the ears excessively long, but even in them they do not droop as in most domestic dogs. The length and quality of the fur often varies much, even in the same species, according to the season, as has been already mentioned. In no natural form is the skin hairless, as in some American domesticated breeds, and the so-called "Turkish" breed of dog.

Abnormalities, of course, may from time to time be met with, as a Fox has been found with a muzzle so deformed as to resemble that of a Pug Dog.

The tip of the nose is always naked, and the pads beneath the feet also. There is a more or less trilobate cushion beneath the roots of the toes, and a single one beneath the end of each digit, including a minute one beneath the small thumb, or *pollex*, and another beneath the wrist. The hair between the pads is mostly but moderately developed; but in some forms in winter, especially in the Arctic Fox (*C. lagopus*), the feet (as its scientific name implies) are densely furred below.

No *hallux* (*i. e.* no digit answering to our great toe) is visible externally on the hind foot of any wild species, though in domestic breeds it is often developed, frequently in an imperfect manner, its component bones not being directly connected with those of the rest of the foot, so that it hangs loosely, and is familiarly known as a "dew-claw."

In the fore foot, a short thumb or *pollex* (not reaching the ground) is always present, save in the genus *Lycaon*, which has but a rudiment of it concealed beneath the skin. The toes are each provided with a slightly curved, non-retractile, and more or less blunt claw.

All the *Canidæ* are "digitigrade," that is they walk upon their toes, and not upon the soles of the feet as we do, and as do various Carnivorous animals, such, *e. g.*, as the Bear and the Coatimondi, which are said to be "plantigrade." In plantigrade animals the parts on

INTRODUCTION.

which they walk are naked, but in digitigrade animals the corresponding parts—the *metacarpus** of the fore limb, and the *metatarsus* of the hind limb,—which are raised above the ground, are hairy.

Fig. 1.   Fig. 2.

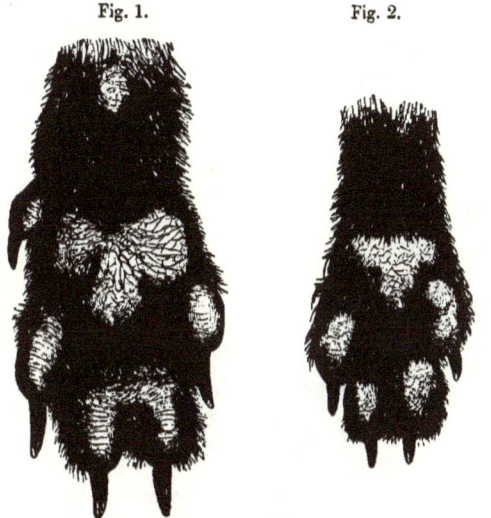

Fig. 1.—Under surface of right fore foot of *Icticyon venaticus*. (Natural size.)
Fig. 2.—Under surface of right hind foot of same. (Natural size.)
(After Flower.)

The Skeleton.

The bones which compose the vertebral column, spine or "backbone," consist of seven cervical vertebræ (as in almost all mammals), thirteen dorsal, seven lumbar (rarely six, as we have found in *C. jubatus*), three or four sacral, and from eleven to twenty-two caudal vertebræ.

---

* For an explanation of these terms the reader is referred to the Author's book on 'The Cat,' pp. 98 and 115, and therein will be found full particulars as to the names of the bones, parts of bones, muscles, and other organs and anatomical structures herein referred to. Space cannot be afforded for such explanations in the present work.

INTRODUCTION.

The bones of the neck, or cervical vertebræ, are larger than in feline beasts of the same size. Certain processes, known as *hyperapophyses*, are strongly marked in them, while others, termed *metapophyses* *, may be traced forwards from the lumbar region to the third cervical vertebra.

The most anterior (or *atlas*) vertebra has its large transverse processes perforated towards its hinder margin by the vertebral artery.

Fig. 3.

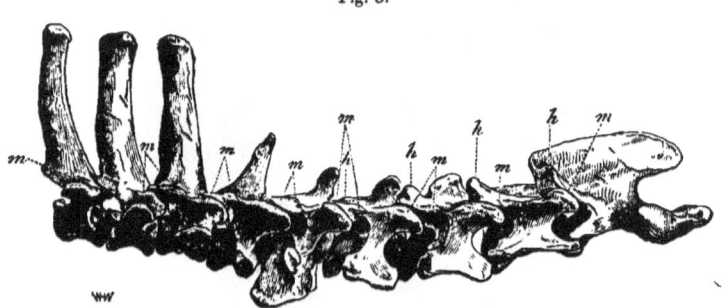

The cervical vertebræ (except the atlas) and first three dorsal vertebræ of *C. dingo*, seen laterally. *m*, metapophyses; *h*, hyperapophyses.

The *skull* has its facial portion or snout much more elongated than in the Cat family. The lateral arches of the skull, or *zygomata*, project strongly outwards, and a transverse elevated ridge of bone, the lambdoidal ridge, crosses transversely the hinder part of the cranium. There may or may not be an antero-posteriorly directed ridge, called a *sagittal* ridge, projecting upwards from the middle of the cranium. It is well-marked in the Wolf. In its place there may be a flattened tract of bone, as in *C. virginianus*.

The bony orbits never form a complete ring, or arch, enclosing the eyeball externally, but the postorbital process of the frontal bone always

---

* For full details as to these structures, see the Proc. Zool. Soc. 1863, pp. 574 & 579, fig. 9.

INTRODUCTION. xvii

remains widely separated from any postorbital process sent upwards from the malar bone. The nasal bones are considerably elongated, and

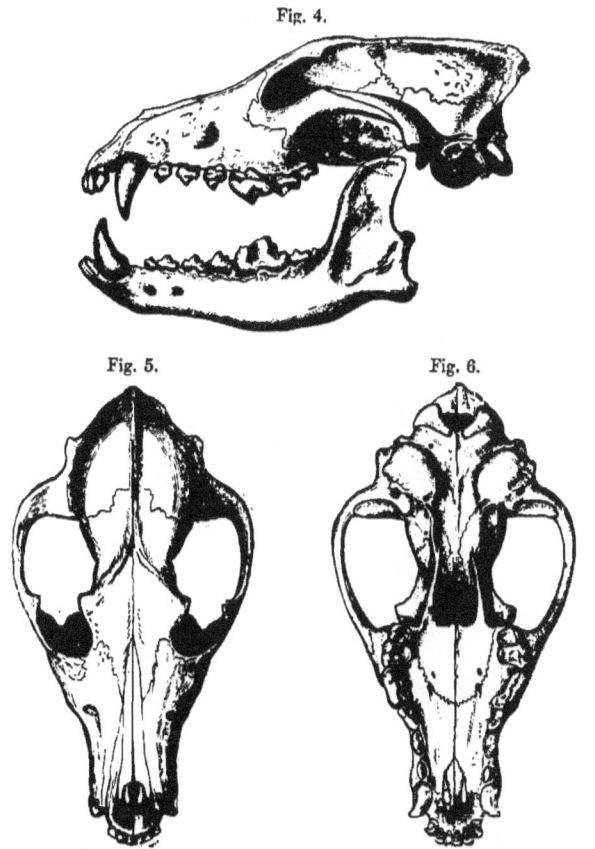

Fig. 4.—Side view of the skull of the Wolf.
Fig. 5.—Dorsal view of the skull of the Wolf.
Fig. 6.—Ventral aspect of the same.

may or may not extend further backwards than do the orbital processes of the maxillary bones. They are never entirely separated from the

d

maxillæ by the junction of the premaxillæ with the frontals. When the skull is viewed in profile, the interorbital region is generally prominent, with a marked concavity in front of it, though this may be absent.

On the *basis cranii* there is to be noted a simple, smooth, and rounded auditory bulla*. As a rule its size varies inversely with that of the species, and thus it is exceedingly prominent in *C. zerda* †. It is

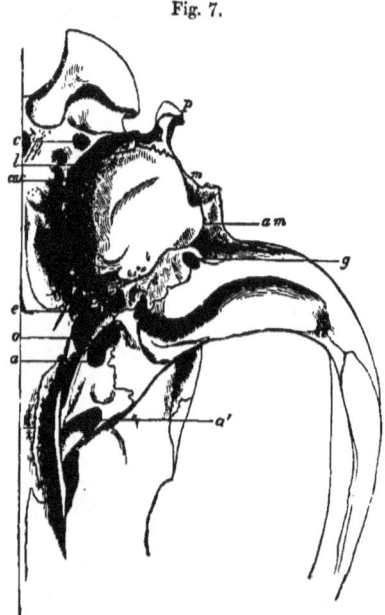

Fig. 7.

Skull of the Wolf (after Flower).

a, alisphenoid canal, its hinder end; *a'*, ditto, its anterior end; *am*, external auditory meatus; *c*, condyloid foramen; *car*, carotid canal; *e*, Eustachian canal; *g*, glenoid foramen; *l*, foramen lacerum posterius; *m*, mastoid process; *o*, foramen ovale; *p*, paroccipital process.

always partially divided within by a very incomplete septum (fig. 8, *s*) which springs from its anterior wall in exactly the same situation as does

---

* See 'The Cat,' p. 57.   † See below, description of the species.

that of the Cat *. The *meatus auditorius externus* has a rather prominent inferior margin at its outer aperture. There is no conspicuous carotid foramen, because the carotid canal † opens posteriorly into the *foramen lacerum posterius* ‡. Thence it runs forwards through the inner wall of the bulla, and opens anteriorly close to the inner side of the groove for the Eustachian tube §. Upon emerging from the anterior end of the canal, the artery turns upwards, and, after forming a loop, enters the skull through the *foramen lacerum medius*. The paroccipital process (*p*) is very peculiar in shape. It is long, prominent, and laterally compressed. It is somewhat applied to the bulla, though to a less extent than in the Cats or *Felidæ* ‖. The mastoid is moderately prominent. The condyloid foramen is very conspicuous, opening as it does on a ridge which extends from the paroccipital to the condyle ¶. That small channel in the skull, known as the *alisphenoid canal* **, is

Fig. 8.

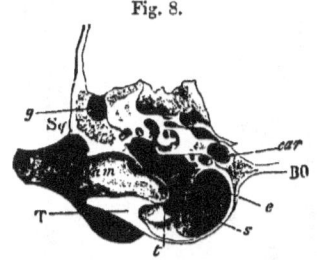

Section of auditory bulla of Dog (Flower).

am, external auditory meatus ; *BO*, basioccipital bone ; *car*, carotid canal ; *e*, Eustachian canal ; *g*, glenoid foramen ; *s*, septum ; *Sq*, squamosal bone ; *T*, tympanic bone : *t*, tympanic ring.

constantly present, and there is also a large glenoid foramen. The bony palate is but very rarely prolonged backwards beyond the hindmost molars. The ethmoid and ethmoturbinal bones are always very large and extremely convoluted (in relation with the highly developed

* *Op. cit.* p. 67, fig. 30. † *Op. cit.* p. 83.
‡ *Op. cit.* p. 62. § *Op. cit.* pp. 66 & 208.
‖ *Op. cit.* p. 82. ¶ *Op. cit.* pp. 57 & 58, fig. 29.
** *Op. cit.* p. 447.

faculty of smell), but the frontal bones may or may not contain air-cavities or "frontal sinuses."

The bone of the lower jaw, or mandible, may * or may not present the appearance of a lobe or process at its postero-inferior margin, causing it to look as if the angle of the mandible had been pushed up towards the mandibular condyle.

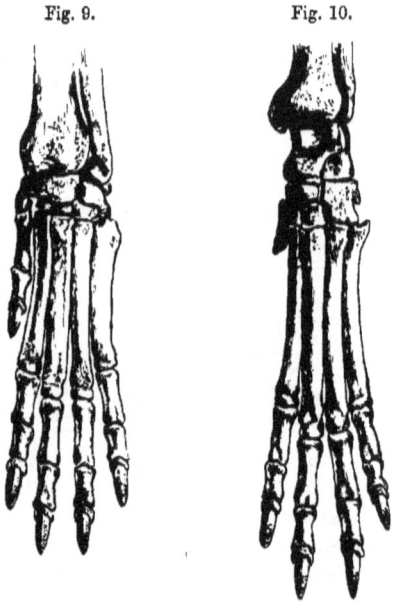

Fig. 9.   Fig. 10.

Bones of the extremities of *Canis dingo*.
Fig. 9.—Skeleton of the manus or fore paw. (RIGHT)
Fig. 10.—Skeleton of the pes or hind paw. (RIGHT)

Bones of the Limbs.—The blade-bone, or scapula, is narrower in proportion to its length than in the *Felidæ*, and the fossa for the supra-spinatus muscle is relatively smaller, while the metacromion process † is quite rudimentary. The collar-bone, or clavicle, is, almost always,

---

* See below, the description and figure of the skull of *C. procyonoides*.
† *Op. cit.* pp. 90 & 91, figs. 51 & 52.

only represented by a small cartilage imbedded in the flesh, but it may be considerably larger in *Lycaon pictus* *.

The upper arm-bone, or humerus, has a large olecranal perforation, but no supra-condyloid canal †. In the forearm the radius and ulna are placed more one in front of the other than in Feline animals, the paw in the *Canidæ* not being susceptible of being so turned in different directions as in the Cat, which in this matter more approximates to the human structure.

The bones of the wrist and ankle, the carpus and the tarsus, are much as in most Carnivora ‡, but the metacarpal and metatarsals § are relatively long, and the terminal bone, or phalanx, of each digit has a much less prominent lamella for sheltering the root of the claw than have those Carnivora the claws of which are retractile.

The pollex has always two phalanges, save in *Lycaon*. The hallux is generally represented by a rudimentary metatarsal bone, and still more rudimentary phalanx, which latter may be wanting altogether. By rare exception there may be two phalanges, the metatarsal being attached to the tarsus as usual. In that abnormal structure called a "dew-claw," often found in Domestic Dogs, there is a rudimentary metatarsal bearing two phalanges, the whole being detached from the tarsus, and lying beside the median part of the second, or index, metatarsal.

A triangular plate of fibro-cartilage, or of dense fibrous structure only, is often or always attached to the anterior margin of the pubis, and is a noteworthy and interesting structure ∥.

* See Hartmann in Sitzungsb. d. Gesellsch. natur. Freunde Berlin, 1876, p. 168.

† See 'The Cat,' pp. 91 & 92, fig. 53.

‡ The extra carpal ossicle has been found, by Professor Flower, between the scaphoid and lunare and the more distal carpals (see 'Journal of Anatomy and Physiology,' 1871, p. 62). See also a paper on the Carpus by Dr. Burt G. Wilder in the Bulletin of the Cornell University (Science), vol. i. no. 3, p. 301 (1874).

§ See 'The Cat,' pp. 96 & 113.

∥ It was described by Professor Huxley (see his 'Anatomy of Vertebrates,' p. 417) as a fibro-cartilage. He subsequently found this represented by fibrous tissue only, in a male and female Dog and a male and female Fox (see Proc. Royal Soc. vol. xxx. 1881, p. 162). He also found it in *C. mesomelas* and *C. bengalensis* (see Proc. Zool. Soc. 1880, p. 264).

Proportional dimensions of the Skeleton, the length between the front of the atlas and the hinder end of the sacrum being taken as 100.

	C. lupus.	C. jubatus.	C. latrans.	C. vulpes.	C. zerda.	C. dingo.	Cyon.	Icticyon.	Lycaon.	Otocyon.
Length of cervical region	30·0	26·0	27·1	27·2	24·7	25·1	25·9	26·2	24·3	24·6
,, dorsal ,,	37·0	36·6	36·4	36·2	38·8	37·7	37·7	38·7	41·2	39·0
,, lumbar ,,	27·9	31·6	30·5	30·5	30·9	29·1	29·9	28·7	29·8	31·0
,, caudal ,,	57·3	54·6	61·0	85·0	120·2	59·0	47·2	32·0	49·1	72·3
,, fore limb	93·7	85·7	75·4	75·0	79·0	74·0	58·2	?	75·4	80·0
,, hind limb	102·6	98·7	86·4	87·5	93·4	85·0	74·8	?	86·8	105·3
,, humerus	30·7	28·9	25·4	25·7	27·4	25·9	21·2	20·2	25·6	27·6
,, radius	30·0	31·1	25·7	23·7	27·1	25·1	18·8	16·7	25·8	28·9
,, pollex	8·8	6·9	5·7	6·7	6·5	6·7	5·3	6·5	2·2	7·3
,, second metacarpal	12·1	11·1	9·4	8·5	8·2	8·9	8·9	6·5	8·8	10·4
,, femur	33·8	32·5	27·9	23·2	27·8	28·3	24·4	23·0	29·0	33·5
,, tibia	33·5	33·6	28·8	29·0	33·6	27·7	22·5	20·5	27·7	33·8
,, hallux	4·1	1·7	3·2	3·1	2·4	2·8	2·5	1·5	3·1	4·0
,, second metatarsal	13·0	13·9	11·6	11·5	13·4	9·9	8·6	7·0	10·2	14·1
,, cranium *	7·8	6·3	7·2	8·2	?	8·0	8·9	9·7	7·4	8·9
,, face †	22·7	18·7	21·1	21·2	?	20·7	17·0	18·0	17·8	22·4

* Estimated by a line drawn from the most anterior point of the margin of the foramen magnum to the junction of the basi-sphenoid with the presphenoid on the *basis cranii*. This point of junction we have termed the sphenoideum. Prof. Huxley's "basicranial axis" (Proc. Zool. Soc. 1880, p. 240) we have found to be practically very inconvenient.

† Estimated by a line drawn from the sphenoideum to the front of the premaxilla.

Proportional dimensions, the distance from the basion to the sphenoideum being taken as 100.

	C. lupus.	C. jubatus.	C. latrans.	C. vulpes.	C. zerda.	C. dingo.	Cyon.	Icticyon.	Lycaon.	Otocyon.
Length of palate.	181·3	209·8	202·2	190·9	180·0	194·1	170·4	141·0	176·3	179·3
Breadth "	100·0	107·3	106·6	112·1	96·0	119·6	115·9	92·3	123·6	79·3
Length of $\frac{P.4}{}$*	40·6	35·2	44·4	27·2	30·0	41·1	43·1	28·2	36·3	17·2
" $\frac{M.1}{}$	27·0	29·4	26·6	18·1	24·0	29·4	25·0	15·3	27·2	17·2
" $\frac{M.2}{}$	14·4	19·6	13·3	13·6	18·0	15·6	13·6	7·6	12·7	15·5

* $\frac{P.4}{}$ represents the fourth upper premolar. The teeth of the lower jaw are represented with the horizontal line above the letter and numeral.

INTRODUCTION.

Dentition.—The *Canidæ*, in common with almost all Carnivora, have six incisors and two canines* above and below. They have also four premolars on either side of either jaw. One true molar†, at least, is present in the upper jaw, and at least two in the lower. There may be no more, as is normally the case in *Icticyon*. In *Cyon* we find two true molars, both above and below; while in *Otocyon* there are three, or even four, true molars above and four below. In all the rest (that is, the overwhelming majority of the *Canidæ*) there are two true molars above and three below, so that their dentition may be thus expressed:

I. $\frac{3}{3}$, C. $\frac{1}{1}$, Pm. $\frac{4}{4}$, M. $\frac{2}{3} = \frac{10}{11}$.

In the dentition, however, as in every part of the body, abnormalities are occasionally to be met with. Thus we have found a specimen of

Fig. 11.

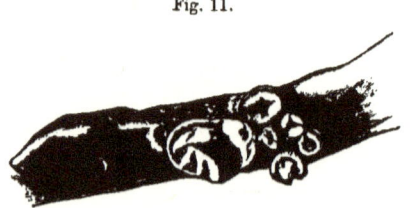

Abnormal denticles in *C. cancrivorus*. (Twice the size of nature.)

Cyon javanicus to be destitute of the second upper molar on each side; a *C. lateralis* with five premolars on one side; and both a *C. magellanicus* and a *C. cancrivorus* with one extra molar on each side of the lower jaw.

---

* For an explanation of all terms used in describing the dentition, see 'The Cat,' pp. 27–33, and figs. 12–15.

† A true molar is a tooth which has no milk predecessor, but is behind other teeth, the premolars, which (except the first) have milk predecessors. A "true molar" is often called a "molar" simply.

In another specimen of *C. cancrivorus* there was no third lower molar, but a rosette made up of five very small denticles in its place (fig. 11, p. xxiv). A third upper molar has also been found in *C. cancrivorus*, and Professor Flower, C.B., has observed a second upper molar in a specimen of *Icticyon venaticus*.

In Domestic Dogs abnormalities are more frequent, especially in the form known as the Japanese Pug, in which the teeth may be extraordinarily defective, as will be noted when we come to treat of the domestic Dog.

Almost always the fourth upper premolar and the first lower molar are larger than the others, with sharp cutting-blades which play one against the other, on which account they are often spoken of as the "sectorial" or "carnassial" teeth. In *Otocyon*, however, they hardly differ in this respect from those adjacent to them. Taking the teeth of

Fig. 12.

Side view of the teeth of a Wolf.

such a form as the Dingo or the Wolf as a type of the *Canidæ*, we find, if we compare it with the teeth of one of the *Felidæ*, or Cats, that the incisors are larger relatively both above and below. The four median

e

teeth in each jaw have each a crown consisting of one median and two small lateral lobes; but in either outermost incisor the inner lobe is obsolete. In the upper jaw the first premolar has but a single fang. All the teeth behind it have two fangs each, while the last three upper teeth have each three. In the lower jaw the first premolar and the third molar have each only one fang, while all the intermediate teeth have two fangs.

The upper sectorial tooth has a very large anterior external cusp, the apex of which is directed backwards as well as downwards, while on its inner side is a very small antero-internal cusp. A second, broad, external cusp is placed behind the anterior one, but does not extend so far downwards. In the *Felidæ*, however, there are three external cusps, whereof the most anterior is obsolete in the Dog.

The first upper true molar has a very extensive grinding-surface, with two large external cusps, two smaller internal ones, with also a very large internal band of tooth-substance or "cingulum." The second upper true molar is formed like the first, but is only about half its size.

The first lower premolar consists of one conspicuous cusp with a rudimentary one behind it. The next three teeth have each a large anterior cusp with two small ones behind it, whereof the anterior is the larger and more elevated.

The lower sectorial tooth consists of a large anterior cusp, followed by one still larger (whereas in the *Felidæ* they are of nearly equal size), with a minute cusp postero-internal to it. These last two cusps play against the inner surface of the two large cusps of the upper sectorial. Behind the three cusps just described, the lower sectorial possesses a very large posterior prolongation, or "talon," which bears two cusps, whereof the external one is the larger. The surface of the talon bites against that of the anterior, upper true molar.

The second true molar of the mandible has a quadrate grinding-surface with two transverse ridges, the anterior one being divided into two subequal cusps. The third true molar is very small with a rounded crown.

Each milk-molar resembles, not the tooth which replaces it, but the one which comes behind it in the permanent dentition. The first premolar above and below, and the true molars, have no milk-predecessors.

In most species the upper sectorial is much longer than the first upper molar, but in this respect there are many degrees of difference; nor are the relative sizes of the various teeth always quite constant even in the same species.

Myology.—The muscles * of the Dog are formed and arranged, for the most part, as in the Carnivora generally. Comparing them with those of the Feline Carnivora, it may be mentioned that there is but a single *dorso-epitrochlear* and no *supinator longus*. The latter fact is in harmony with the habitual action of the Dog's fore limb, which is almost exclusively used for running and walking, and not for climbing or movements which require the paw to be bent sole upwards. The *extensor communis digitorum* gives off only four tendons. The *plantaris* is large, and its tendon gives origin to the *flexor brevis*. The tendons of the *flexor longus digitorum pedis* and of the *longus hallucis* unite together as in the Cats, and, as in them, an elastic ligament connects the last phalanx of each digit with the penultimate phalanx, so that when the foot is dissected the claws are seen to be slightly retracted in fact, although their retraction is not visible externally.

The *rectus* muscle takes origin from the triangular fibrous or fibro-cartilaginous structure before described † as attached to the brim of the pubic part of the pelvis. The tendons of both the *external* and *internal oblique* muscles—forming the inner pillar of the abdominal ring—are inserted into the inner side of the same fibrous structure, while the outer pillar of the abdominal ring is formed by part of the external oblique inserted into the outer margin of the same, the *pectineus* being attached to its ventral surface.

Splanchnology ‡.—The mucous membrane of the edges of the lips, especially of the lower lip, is developed into a number of delicate sensitive processes. The lower lip is firmly bound down to the gum in

---

* For information concerning muscles, see 'The Cat,' chapter v.

† See above, p. xxi.

‡ See 'The Cat,' chapters vi. to ix. The viscera have been described by Professor Flower, C.B., in the 'Medical Times' for 1862, p. 621.

xxviii   INTRODUCTION.

the interval between the canine and the first premolar. The hard palate has curved transverse ridges, notched at the edge. The thin soft palate hardly forms a uvula.

The tongue is long and very movable. It is narrow towards its hinder end, rounded in front, with thin edges and a median longitudinal depression. The conical papillæ are generally small and closely set, but are larger at the tip, edges, and base of the tongue. The fungiform papillæ are numerous, and scattered over the sides and front of the tongue, but they are not conspicuous. There are but two, moderate-sized circumvallate papillæ. Beneath the front of the tongue is what is known as the "worm" or Lytta*. It is about a quarter of the length of the tongue. The belief that this structure is in any way prejudicial, and that it should be removed is, of course, utterly absurd and groundless.

The *œsophagus*, or gullet, extends about two inches (in a good-sized dog) beyond the diaphragm. The stomach has its cardiac and pyloric

Fig. 13.

Cæcum of Dog
(as in most species).

Fig. 14.

Cæcum of *Icticyon venaticus*.
(After Flower.)

---

* For a description of the structure of this organ, see a paper by Dr. Scott in the 'Journal of Anatomy and Physiology,' vol. xiv. p. 288.

portions separated by a well-marked constriction, and there are many permanent folds in the pylorus. Generally, the small intestine is nearly six or seven times the length of the large intestine, which is about as long as the body. The length is increased by domestication in the Dogs, as in various other beasts. The small intestine is lined with long, filiform villi. Peyer's patches are usually small and confined to the middle of the intestine. The cæcum is a moderate-sized, cylindrical body, rounded at its end, and in the great majority of species curiously contorted (fig. 13). In some species, however, as in *C. jubatus*, *C. cancrivorus*, *C. azaræ*, *C. procyonoides*, and *Icticyon venaticus* (fig. 14), it is almost or quite straight.

The *liver* has an undivided left lateral lobe, and slightly smaller left central one, compared with that of the Cat, and a very much smaller right central lobe as regards that part of it which is placed on the right side of the gall-bladder. The right lateral lobe, however, is much larger. The caudate lobe is also relatively larger, and the Spigelian lobe is divided into two lobules by a notch[*].

The *brain* shows four generally distinct and regular gyri surrounding the short, nearly vertical Sylvian fissure. The first and second gyri have their limbs—anterior and posterior to the Sylvian fissure—nearly equal. The parietal (often called the "middle lateral") gyrus has its posterior limb broad and bifurcate. The sagittal gyrus (often called the "superior lateral gyrus") is single. The hippocampal gyrus is divided from the sagittal one by the junction of the calloso-marginal sulcus with the largely developed crucial sulcus. The crucial sulcus, so characteristic of the Carnivora[†], is very plainly marked (figs. 15 & 16).

Some individual variation exists as to the extent of the bifurcation of the parietal gyrus (*m*), and the separation between the first and second

---

[*] In *C. procyonoides* the Spigelian lobe is very large, and various small differences exist in different species. See Proc. Zool. Soc. 1878, pp. 374 and 375, and 1880, p. 74.

[†] For further information on this subject, see our paper in the 'Journal of the Linnean Society,' vol. xix., Dec. 18, 1884, "Notes on the Cerebral Convolutions of the Carnivora."

INTRODUCTION.

Sylvian gyri (i, i') may be incomplete, as was found to be the case on one side of a brain of *Icticyon venaticus*, as here figured, and sometimes the sagittal gyrus is longitudinally grooved on its dorsum (as on one side in the figure) or on its inner side. The olfactory lobes are very large, as might be expected in animals with so acute a power of smell.

Fig. 15.   Fig. 16.

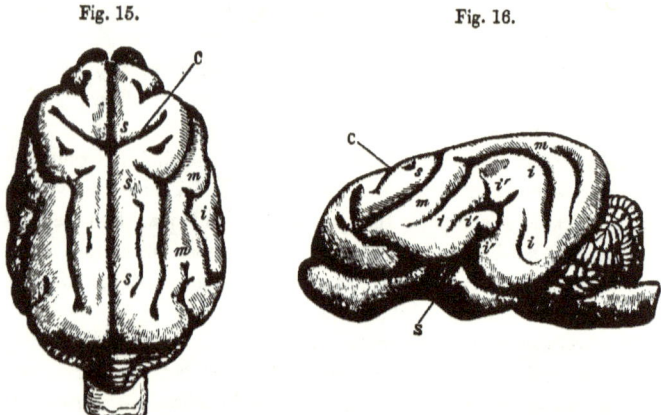

Fig. 15.—Brain of *Icticyon venaticus*, nat. size (after Flower). Dorsum: C, crucial sulcus; s, sagittal gyrus; m, parietal gyrus; i, second gyrus.

Fig. 16.—Brain of *Icticyon venaticus*, nat. size (after Flower). Lateral view: C, crucial sulcus; S, Sylvian fissure; i', first gyrus; i, second gyrus; m, parietal gyrus; s, sagittal gyrus.

The generative organs are remarkable for their salient prostate, and for not possessing Cowper's glands. The ossicle is of considerable size, straight and grooved.

The ovum is spindle-shaped at an early period, as is also the umbilical vesicle.

The placenta has the form and structure normal in the Carnivora, but its maternal portion cannot be so well defined and separated as in the *Felidæ*.

For further anatomical details, to describe which would be foreign to the purpose of this Monograph, the reader is referred to the various publications, the titles of which he will find given in the Bibliography and in the notices of the various species herein described.

PALÆONTOLOGY AND AFFINITIES OF THE CANIDÆ.

The Dog has been a domestic animal from time immemorial. Remains in Denmark and Switzerland prove that such was the case in the Neolithic and Bronze periods, as also that one kind of domestic Dog was succeeded at a later period by a larger one of a distinct breed. Moreover, in very ancient times, as also in the Pacific Islands and elsewhere recently, the Dog was used for human food. But a yet greater antiquity for this species as a companion of man seems implied by the fact that the remains of the Dingo have been obtained* from Pleistocene deposits, which have also yielded us the relics of various extinct animals. Of course it is probable that the animal may have found its way to Australia in some way independent of man, but it seems impossible to imagine such, while if it did owe its introduction to human agency, such a fact is enough to prove that even when its fossil contemporaries existed, man was in a relatively advanced social and intellectual condition.

Remains of other *Canidæ* have been found in caverns of the Quaternary period and in strata of Pleistocene times, and relics of the Common Fox (*C. vulpes*) have been found in the Upper Pliocene †. The African genus *Lycaon* seems then to have existed in Glamorganshire; and still surviving species of the genus *Canis*, as well as the yet living species *Icticyon venaticus*, existed in Brazil. The genus *Cyon* has been found in Pleistocene deposits in a cavern in Europe.

For the latest account known to us of fossil *Canidæ*, the reader is referred to the labours of Max Schlosser, Woldrich, Lydekker, Filhol, and Cope, as also to the well-known works of Cuvier, De Blainville, Gervais, Gaudry, Lund, Leidy, and others‡.

* See below, our description of the Dingo.
† In the Suffolk Crag. See Lydekker, Geological Mag. decade iii. vol. ii. p. 443 (1884).
‡ See below, the Palæontological section of our Bibliography.

A great number of fossil forms, presumed to be distinct species, have been distinguished by many specific and some generic names. But we must exclude their consideration from the present work as not coming within its professed scope. Moreover, without any disrespect to the distinguished palæontologists who have described them, we must also confess to a good deal of scepticism with respect to various fossil species. The examination of many skulls belonging to one existing kind has convinced us that though the form of the teeth is about the most constant character, it is nevertheless so subject to individual variation that definitions reposing upon almost any single, more or less imperfectly preserved, skull have little value in our eyes. But we by no means intend by this remark to slight or undervalue the labours of Palæontologists. They must work, with the relatively poor materials they have, in the only way possible to them, *i. e.* by most careful discrimination between all the fossil specimens they can procure. Palæontology and the Zoology of living forms seem to us such very distinct, though closely allied, sciences, that the mental attitude of the student of the one must necessarily diverge from that of the other, in spite of the single aim common to them both.

A genus of Mammals named *Cynodictis* (in which the genera *Galecynus* of Cope * and *Cynodon* of Filhol should probably be included) is found in the Lower Miocene and Upper Eocene of Europe, and in the Miocene strata of North America. This genus, however, cannot be affirmed to belong to the *Canidæ*, as it seems to be intermediate between the Dogs and the Civets.

The genus *Amphicyon*†, the dentition of which has much resemblance to that of the Dogs, differs greatly from them in the structure of its feet, which approach those of the Bears and are plantigrade.

The interest of the Palæontology of the group largely reposes upon any light which may thence be thrown upon the origin and evolution of the *Canidæ*.

We have ever affirmed our conviction in the truth of Evolution, and

---

* The *Galecynus* of Owen is merely *Canis*. It is the well-known fossil Fox of Œningen.
† See below, Bibliography.

our belief in it tends to increase with study and experience. Simultaneously with the growth of that conviction, however, we also experience a simultaneous growth of scepticism with respect to our power of determining the precise course which specific evolution has followed. Phylogeny, or the science of such evolution of forms of life, seems to us to be not merely in its infancy but rather at a low stage of embryonic development. We have already seen the overthrow of a great many promising and carefully drawn out genealogical trees of life, and therefore feel little inclined to attempt now to construct the pedigree of the Dog family.

The palæontological history of the *Canidæ* is as yet very incomplete and unsatisfactory, and only permits the formation of speculative opinions which appear to us to be of very doubtful value. Moreover, as we have said, this work is intended to make known living *Canidæ*—that is to say, the most divergent forms into which the group, whatever its origin, has become differentiated. For this end, Palæontology affords no help, since the further we go back the less differentiated we must expect such remains, as may be discovered, to be. So far as we yet know, no fossil *Canidæ* present us with nearly such exceptional forms as are found amongst fossil Feline animals*. Had such been found, they would have demanded careful description here.

The most diverging groups of the existing terrestrial Carnivora, besides the Dogs, are the Bears, Weasel-group, Civets, Hyænas, Raccoon-group, and Cats. In the world as we see it, the Dogs stand quite aloof from all the others. The once supposed affinity of the Hyæna-Dog (*Lycaon pictus*) to the Hyæna, and the Raccoon-Dog (*Canis procyonoides*) to the Raccoon, was due to mere superficial resemblances in external aspect. But the triangular fibrous structure attached to the pubis strongly reminds us of the marsupial bones of the Opossum Order (*Marsupialia*), and it has been suggested that since the Dogs diverge so much from the existing *Carnivora* they may be survivors of very early forms which had a close genetic affinity with the *Marsupialia*. The idea is supported by the facts (1) that there is a considerable resemblance in form, and in

---

* Such as the extremely modified forms *Machærodus* and *Eusmilus*. See 'The Cat,' pp. 432 & 437, figs. 184 & 190.

f

the structure of some of the teeth, between the largest existing predatory Marsupial, the so-called Tasmanian Wolf (*Thylacinus*), and the true Wolf; and (2) that this large Marsupial is one which is most exceptional in its order, through having the Marsupial bones represented by mere cartilages. We, however, do not attach any importance to these coincidences, but believe that the resemblances referred to have arisen independently.

As to speculations concerning the origin of different Canine forms, M. Marcellin Boule* expresses the opinion that *Amphicyon* was the ancestor of both the Bears and the Dogs, while *Cynodictis* was the ancestor of both the Civets and Foxes. This appears to us to be a mere speculation, which, while we have no desire to contest its truth, we cannot give an express adherence to. Should it, however, turn out to be a well-founded belief, it would form another interesting example of that independent origin of similar structures for which we have so long contended. M. Boule very sensibly remarks † that if Dogs and Foxes did have so diverse an origin, such a fact would constitute no reason why their descendants should not now be grouped in one single genus.

Indeed, we cannot reasonably arrange our classification of the organic world upon a basis of what its parts may have been or actually once were. On the view of Evolution which is as yet most popular, every kind of intermediate form must have existed at one time or another; and if every such form had to be included, no kind of classification whatever would be possible for us.

The Carnivora were classified by the late H. N. Turner, jun.‡, as a family *Ursidæ* of Bears, Raccoons, and Weasels, a family *Felidæ* of Civets, Hyænas, and Cats, and the family *Canidæ*. These three families Professor Flower has proposed § to raise to the rank of three suborders, called respectively *Arctoidea*, *Æluroidea*, and *Cynoidea*, a proposal which we have ourselves accepted ||, and which has met with a very

---

* See Bulletin de la Société Géologique de France, 3ᵉ série, t. xvii. p. 321.
† P. 330. ‡ P. Z. S. 1848, p. 86.
§ P. Z. S. 1869, pp. 4–37.
|| 'The Cat,' p. 474; and Proc. Zool. Soc. 1882, p. 138.

general acceptance. Schlosser objects to it as receiving very little support from Palæontology, and regards the Dogs as very closely related to the Bears, a view which receives support from both Gaudry * and Lydekker †. Scott ‡ also deems the Bears and Dogs to be nearly allied, while he regards the Civets and Hyænas as being more allied to the Weasel-group than to the *Felidæ*; while Schlosser considers the Cats to be most widely separated from all the other groups of existing Carnivora, and to have had an origin independent of them. Garrod, on account of the form of the brain, represented § the *Canidæ* as an offshoot from the *Felidæ*.

Such conflicting opinions suffice to make plain, to everyone who reflects on them, how speculative and uncertain such phylogenetic statements are.

Maintaining, then, still that system of classification for the Carnivora which we before made use of, it but remains for us to note here the characters by which the *Canidæ*, or *Cynoidea*, differ from the Arctoid Mammals on the one hand, and from the Æluroids on the other.

That the Dog-group (excepting domestic forms) is singularly uniform in structure compared with the others, will be evident if we compare the amount of divergence between *C. lupus* and *Otocyon megalotis*, with the great contrast which exists between such species as a Lion and a Mongoose amongst the Æluroid forms, and between a Raccoon and an Otter amongst the Arctoids.

The characters by which the *Canidæ* differ from the *Arctoidea* are the following:—

They are always digitigrade.

They possess a smooth auditory bulla which tends to be divided internally by a bony septum, which nevertheless remains very incomplete.

* See his 'Les Enchaînements,' chap. ix.
† Palæontologia Indica, ser. 10, p. 202; and Cat. of Fossil Mammalia, part i. p. 106.
‡ Notes on the Osteology and Systematic Position of *Dinictis felina*, p. 242.
§ See Proc. Zool. Soc. 1878, p. 377.

There is a long and prominent paroccipital process, which is applied to the bulla.

There is no long, outwardly projecting process beneath the opening of the *meatus auditorius externus*.

The mastoid is small and not prominent, and the condyloid foramen opens on a bony ridge.

There is a cæcum which, in the great majority of species, is curiously contorted and coiled.

The prostate is salient.

The bone in the *corpus cavernosum* is grooved and not dilated and bilobed anteriorly.

Except in *Otocyon* there are not * more than two true molars above and three below, while, except in *Icticyon*, there are never less than two true molars above and two below.

The characters by which the *Canidæ* differ from the *Æluroidea* are :—

They have an auditory bulla which is but very incompletely subdivided by a bony septum.

They have a long and prominent paroccipital process, and a large glenoid foramen.

There is a relatively longer *meatus auditorius externus*.

The condyloid foramen opens on a bony ridge and is conspicuous.

There is always an alisphenoid canal.

The orbit is never enclosed by bone.

There is a cæcum which, in the great majority of species, is curiously contorted and coiled.

There are no Cowper's glands.

There is a large, symmetrically-shaped bone in the *corpus cavernosum*.

There are generally four premolars and two true molars above, and four premolars and three true molars below, while there are generally two tubercular teeth (devoid of a cutting-blade) behind the sectorial tooth both above and below.

* Abnormalities of course excepted.

INTRODUCTION. xxxvii

BIBLIOGRAPHY.

General Zoology of the Group, or notices of a considerable number of the Species contained within it.

BUFFON, Histoire Naturelle, vols. v., vii., xiii., and Supplément, vii.
SHAW, General Zoology, vol. i.
DESMAREST, Mammalogie.
F. CUVIER, Histoire Naturelle des Mammifères.
J. A. WAGNER, Supplement to Schreber's Säugthiere, 2nd Abtheilung.
PALLAS, Zoographia Rosso-Asiatica.
HARLAN, Fauna Americana.
RICHARDSON, Fauna Boreali-Americana.
JARDINE's Naturalist's Library, vols. ix. and x.
PAUL GERVAIS, Mammifères, vol. ii.
AUDUBON and BACHMAN, Quadrupeds of North America.
TEMMINCK, Siebold's ' Fauna Japonica.'
DARWIN, Animals and Plants under Domestication.
BURMEISTER, Fauna Brasiliens.
BURMEISTER, République Argentine, vol. iii.
HARTING, The Zoologist, vol. viii.
HUXLEY, Proceedings of the Zoological Society, 1880.
FLOWER, Article "Mammalia," ' Encyclopædia Britannica '*.
GRAY, Catalogue of Carnivorous Mammalia in the British Museum.
JERDON, Mammals of British India.
BLANFORD, Fauna of British India.
ALSTON, Biologia Centrali-Americana (Mammals).
RÜPPELL, Zoological Atlas.
RÜPPELL, Neue Wirbelthiere.
RENGGER, Naturgeschichte der Säugethiere von Paraguay.
AZARA, Essais sur l'histoire naturelle des Quadrupèdes.
HODGSON, Asiatic Researches.
BAIRD, Mammals of North America.
DE BLAINVILLE, Ostéographie *(Canis)*.
LEURET, Anatomie comparée du Système nerveux.
CUVIER, Leçons d'Anatomie comparée.
MECKEL, Anatomie comparée.

(The works and papers which relate to single kinds or varieties will be referred to in the description separately assigned to each reputed species.)

* Shortly to appear in an expanded form as a work on Mammalia, by Flower and Lydekker.

g

Palæontology of the Group.

CUVIER, Ossemens fossiles.
DE BLAINVILLE, Ostéographic (*Canis*).
PAUL GERVAIS, Zoologie et Paléontologie Française.
OWEN, Palæontology.
GAUDRY, Enchaînements du Monde Animal.
NICHOLSON and LYDEKKER, Manual of Palæontology.
LYDEKKER, Palæontologia Indica.
LYDEKKER, Catalogue of Fossil Mammalia in the British Museum.
BOURGUIGNAT, Recherches sur les Oss. des Canidæ quatern.
MAX SCHLOSSER, Die Affen, Lemuren, Chiropteren, Insectivoren, Marsupialien, Creodonten und Carnivoren des Europäischen Tertiärs.
Numerous papers by LUND, COPE, LEIDY, FILHOL, ALLEN, MARSH, NEHRING, WALDRICH, POWEL, F. MAJOR, BOSE, and others.

Amongst the specific names which have been given to fossil specimens described of the genus *Canis* are :—*europæus, edwardsianus, nemesianus, hercynicus, sussii, sævus, cautleyi, neschersensis, cadurcensis, filholi, falconeri, etruscus, haydenii, dirus, wheelerianus, projubatus, cultridens, indianensis, brachypus, avus, robustior, lycodes, troglodytes, validus, fossilis, borbonicus, æningensis, gypsorum, temerarius, curvipalatus, palustris, robustus, parisiensis, viverroides, issiodorensis, brevirostris,* and *palæolycos*. A European *Cyon* and an English *Lycaon* have also been described.

A

MONOGRAPH OF THE CANIDÆ.

CANIDÆ.

Characters of the Family.—The Canidæ are Carnivorous Mammals, with only four complete digits behind and four or five in front; premolars four above and four below; molars generally two above and three below on each side; auditory bulla smooth, rounded, with a very incomplete internal septum; paroccipital process projecting and applied against the bulla; mastoid distinct but small; condyloid and glenoid foramina conspicuous; a well-developed alisphenoid canal; brain with four convolutions around the Sylvian fissure; cæcum always present, and mostly coiled on itself; bone of corpus cavernosum straight, wide, and grooved; prostate salient; no Cowper's glands.

Subdivisions of the Family.

CANIDÆ. $\begin{cases} \text{Digits 5—4} \begin{cases} \text{M.} \frac{2}{3} & \ldots \ldots \text{CANIS.} \\ \text{M.} \frac{2}{2} & \ldots \ldots \text{CYON.} \\ \text{M.} \frac{1}{2} & \ldots \ldots \text{ICTICYON.} \\ \text{M.} \frac{3}{4} & \ldots \ldots \text{OTOCYON.} \end{cases} \\ \text{Digits 4—4} \quad \ldots \ldots \text{LYCAON.} \end{cases}$

Genus CANIS, Linneus (1766).

Canis, Linneus, Systema Naturæ, 12th ed. vol. i. p. 56 (1766).

Generic characters.

Digits 5—4. Pm. $\frac{4}{4}$, M. $\frac{2}{3}$.

Nasals extending backwards beyond frontal process of maxillæ, or not so extending; outer margin of nasals not strongly sigmoid; anterior palatine foramina not very large; first upper premolar decidedly smaller than the second; inner portion of first upper molar well developed, the cingulum not coalescing with the inner tubercles; cæcum generally coiled and contorted.

THE COMMON WOLF.
Canis lupus.

Mintern Bros. imp

THE COMMON WOLF.

CANIS LUPUS.

Canis lupus, Linneus, Syst. Nat. 12th ed. vol. i. p. 58 (1766); Schreber,
Säugthiere, Theil iii. p. 346, pls. 81 & 88 (1778); Cuvier,
Règne An. vol. i. p. 153 (1817); Desmarest, Mammalogie,
p. 197 (1820); Pallas, Zoographia, vol. i. p. 36 (1831);
J. A. Wagner, Supplement to Schreber's Säugth., Abtheil.
ii. p. 366 (1840); Alston, Biologia Centr.-Amer., Mamm.
p. 65; Blanford, Fauna British India, Mammalia, p. 135.
Lupus vulgaris, Brisson, Regnum An. 4to (Paris), p. 235 (1756); id.
ibid. 8vo (Leyden), p. 170 (1762); Gray, Proc. Zool. Soc.
1868, p. 501; id. Catalogue of Carnivorous Mammalia in
Brit. Mus. p. 186.
Canis occidentalis, Richardson, Fauna Boreali-Americana, p. 60 (1829);
Baird, Mammals North America, p. 104 (1857); De Kay,
Nat. Hist. New York, vol. i. p. 42, pl. 27 (1842); Gray,
Catalogue of Carnivorous Mammalia, p. 187.
Canis griseus, Audubon & Bachman, Quadrupeds of N. Amer. vol. iii.
p. 279 (1854).
Lupus griseus, Richardson, Fauna B.-Americana, p. 66 (1829).
Canis mexicanus, Brisson, Reg. An. 4to (Paris), p. 237; Schreber,
Säugth. Th. iii. p. 352; Desmarest, Mamm. p. 199.
Lupus laniger, Hodgson, Calcutta Journ. Nat. Hist. vol. vii. p. 474
(1847); Horsfield, Ann. & Mag. Nat. Hist. 2nd series,
vol. xvi. p. 107 (1855).
Canis chanco, Gray, Proc. Zool. Soc. 1863, p. 94.
Canis pallipes, Sykes, P. Z. S. 1831, p. 101; Jerdon, Mammals of Brit.
India, p. 139; Blanford, Fauna Brit. India, p. 139.
Canis hodophylax, Temminck, Siebold's Fauna Japonica (Mammalia),
p. 38, pl. 9 (1847); Brauns, The Chrysanthemum (Yoko-
hama), vol. i. p. 66 (1881).
Canis nubilus, Say in Long's Expedition to the Rocky Mountains, vol. i.
p. 169 (1823); Richardson, Fauna B.-Americana, p. 69
(1829).
Canis variabilis, Maximilian, Prinz zu Wied, Reise in Nord-America
(Coblenz), vol. ii. p. 95 (1841).

THE COMMON WOLF.

Lupus sticte, Richardson, Fauna B.-Americana, p. 68 (1829).
Le Loup, Buffon, Hist. Nat. vol. vii. p. 39 (1758), and Supplément,
    vol. vii. pp. 161-217 (1789); F. Cuvier, Hist. Nat. des
    Mammifères, vol. ii. (1824).

BLACK VARIETY.

Lycaon, Erxleben, Syst. Nat. (Mammalia), p. 560 (1777).
Canis lycaon, Desmarest, Mammalogie, p. 198 (1820); Harlan, Fauna
    Americana, p. 82 (1825); Cuvier, Règne An. vol. i. p. 154.
Lupus ater, Richardson, Fauna B.-Americana, p. 113 (1829); Audubon
    and Bachman, Quadrupeds of N. Amer. vol. ii. p. 126,
    pl. 67 (1851).
Canis niger, Sclater, P. Z. S. 1874, p. 654, pl. 78.
Loup noir, Buffon, Hist. Nat. vol. ix. p. 362, pl. 41; F. Cuvier, Hist.
    Nat. des Mammifères, vol. ii.

WHITE VARIETY.

Canis (Lupus) albus, Sabine, in Franklin's Journey to Polar Sea, p. 655
    (1823); Audubon and Bachman, Quadrupeds of N. Amer.
    vol. ii. p. 156, pl. 72 (1851).
Lupus albus, Richardson, Fauna B.-Americana, p. 68.

THIS animal is the largest and most dreaded of the Canidæ. Its ferocity and the ravages often made by wolves are matters of common notoriety, so that even naturalists, following Buffon, have declared it to be really untamable and incapable of true attachment. We have, however, ourselves seen a Spanish she-wolf of extreme gentleness. She would come to be caressed, wagging her tail, and showing the signs of pleasure a domestic dog would exhibit. F. Cuvier describes one which had been brought up in domesticity, was perfectly tame and very strongly attached to its master, who presented it to the Jardin des Plantes. Thus left, it became for a time gloomy and ate little, but afterwards began to attach itself to its keepers. Eighteen months later its old master came to see it, and at the first sound of his voice it was violently excited. On being set free, it lavished on its master all the caresses a dog would bestow. Being again tried in the same way, for a period of three years, it once more exhibited, in a similar manner, on its master's return, the tenacity of its memory and the vivacity of its attachment. There is no doubt but that wolves are easily tamed when taken young; and even when not caught till fully adult may be tamed, so as to live with dogs and learn from them to bark.

Wolves frequent both forests and open country, and they may be met with by day as well as by night, either singly, in pairs, or in packs. It is especially in winter time that they herd together for predatory purposes, to the great danger of solitary travellers. In 1875 one hundred and sixty-one persons fell victims to wolves in Russia, and the damage to cattle in 1873 was estimated at seven and a half millions of roubles. Wolves destroy horses and cattle by combined attacks, but will singly destroy sheep, goats, or children. They greedily devour birds, and will eat mice, frogs, or almost any small animals. They will also feed on carrion, and are said to even seek nourishment from buds and lichens.

The voice of the wolf is mainly a loud howl, but, as above remarked, wolves will learn in confinement to bark, if they hear dogs do so.

The males fight together in the month of January, and the successful combatant who has thus obtained a female, remains with her till the young are advanced in growth. Gestation lasts 63 days, and from three to nine cubs may be born. The young are suckled for two months, but at the end of the first begin to eat half-digested meat thrown up by the mother for them. She makes her nest in a burrow, small cave, or dense thicket, often furnishing it with moss as well as the hairs of her coat, which she sheds about that time.

In November or December the cubs quit their parents, but may keep together for another six or eight months or longer. They become full-grown the third year after their birth, and live from twelve to fifteen years.

The European Wolf may be considered as a survivor of a group of ferocious beasts of prey—the cave-bear, the cave-hyæna, &c., with which animals prehistoric man had to contend. It still exists in the wilder or more mountainous parts of France, Belgium, and all other European countries except Central and Northern Germany. It is very abundant in many parts of Russia [*].

[*] For details as to its distribution in Russia, see the 'Zoologische Garten,' xxiv. Jahrgang (1883), p. 91.

In England wolves must still have been common in Yorkshire in the reign of Richard II., for in the account-rolls of Whitby Abbey there is an entry * of a payment for dressing wolf-skins. They were probably exterminated in the reign of Henry VII. The last in Scotland is said to have been destroyed in 1743, while one is asserted to have been killed in the Wicklow Mountains in Ireland in 1770. Should these statements, however, be inaccurate, it is, at any rate, certain that Wolves existed in Scotland till 1680, and in Ireland down to 1710.

The size and proportions of the Wolf roughly resemble those of a large mastiff, though individuals, especially from different localities, differ greatly in size.

The prevailing colour is a tawny or rufous grey, and the greyness is apt to increase with old age. The head, back of the neck, shoulders, loins, and crupper are blackish with yellow tints. There is an underfur of a slate or a brown colour, amongst which whitish and black-tipped hairs are intermixed. The thighs and outsides of the legs reddish yellow, as is also the tail, save that the end is black. The inner side of the limbs is of a dirty yellowish grey. The lower jaw, the margin of the upper jaw, the inside of the ears, and the belly are more or less white. A black mark extends vertically from the wrist up the front of the leg, and there is sometimes a V-shaped black mark, with the apex directed backwards, over the shoulders.

The form and proportions of the skull, and the shape and relative development of the different teeth, agree generally with those which have been described in our introductory chapter.

In Plate I. we have a representation of a wolf from the Pyrenees, which is of a somewhat brighter, richer tint than that commonly found in the Wolves of Central Europe; but Spanish wolves are often very much darker, with a great deal of black in the coat, and sometimes are almost entirely black, and but little more than twenty years ago a black wolf was killed † near Dinant, in Belgium. North-European

---

* See J. E. Harting's 'British Animals extinct during Historic Times.' Trübner & Co.: 1880.

† See 'Archives Cosmologiques' (Bruxelles, 1868), p. 78, plate 5.

Wolves are generally greyer with longer fur, and may be of a very light colour. A specimen from Moscow, in the British Museum, has remarkably long, soft hair, of a pale colour, and altogether devoid of a rufous tint on the outside of the limbs.

The Wolf is a striking example of the variability common to so many of the Canidæ. This variability is by no means confined to its furry coat, but also affects the details of the skeleton and dentition, and the general proportions and size of its whole bodily frame.

Various zoologists have regarded different local forms of the Wolf— both in the Old World and the New—as so many distinct species. We have already observed, in our Introduction, that many members of the canine family vary so much that the specific separation of them must be largely a matter of individual opinion concerning which zoologists may reasonably differ. Acting on our principle not to separate as probable species, forms which we have not found to differ by any characters which seem constant *, we feel compelled to treat the various local forms here referred to as varieties of *Canis lupus*.

We have seen that the European Wolf varies greatly—not only in having predominantly either a red or a grey hue, but in being (as sometimes in Spain) almost black, or (as in North Europe) of an extremely light tint.

We might therefore expect to find a similar range of variations in the Wolves of Asia and America.

In Plate II. we give a representation of a black wolf from Thibet. It is not, however, completely black, having a reddish tinge on the hinder part of either thigh, while the margins of the mouth, a patch on the breast, the under surface of the lower jaw, and the paws are white.

The individual figured is one of a pair which the Zoological Society of London received from Lieut. A. A. Kinloch and Lieut. J. Biddulph in August 1867, and which they had obtained from some Tartars in Thibet, at the foot of the Lanak pass. These beasts had shaggy fur, and were uniformly black except on the muzzle, the feet, and a patch on the

* See *ante*, p. v.

breast, which were white. They are the types of Dr. Sclater's * species *C. niger*.

Another black wolf in the British Museum has shorter fur and browner knees than the former. Its face also is not white, but only the lips, while there is some white behind the thigh, as well as brown in front of it.

Our Plate III. represents a fine specimen of a uniformly pale colour, which was shot by Lieut. W. P. Hodnell in Chinese Tartary, and presented by Lady A. Harvey to the British Museum. It was named by Dr. Gray † *Canis chanco*, and is the actual type of his species. Its fur is pale fulvous, the hair of the back having black and grey hairs intermixed. The head is greyish with short black and grey hairs on the forehead.

Its skull and teeth are like those of the Common Wolf.

This is probably the same variety of wolf as that to which the name *C. laniger* has been applied by Mr. B. H. Hodgson ‡, and which he says is common all over Thibet, and he describes it as: "Above, dull earthy-brown; below, with the entire face and limbs yellowish-white. No marks on the limbs. Tail concolorous with the body." He adds that it measures three feet nine inches from snout to tail, and that the tail is one foot four inches long. Mr. Blanford, in his 'Fauna of British India' §, identifies, as we do, this form with the Common Wolf. He is of a different opinion, however, as regards what is called the Indian Wolf, to which the name *C. pallipes* was applied by Sykes ||. But Mr. Blanford only distinguishes it from *C. lupus* as being smaller and slighter, with a shorter coat and little or no underfur. In these characters we have found undoubted specimens of *C. lupus* to differ as much as they differ from the Indian Wolf, and in five skins carefully examined by

---

* P. Z. S. 1874, p. 654, plate lxxviii. An account of the capture of these animals will be found in a work entitled "Large-Game Shooting in Thibet and the North-West." By Alexander A. A. Kinloch. (London, 1869: Harrison.)

† P. Z. S. 1863, p. 94.

‡ Calcutta Journ. Nat. Hist. vol. vii. (1847), p. 474

§ Part I. pp. 135, 136.

|| P. Z. S. 1831, p. 101.

us we found no satisfactory distinctive character, though the V-shaped stripe over the shoulders was more marked than in most European wolves. We at first thought that the skull would provide us with distinguishing characters in its greater concavity above between the orbits, the position of the suture between the palatine and maxillary bones on the palate, and in certain details of dental structure. An extended examination, however, of crania belonging to both varieties convinced us that not one of these differences was constant, and that no other such could be depended on.

Our Plate IV., representing the Indian Wolf, is drawn from a specimen living in the Zoological Gardens.

Its coloration varies from greyish red to reddish white, with a touch of grey, many of the hairs being black-tipped; there is generally black on the back, especially a V-shaped patch behind the shoulders. The limbs are paler than the body. The tail is slightly or decidedly tipped with black. The underparts of the body are more or less white *.

This variety appears to be mainly confined to the plains south of the Himalayas. It is said but rarely to be found west of the Indus or in Lower Bengal, and it is unknown in Ceylon as far as present evidence goes.

As to the habits of the Indian Wolf, Mr. Blanford informs us it does not associate in large packs, but that two or more will combine to attack man, while six or eight sometimes hunt together. A large number of Indian children are carried off each year by them. Their depredations are facilitated by the superstition of the people, who are very averse to killing a wolf, thinking its blood injures the bearing of their fields. Tales are current in India, as in Europe, of male infants reared by wolves, but are of doubtful authenticity at the best.

* A specimen has newly arrived at the British Museum from Pekin. It is a rather small animal, with a well-marked patch of black on the back of the neck, continued backwards as an interrupted dorsal streak. The tail is pale ochre towards its root, but its distal half is redder and it is black at the point. The ears, snout, back of head, and limbs are redder than in *C. pallipes* or than in most specimens of the European Wolf.

It is very rarely that its voice is heard, and it does not howl like the European Wolf. Its breeding-time is from about the middle of October to about the end of December, but mostly in December. The young cubs are blind, and have the ears drooping. Their general colour is sooty brown on the surface, the roots of the hairs being a light tan colour, especially on the head and flanks. They have a milk-white chest-spot, and often the tip of the tail is white. After a time the chest-spot disappears, and is replaced by a temporary dark collar beneath the neck *.

The Indian Wolf is remarkable both for its speed and its powers of endurance. Dr. Jerdon tells us †:—"I have known wolves turn on dogs that were running at their heels and pursue them smartly till close up to my horse. A wolf once joined with my greyhounds in pursuit of a fox, which was luckily killed almost immediately afterwards, or the wolf might have seized one of the dogs instead of the fox. He sat down on his haunches about sixty yards off, whilst the dogs were worrying the fox, looking on with great apparent interest, and was with difficulty driven away."

The American variety of the wolf, which has been named *Canis occidentalis* ‡, cannot, we are persuaded, be considered a distinct species from that of Europe. The differences which exist between its extreme varieties are greater than any which exist between those forms of European and American wolves which are most alike, as also are the differences which exist between extreme varieties of the European Wolf.

We have examined a number of skins, endeavouring with the greatest care to detect specific characters. We have found the American forms less red than most European ones, especially on the legs and hinder part of the head; but in this they agree with specimens from Northern Europe. The American skins have generally more black on the back than most European ones, yet not so much as may be found in many Spanish wolves.

* See E. Bonavia in 'Nature,' vol. xii. (1875), p. 67.
† *Loc. cit.* p. 141.
‡ Richardson, 'Fauna Boreali-Americana' (Murray, 1829), p. 60.

We have carefully measured skulls and teeth of a number of American wolves, and compared them with the skulls and teeth of European forms, but could not detect the slightest constant difference between them, any more than between the skins of specimens of the two races.

In our Plate V. we have had represented what appears to us to be a normal specimen of the American variety, *C. occidentalis*.

The enormous and rapid spread of population and tillage in the United States have greatly restricted the range of this formidable animal; yet Allen * refers to it as still an inhabitant of Massachusetts a little more than twenty years ago. In 1829 they used to be very numerous on the sandy plains eastward of the Rocky Mountains, where they would hang on the skirts of herds of the Bison, and prey on the sick or on straggling calves. But they would not venture to attack any vigorous full-grown Bison. Hunters informed Mr. Richardson that they had often seen wolves walking through a herd of bulls without exciting the least alarm amongst them. The hunters used to rely upon the wary and suspicious nature of the wolf, to preserve the game they had obtained. For this purpose it was generally found sufficient to tie a handkerchief, or an inflated bladder, to the branch of a tree. The ferocity of these animals is, however, vouched for by Audubon, who relates an instance of two negroes who, though armed with axes, were set upon while travelling at night, when one, after fighting as long as he could, saved himself by climbing into a tree, while the other was killed and eaten. In spite of its carnivorous, predatory habit, this variety sometimes feeds on berries †.

The American Wolf burrows, and its earths have several outlets, as was observed by Richardson, who saw some of them on the plains of the Saskatchewan, and also on the banks of the Coppermine river.

In the present day I learn, through the kindness of Dr. Elliott Coues,

* See his "Mammals of Massachusetts" in Bulletin of the Museum of Comp. Zoology of Harvard Coll. 1863–69.

† See a note by J. C. Hughes in the 'American Naturalist,' vol. xvii. (1883), p. 1192.

12   THE COMMON WOLF.

on the authority of Mr. Allen, that the wolf is found east of the Mississippi and south of Canada only in the still nearly unsettled parts of the country, as the northern portion of New England and New York, portions of the Alleghanies, Southern Florida, and possibly in the sparsely settled parts of the interior States south of the Ohio. It is only abundant in the remote districts of Maine. West of the Mississippi its numbers are very small in comparison with its former abundance, while over vast areas it has been wholly extirpated. North of the United States, except in the more settled parts of Canada, it is probably still more or less common.

Mr. S. F. Baird justly observes *, with respect to the unity or multiplicity of species of Wolf:—" It is difficult to occupy a middle ground between considering all our wolves as one species with many varieties, or making all these varieties into as many distinct species. Thus, we have the pure white wolf of the Upper Missouri; the dusky blackish plumbeous wolf of the Missouri; the entirely black wolf of Florida and the Southern States, and the entirely red or rufous wolf of Texas. These vary, too, in shape as well as colour, the more southern ones appearing usually more slender †, and standing higher on the legs, in consequence, perhaps, of the comparative shortness and compactness of the fur." The wolf descends so far south in Mexico as the State of Guanajuato, but these southern wolves are greatly inferior in size to the northern, and especially the subarctic forms ‡.

We have examined a black wolf-skin from America, and a perfectly white one also from America, not an albino, was seen at Liverpool a short time ago by Mr. A. D. Bartlett. At the British Museum there is a specimen brought from North America by Dr. Rae, which is most remarkable on account of its long white hair, being an example of a

* *Loc. cit.* p. 105.
† This remark is interesting because the Southern Old-World form *pallipes* is distinguished by its greater slenderness from the wolves of northern parts of the Palæarctic region.
‡ Alston, *loc. cit.* p. 66.

very pale variety from the far North. Along the middle of the back this specimen has its long light hairs dark towards their roots.

Thus in both hemispheres we may meet with red, or grey, or black, or white wolves, as well as wolves of very sturdy, or of slender build, and either with long and woolly, or very short fur. Moreover, a great number of intermediate varieties exist, so that species must be greatly multiplied, without any really distinctive characters; or else all these forms must be taken to be (as we take them to be) but local or climatic varieties of one and the same species. On this account we have, in our list of synonyms, united under the one head, *Canis lupus*, the great number of different names therein cited.

The American Wolf ranges from Mexico to the North of Canada, and to Greenland [*].

There now remains but one form to consider, which is the variety, or species, named by Temminck *Canis hodophylax*, which he tells us is called "Jamainu" by the natives. It is said to inhabit woody and mountainous parts of Japan, where it hunts in small troops or families, and is greatly dreaded by the Japanese, who even consider its flesh unwholesome to eat.

As to its specific distinctness, Temminck admits that it is very like the Common Wolf, but asserts it to differ therefrom not only by its smaller size, but also, and above all, by the shortness of its legs. Nevertheless, we have seen undoubted specimens of *C. lupus* with legs as short as those of the animal represented in Temminck's plate.

Prof. D. Brauns [†], however, considers the variety a distinct species, and his figure, which we here reproduce (fig. 17, p. 14), does show limbs which are relatively short, but the tail is hardly so, although he makes its shortness a distinctive character as well as the greater elongation of the muzzle. But he remarks: "There can be no doubt as to the existence of only one kind of wolf in Japan."

[*] See a letter from Dr. Robert Brown in the Ann. of Nat. Hist. 4th series, vol. vii. (1871), p. 65.

[†] See 'The Chrysanthemum,' vol. i. (1881), p. 66.

14   THE COMMON WOLF.

In the British Museum, however, there are two skulls of wolves from Japan. Neither skull exhibits any character by which it can be specifically distinguished from *C. lupus*, but the two differ very much

Fig. 17.

CANIS HODOPHYLAX.
(Facsimile from 'The Chrysanthemum.' See note, p. 13.)

in size, though both are fully adult. If, then, so great a difference can exist between the size of the head of adult Japanese wolves, it is difficult to think that the length of the limbs may not have varied from that found in the Continental wolves. Moreover, Prof. Brauns lets us know that the Japanese variety (*hodophylax*) does vary much, since he expressly says that in the Museum at Tokio there are very differently coloured skins, namely "yellowish," "brownish," and "whitish grey."

Of the two skulls in the British Museum, the larger one comes from the province of Yesso—a region which has Palæarctic affinities. The small one is from the province of Kotsuke, which is more Oriental in its zoological character. They may well therefore be nothing more than local varieties, differently modified in harmony with their respectively diverse environments. This quite agrees with what we find in the American continent, where the difference of the lengths of the skull of a number of North-Mexican and Hudson-Bay wolves amounts to no less than twenty-five per cent. of the average size in the whole series *.

Altogether, we cannot yet see our way to advancing the Japanese variety to the rank of a species. Our view is in harmony with the opinion expressed by Professor Huxley, who, when specially studying the Canidæ, had the advantage of seeing a living specimen of this form. He says † :—"The Japanese *C. hodophylax*, of which there is a fine specimen now living in the Gardens, appears to be simply a small form of wolf; but in the absence of any accessible skulls of this form, I refrain from giving any definite opinion." Having ourselves now had the opportunity of examining two skulls, we are in a position to confirm the provisional opinion above quoted, based on the inspection of a living specimen.

Habitat. Treating, then, all the herein noted forms of the Wolf as mere varieties of the one species, *C. lupus*, we may say that the animal has an exceedingly wide geographical range, extending, as it appears to do, throughout the whole of the Palæarctic region, with the single exception of Africa north of the Sahara, and ranging southwards over Hindostan, without, however, extending to the island of Ceylon, nor into Burmah or the Indian Archipelago. In America it ranges over the whole continent northwards from the State of Guanajuato in Mexico.

* Alston, *loc. cit.* p. 66.
† P. Z. S. 1880, p. 274.

THE COMMON WOLF.

Dimensions (in centimeters) of the large Wolf from Moscow in the British Museum.

Length from end of snout to root of tail	122·0
,, of tail	38·0
,, from heel to end of longest digit	25·0
,, of ear	10·0

Skeletal and dental dimensions (in centimeters) of a specimen of the American variety.

Length of the cervical vertebræ	21·5
,, dorsal ,,	26·0
,, lumbar ,,	20·0
,, sacral ,,	4·0
,, caudal ,,	41·0
Length from front of atlas to hinder end of sacrum	71·5
Length of whole pectoral limb *	67·0
,, whole pelvic † ,,	76·0
,, humerus ‡	22·0
,, radius §	21·5
,, femur ‖	24·2
,, tibia ¶	24·0
,, index metacarpal	8·7
,, third ,,	9·8
,, metacarpal of pollex	3·0
,, whole pollex	6·3
,, last phalanx of third digit (manus)	2·6
,, index metatarsal	9·3
,, metatarsal of hallux	1·4
,, whole hallux	3·0
,, last phalanx of third digit (pes)	2·3
Basion to ovalion **	5·6
,, anterior end of basiphenoid, or sphenoideum	5·6
Sphenoideum to gnathion ††	16·1

---

* From upper end of humerus to distal end of manus.
† From upper end of femur to distal end of pes.
‡ From head of humerus to end of capitellum. § To root of styloid process.
‖ From head to condyloid surface. ¶ To root of malleolus.
** That is, from anterior margin of foramen magnum to the middle of a line joining the posterior margins of the oval foramina.
†† That is, to the anterior end of the premaxillæ.

CANIS LUPUS.

Dimensions (in centimeters) of the Skull and Teeth of a European Wolf.

Basion to ovalion . . . . 4·0
Basion to sphenoideum . . . . 5·9
Sphenoideum to gnathion . . . . 14·4
Length* of palate . . . . 10·7
Breadth † of palate . . . . 5·9
Length of nasals . . . . 8·9
Greatest breadth of nasals . . . . 2·0
Breadth of brain-case . . . . 6·3
„   zygomata . . . . 11·5
Length of first upper premolar, or $\underline{P.\,1}$ . . . . . . 0·7
„   second „   „   or $\underline{P.\,2}$ . . . . . . 1·4
„   third „   „   or $\underline{P.\,3}$ . . . . . . 1·55
„   fourth „   „   or $\underline{P.\,4}$ . . . . . . 2·4
„   first upper molar, or $\underline{M.\,1}$ . . . . . . 1·65
„   second „   „   or $\underline{M.\,2}$ . . . . . . 0·85
Breadth of fourth upper premolar, or $\underline{P.\,4}$ . . . . . . 1·1
„   first upper molar, or $\underline{M.\,1}$ . . . . . . 2·0
„   second „   „   or $\underline{M.\,2}$ . . . . . . 1·4
Length of first lower premolar, or $\overline{P.\,1}$ . . . . . . 0·5
„   second „   „   or $\overline{P.\,2}$ . . . . . . 1·25
„   third „   „   or $\overline{P.\,3}$ . . . . . . 1·35
„   fourth „   „   or $\overline{P.\,4}$ . . . . . . 1·5
„   first lower molar, or $\overline{M.\,1}$ . . . . . . 2·6
„   second „   „   or $\overline{M.\,2}$ . . . . . . 1·2
„   third „   „   or $\overline{M.\,3}$ . . . . . . 0·5
Breadth of first lower molar, or $\overline{M.\,1}$ . . . . . . 1·05
„   second „   „   or $\overline{M.\,2}$ . . . . . . 0·75
„   third „   „   or $\overline{M.\,3}$ . . . . . . 0·5

* Backwards to the base of the process projecting backwards from the middle of the posterior margin of the palate.

† Taken within the angle formed by the approximation of the fourth premolar and first molar tooth of either side.

THE ABYSSINIAN WOLF.

CANIS SIMENSIS.

Canis simensis, Rüppell, Neue Wirbelthiere z. d. Fauna von Abyssinien
gehörig (Frankfurt, 1835-1840), p. 39, pl. 14 (1835);
J. A. Wagner, Supplement to Schreber's Säugth., Abth. ii.
p. 382.
Simenia simensis, Gray, Proc. Zool. Soc. 1868, p. 506; id. Catalogue of
Carnivorous Mammalia, p. 192.

THE animal we have next to consider is plainly a very distinct species, and has no special affinity to any of the numerous varieties of the Common Wolf. It was discovered by Dr. Edward Rüppell during his travels in Abyssinia, in most of the provinces of which country it is, he says, to be met with. It hunts in packs, preying upon domestic sheep and small wild animals, but it is regarded as never being dangerous to man. The individual captured was taken in the mountains of Semyen (Samen or Simen), and is now in the British Museum. This specimen, which is the type of the species, is figured in our Plate VI.

The animal is about the size of a large sheep-dog.

The Abyssinian Wolf is remarkable for the great length and slenderness of its snout.

Its colour is a light yellowish reddish brown on the whole of the upper and almost all the outer parts. It is white round the mouth, more or less round the eyes, on the inner margins of the ears, on the chest, on the front of the fore legs below the wrist, on the front of the hind legs below the knee, around the vent, beneath and at the sides of the proximal half of the tail, inside the thighs, and on the hinder half of the belly. The distal half of the tail is blackish. Those lower

THE ABYSSINIAN WOLF.
Canis simensis.

parts which are not white (beneath the throat, the fore part of the belly, &c.) are lighter in colour than the upper parts. There is much black on the dorsum of the proximal half of the tail, and many of the hairs of the sides of the body and haunches are black for a considerable part of their length. There are also white hairs intermixed with them.

Habitat. Abyssinia.

	Centimeters.
Length from end of snout to root of tail	99
,, of tail	25
,, from heel to end of longest digit	20
,, of ear	11

Fig. 18.

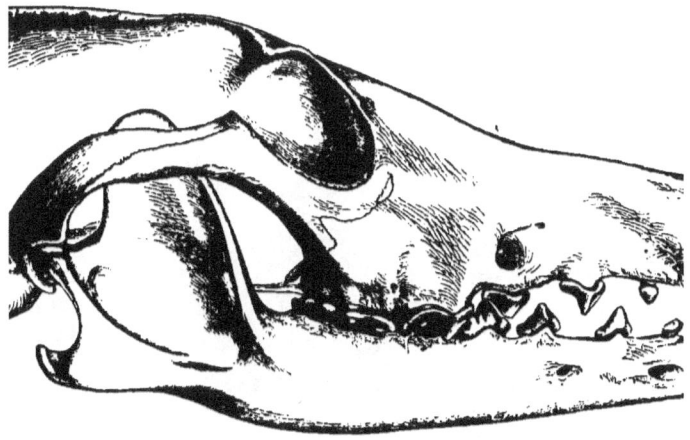

CANIS SIMENSIS.

Cranial and Dental Characters.

The skull of this species presents a great contrast to that of the Common Wolf, its facial part being so exceedingly long and slender.

The dentition is remarkable for the small size of the fourth upper premolar compared with the upper molars.

THE ABYSSINIAN WOLF.

Dimensions of Skull and Teeth.

	Centimeters.
Basion to ovalion	3·5
,, to sphenoideum	5·0
Sphenoideum to gnathion	13·8
Length of palate	10·2
Breadth of ,,	4·9
Length of nasals	8·8
Breadth of ,,	1·8
,, brain-case	6·2
,, zygomata	10·5
Length of $\overline{P.1}$	0·4
,, $\overline{P.2}$	0·85
,, $\overline{P.3}$	1·0
,, $\overline{P.4}$	1·6
,, $\overline{M.1}$	1·2
,, $\overline{M.2}$	0·8
Breadth of $\overline{P.4}$	0·6
,, $\overline{M.1}$	1·3
,, $\overline{M.2}$	1·0
Length of $\underline{P.1}$	0·4
,, $\underline{P.2}$	0·8
,, $\underline{P.3}$	0·9
,, $\underline{P.4}$	1·05
,, $\underline{M.1}$	1·9
,, $\underline{M.2}$	1·0
,, $\underline{M.3}$	0·4
Breadth of $\underline{M.1}$	0·7
,, $\underline{M.2}$	0·6
,, $\underline{M.3}$	0·4

THE MANED WOLF.

CANIS JUBATUS.

Canis jubatus, Desmarest, Mammalogie, p. 198; Rengger, Naturgesch.
 der Säugethiere von Paraguay, 1830, p. 138; Sykes, Proc.
 Zool. Soc. 1838, p. 111; J. A. Wagner's Supplement to
 Schreber's Säugth., Abth. ii. p. 380; Burmeister, Fauna
 Brasiliensis, p. 25, pls. 21 & 26; id. République Argentine,
 vol. iii. p. 140 (1879); Hensel, Zool. Garten, xiii. Jahrg.
 (1872), p. 76; Sclater, P. Z. S. 1877, p. 806, pl. 81;
 Flower, P. Z. S. 1879, p. 766.
Canis campestris, Maximilian, Prinz zu Wied, Beiträge, vol. ii. p. 334.
Chrysocyon jubatus, Hamilton Smith, Naturalist's Library, vol. ix. p. 242
 (1839).
Chrysocyon jubata, Gray, P. Z. S. 1868, p. 506; id. Catalogue of Carni-
 vorous Mammalia, p. 192.
Agouara gouazon, Azara, Essais sur l'histoire naturelle des Quadrupèdes
 du Paraguay, vol. i. p. 307 (1801).

This Wolf is not well named, since the rather long hair of the nape of the neck hardly merits to be called a "mane." The animal, however, is a very interesting one, and, like the Abyssinian Wolf, constitutes an exceedingly marked and distinct species. It is the largest of the *Canidæ* found in South America, where it inhabits Paraguay and parts adjacent, and notably the Province of Minas Geraes in Brazil. Its long limbs, long and large ears, and conspicuous coloration cause it to be easily recognized.

In spite of its large size, the Maned Wolf is by no means a dangerous animal, never attacking man. It is described by Azara as inhabiting low and moist situations, and as being of solitary habit, never hunting in packs. Although it may pursue wild deer, he declares that it commits no depredations on herds or flocks of domestic animals. It does, however, appear sometimes to pursue sheep*. An individual kept by Azara was very fond of rats, small birds, sugar-cane, and oranges, yet it never attempted to seize the domestic fowls, which from time to time came within its reach, and it agreed well with other domestic animals. In a wild state this Wolf devours pacas, agoutis, birds, reptiles, and even some insects. It will also eat plants, and is especially fond of the fruit of *Solanum lycocarpum*. It is said by Rengger to frequent the outskirts of the forests in Paraguay, near water; but it is also found amidst the high grass of the plains, but being an exceedingly timid animal—afraid even of small dogs—there is little opportunity of observing it save in confinement. Except in uninhabited regions, it passes the day in cover, sallying forth at night. The sexes approach each other in the autumn, at which season their loud cry is most frequently heard. Its local name " A-gua-a " is doubtless derived from the sound of this cry.

One reared in captivity came to recognize its name, even when pronounced by strangers, as also its master's voice. It avoided the light of midday, and generally slept from ten in the morning till five in the afternoon, and also for a time after midnight.

It will breed with the domestic dog, and the mongrel so produced is said by Dr. Lund to be an excellent animal for the chase. The female brings forth three or four young in the month of August.

The species seems to have been first made known, under the name of "Aguaria," by M. Dobritzhofer ('Geschichte der Abiponer,' i. p. 404 : Vienna, 1783), and to have been first brought alive to Europe in 1877, when it was exhibited in the Gardens of the Zoological Society of London.

The animal represented in our Plate VII. is one the skin of which is preserved in our National Collection, and which came from the Zoological Society after having lived some time in that Society's Gardens.

The body is clothed with long hairs, which are predominantly of a light yellowish reddish tinge. A median longitudinal patch from the nape of the neck backwards over the shoulders is black, as is also most

---

* According to Hensel, *loc. cit.* p. 77.

of the under surface of the lower jaw. There is also a black patch on the front of the lower part of each fore leg, and also from the heel downwards, on the middle of the posterior part. There is a good deal of black about the jaws generally, but the upper surfaces of the toes are clothed with whitish hairs. There are also many black hairs about the head. The front of the upper part of the throat and the hinder part of the under surface of the lower jaw are white. There are long white hairs within the ears, and a tuft of white hairs terminates the tail. The rest of the body is of a reddish-yellow colour, which may be darker across the shoulders, along the middle of the back, and on the outside of the ears.

The coloration of this animal is evidently subject to variation. The specimen figured by Burmeister is much more dull in colour than that represented by us, or than is shown in the plate in the 'Proceedings of the Zoological Society.' The latter has white around the mouth, no white patch on the front of the throat, and no transverse darkening across the shoulders. Burmeister's specimen has the white throat, but immediately beneath is a curiously shaped longitudinal black patch (wanting in our specimen and that figured by the Zoological Society) passing downwards and backwards, ending in a point on the front of the chest. The muzzle also is black.

Habitat. Brazil, Paraguay, and probably Uruguay and the northern parts of the Argentine Republic.

		Centimeters.
Length from the snout to the root of the tail	. . . .	120
,, of the tail	. . . .	25
,, from heel to end of longest digit	. . . . . .	20
,, of ear	. . . .	11

Skeletal and Dental Characters and Dimensions.

The skull is much elongated, and the angle of the mandible very small. The fourth upper premolar is exceptionally short, and the two true upper molars, taken together, exceptionally long in proportion.

Our woodcut is a representation of the skull which was extracted from the skin we have had figured.

The thorax is relatively small.

The radius, manus, and pes are very long.

The pollex is remarkably short, compared with the index of the manus, and the hallux still more so, compared with the index of the pes.

Fig. 19.

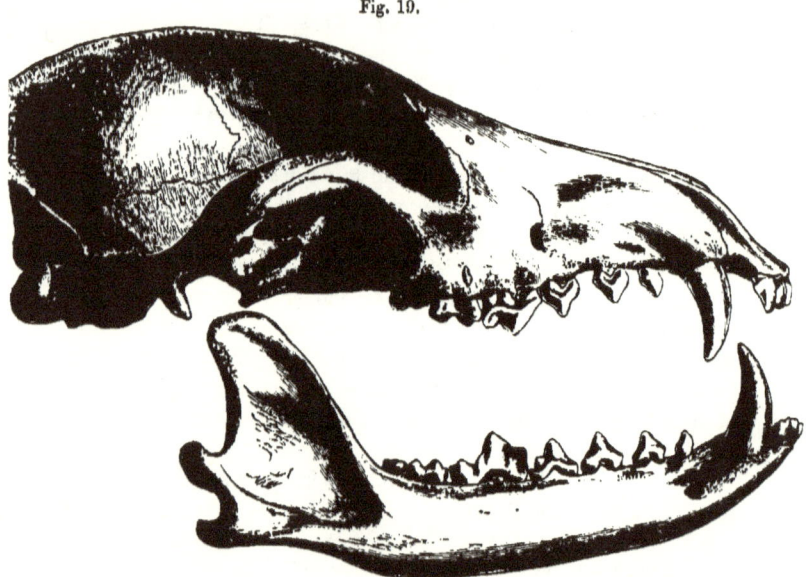

CANIS JUBATUS.

	Centimeters.
Length of cervical vertebræ	21·0
„ dorsal „	29·5
„ lumbar „	25·5
„ sacral „	4·5
„ caudal „	44·0
Length from front of atlas to hinder end of sacrum	80·5
Length of pectoral limb	69·0
„ pelvic „	79·5
„ humerus	23·3
„ radius	25·1

CANIS JUBATUS.

	Centimeters.
Length of femur	26·2
,, tibia	27·1
,, index metacarpal	9·0
,, third ,,	10·2
,, metacarpal of pollex	3·1
,, whole pollex	5·6
,, last phalanx of third digit (manus)	2·0
,, index metatarsal	11·2
,, metatarsal of hallux	1·4
,, whole hallux	2·2
,, last phalanx of third digit (pes)	1·8
Basion to ovalion	3·6
,, sphenoideum	5·1
Sphenoideum to gnathion	15·0
Length of palate	10·7
Breadth of ,,	5·5
Length of nasals	8·9
Greatest breadth of nasals	1·9
Breadth of brain-case	6·5
,, zygomata	12·7
Length of $\underline{\text{P. 1}}$	0·6
,, $\underline{\text{P. 2}}$	1·0
,, $\underline{\text{P. 3}}$	1·15
,, $\underline{\text{P. 4}}$	1·8
,, $\underline{\text{M. 1}}$	1·5
,, $\underline{\text{M. 2}}$	1·0
Breadth of $\underline{\text{P. 4}}$	0·7
,, $\underline{\text{M. 1}}$	1·6
,, $\underline{\text{M. 2}}$	1·2
Length of $\overline{\text{P. 1}}$	0·5
,, $\overline{\text{P. 2}}$	0·9
,, $\overline{\text{P. 3}}$	1·2
,, $\overline{\text{P. 4}}$	1·3
,, $\overline{\text{M. 1}}$	2·2
,, $\overline{\text{M. 2}}$	1·1
,, $\overline{\text{M. 3}}$	0·5
Breadth of $\overline{\text{M. 1}}$	0·85
,, $\overline{\text{M. 2}}$	0·80
,, $\overline{\text{M. 3}}$	0·45

THE ANTARCTIC WOLF.

CANIS ANTARCTICUS.

Canis antarcticus, Shaw, Gen. Zoology, vol. i. p. 331 (1800); Desmarest,
  Mammalogie, p. 199 (1820); Waterhouse, Zool. of H.M.S.
  'Beagle,' Mammalia, p. 7, plate 4 (1839); J. A. Wagner,
  Supplement to Schreber's Säugth., Abth. ii. p. 402; Burmeister, République Argentine, vol. iii. p. 142.
Dasicyon antarcticus, Hamilton Smith, Naturalist's Library, vol. ix.
  p. 252, pl. 23 (1839).
Pseudalopex antarcticus, Gray, Proc. Zool. Soc. 1868, p. 531; id. Catalogue of Carnivorous Mammalia, p. 200.
Antarctic Dog, Pennant, Quadrupeds, 1st edition, p. 240 (1781), 3rd
  edition, p. 257 (1793).
Loup-renard, Bougainville, Voyage autour du Monde, p. 65 (1771).

This small species of Wolf, only found in the Falkland Islands, where its numbers are rapidly diminishing, appears to have been first described by Dom. Pernetty in his 'Histoire d'un voyage aux isles Maloaines,' in 1763 and 1764[*]. The explorers of that expedition, seeing that the animals advanced towards them, were inclined to regard them as ferocious creatures; but Pernetty sagaciously observes:—" Peut-être cet animal n'est-il pas féroce, et ne venait-il se présenter et s'approcher de nous, que parce qu'il n'avait jamais vu d'hommes."

The sailors of Commodore Byron's expedition[†] were similarly astonished and not a little alarmed. "The master having been sent one day to sound the coast upon the south shore, reported at his return that four creatures of great fierceness, resembling wolves, ran up to their bellies in the water to attack the people in the boat, and that as

---

[*] See second edition, vol. i. p. 355.
[†] Voyage Round the World in H.M.S. 'Dolphin,' 1767.

they happened to have no fire-arms with them, they had immediately put the boat off in deep water."

In his account of the Voyage of the 'Beagle,'* Mr. Darwin observes :—" To this day their manners remain the same. They have been observed to enter a tent, and actually pull some meat from beneath the head of a sleeping seaman. The Gauchos, also, have frequently killed them in the evening by holding out a piece of meat in one hand, and in the other a knife ready to stick them."

The species was found in both the East and West Falkland Islands, but at the time of the visit of the 'Beagle' their numbers had already so decreased that they had altogether disappeared from the neck of land between San Salvador Bay and Berkeley Sound in the Eastern Island.

They largely feed on native geese, which, to escape them, have taken to build on outlying islets. Mr. Darwin also tells us that they do not go in packs, and are not nocturnal, though they wander about more in the evening than in broad day. Except during the breeding-season, they are generally silent.

They burrow in the ground like a fox, and Byron noticed pieces of seals they had mangled, and skins of penguins, scattered about the mouths of their holes. "To get rid of these creatures," he tells us, " our people set fire to the grass, so that the country was in a blaze as far as the eye could reach for several days, and we could see them running in great numbers to seek other quarters." Our figure, Plate VIII., is drawn from a specimen brought from East Falkland Island by Sir W. Burnet.

The fur of this animal is moderately long, with no very abundant underfur, which is of a pale brown colour. The hairs are yellow, commonly black at the apex, annulated with white on the upper parts of the body; those of the hinder part of the belly of a nearly uniform dirty white, and those of the chest yellowish, with black tips and greyish at the base.

The hairs of the lips, chin, and throat are white, and also the inner margins of the ears. The insides of the thighs are whitish. The limbs are fulvous externally, the feet somewhat paler. There may be a

* First edition, vol. iii. p. 250.

blackish tint on the crown of the head; the muzzle is somewhat lighter in colour. The tail, which is rather bushy, is coloured like the body for the proximal two fifths of its length, the next two fifths are black and its terminal fifth is white.

There are no special markings on the body except a black patch outside the lower part of the hind leg, just above the heel. There is also a darkening of the fur at the side of the lower part of the neck, so as to form an approach to a collar. The individuals inhabiting the Eastern Island are smaller and redder than those of West Falkland. The ears are always rather short.

Habitat. The Falkland Islands.

	Centimeters.
Length from snout to root of tail	97·0
,, of tail	28·5
,, from heel to end of longest digit	18·0
,, of ear	6·5

Skeletal and Dental Characters.

The sagittal ridge is flattened, and this flattened tract has a lyrate margin.

The suture between the palatine and maxillary bones does not advance so far forwards as a line joining the hinder margins of the inner tubercles of the fourth upper premolar.

In the skull examined the hind part of the third upper premolar is placed rather within the anterior part of the fourth premolar, but this may be an individual peculiarity.

Dimensions of Skull and Teeth.

	Centimeters.
Basion to ovalion	3·0
,, sphenoideum	4·2
Sphenoideum to gnathion	11·0
Length of palate	8·35
Breadth of ,,	5·0
Length of nasals	6·1
Greatest breadth of nasals	1·2

CANIS ANTARCTICUS.

	Centimeters.
Breadth of brain-case	5·2
,, zygomata	9·1
Length of $\underline{P.1}$	0·55
,, $\underline{P.2}$	0·95
,, $\underline{P.3}$	1·05
,, $\underline{P.4}$	1·8
,, $\underline{M.1}$	1·2
,, $\underline{M.2}$	0·65
Breadth of $\underline{P.4}$	0·8
,, $\underline{M.1}$	1·5
,, $\underline{M.2}$	0·9
Length of $\overline{P.1}$	0·4
,, $\overline{P.2}$	0·9
,, $\overline{P.3}$	1·0
,, $\overline{P.4}$	1·1
,, $\overline{M.1}$	1·9
,, $\overline{M.2}$	0·8
,, $\overline{M.3}$	0·4
Breadth of $\overline{M.1}$	0·8
,, $\overline{M.2}$	0·6
,, $\overline{M.3}$	0·4

THE PRAIRIE-WOLF OR COYOTÉ.

CANIS LATRANS.

Canis latrans, Say, Long's Expedition to Rocky Mountains, vol. i. p. 168
(1823) ; Harlan, Fauna Americana, p. 83 (1825) ;
Richardson, Fauna Boreali-Americana, p. 73, pl. 4 (1829) ;
J. A. Wagner, Supplement to Schreber's Säugthiere,
Abth. ii. p. 397 (1840) ; Maximilian, Prinz zu Wied,
Reise in Nord-America, vol. ii. p. 96 (1841) ; Audubon,
Quadrupeds of North America, vol. i. p. 150, pl. 71
(1851) ; Baird, Mammals of N. America (in Reports of
Mississippi Railroad), p. 113 (1857) ; id. Report of Mexican
Boundary, vol. ii. Mammals, p. 15 (1858); Coues,
American Naturalist, vol. i. p. 289 (1868) ; id. ibid. vol.
vii. p. 385 (1873) ; Alston, Biologia Centrali-Americana,
Mammals, p. 66.
Canis ochropus, Eschscholtz, Zool. Atlas, Heft iii. p. 1, pl. 11 (1829) ;
Gray, Zool. of H.M.S. ' Sulphur,' vol. i. p. 32, pl. 10 (1844).
Canis frustror, Woodhouse, Proc. Acad. N. Sc. Philadelphia, vol. v.
1850-51, p. 147.
Lyciscus latrans, Hamilton Smith, Jardine's Naturalist's Library, vol. ix.
p. 162, pl. 5 (1839); Frantzius, Archiv f. Naturg.
Jahrg. xxxv. vol. i. (1869).
Chrysocyon latrans, Gray, Proc. Zool. Soc. 1868, p. 506 ; id. Gray, Cat.
of Carnivorous Mammalia, p. 192.

THE Prairie-Wolf is an animal to be met with in large numbers and extends over a very wide range of country.

In reply to our inquiries, Dr. Coues has been kind enough to inform us, on the authority of Mr. Allen, that it has now been extirpated over a considerable portion of the United States, and has elsewhere suffered great reduction in numbers. It has probably wholly disappeared from large areas in Kansas, Nebraska, and elsewhere along the plains, where it was abundant half a century ago. Nevertheless, Dr. Coues had himself believed, what we find it difficult to doubt, that it may yet be found in various regions where the Common Wolf has now ceased to exist. Its less dangerous nature must have caused it to be less earnestly pursued, while its smaller size helps it to escape the observation of pursuers. Even nearly seventy years ago, the Coyoté was, Mr. Say tells us, far more numerous than the Wolf. That author (who first named it) has described various instances of its cunning and dexterity in avoiding different kinds of traps.

It appears to be certain that these animals sometimes hunt in packs, though Prinz Wied only happened to meet with them singly. The Coyoté ranges, at the least, as far as the fifty-fifth degree of north latitude, while it extends southwards through Central America into Costa Rica. According to Messrs. Godman and Salvin, it is of very local distribution in Guatemala. It is, however, very abundant in Northern Mexico, New Mexico, and Texas.

The animal has a bad name for its howling habit. As to this, Dr. Coues says, "One must have spent an hour or two vainly trying to sleep, before he is in a condition to appreciate the full force of the annoyance." The howling of two or three wolves gives the impression that a score are engaged, so many and so long-drawn are the notes, and so uninterruptedly are they continued by one individual after another. A short, sharp bark is followed by others, which grow faster and faster, becoming a long-drawn, lugubrious howl. They will give tongue at any time in the night, as well as morning and evening, though they are rarely or ever heard during the day. The Coyoté feeds greedily upon all kinds of animal substances, and has been known to follow for days in the trail of a travelling party, and to rush in each morning just after camp was broken, to obtain whatever eatable refuse was left behind. If it cannot get animal food, it will eat vegetable substances. In the fall of the year it feeds extensively on the fruit of the prickly pear, and eats juniper-berries in the winter.

All means are deemed good to destroy these animals and to obtain their fur; but it is very difficult to trap them, on account of their extreme wariness and cunning. They are therefore commonly enough poisoned by means of a dead carcass or meat left about for them, treated with strychnine. Aassafœtida is often rubbed in to make the bait more attractive, as the Prairie-Wolf is very fond of the odour of the last-named substance.

It is a very common animal in Texas, and thence westwards to the coast. Dr. Kennerly is quoted by Baird as saying that it is not very swift, and can be readily overtaken on the open plains by a horse of ordinary fleetness. He adds:—"I have never known it attack the larger quadrupeds. It seems to depend mostly for subsistence in the desert region in hunting rabbits, rats, young birds, &c. I have never known it to attack a man, unless wounded, when it defends itself with fierceness and desperation." It may, however, be killed by a single good-sized dog, although it has been known to make a very good fight against three. In the time of Richardson (1829) it was common on the plains of Missouri and Saskatchewan, the animals starting from the earth in great numbers on hearing the report of a gun, gathering round in expectation of getting the offal of some slaughtered animal.

Dr. Frantzius has expressed an opinion that it has only become an inhabitant of Central America in recent times. Towards the south of that region it seems of late to have much increased in numbers, and he thinks it probable that it only immigrated from the North after the invasion of the Spaniards had destroyed the polity and diminished the population of the semi-civilized states which were conquered by them.

The Prairie-Wolves breed in retreats among rocks or underground burrows. The young are born in May and June, and number five or six in a litter, and, it is said, sometimes ten. These animals breed readily with domestic dogs.

Our illustration (Plate IX.) is taken from an individual living in the Zoological Society's collection.

The colour of the Prairie-Dog is said by Coues to vary somewhat with the season, from a rather bright tawny brown in summer, to greyish or quite grey in winter, overlaid, in either case, with a clouding of black. This black tint is not uniform, but tends to form stripes along the back and across the shoulders and hips. The underparts are dingy white. The upper surface of the muzzle, the outside of the ears and of all four legs are mostly of a uniform tawny tint. The Coyoté is really a much more slender animal than it appears to be, on account of the long and copious coat with which its body is clothed.

Habitat. From the south of Costa Rica to Canada, in at least 55° N. lat.

	Centimeters.
Length from snout to root of tail	92·0 to 101·0
,, of tail	32·0
,, from heel to end of longest digit	18·0
,, of ear	14·0

Skeletal and Dental Characters.

The skull possesses no distinctive characters, nor have we been able to detect any in the shape of the teeth.

	Centimeters.
Length of cervical vertebræ	16·0
,, dorsal ,,	21·5
,, lumbar ,,	18·0
,, sacral ,,	3·5
,, caudal ,,	36·0
Length from front of atlas to hinder end of sacrum	59·0
Length of pectoral limb	44·5
,, pelvic ,,	51·0
,, humerus	15·0
,, radius	15·2
,, femur	16·5
,, tibia	17·0
,, index metacarpal	5·6
,, third ,,	6·6
,, metacarpal of pollex	3·0
,, whole pollex	3·4
,, last phalanx of third digit (manus)	1·4
,, index metatarsal	6·85
,, metatarsal of hallux	1·1
,, whole hallux	1·9
,, last phalanx of third digit (pes)	1·3
Length from basion to ovalion	2·6
,, ,, to sphenoideum	4·3
,, sphenoideum to gnathion	12·5

THE PRAIRIE-WOLF.

Another specimen.

	Centimeters.
Basion to ovalion	3·1
„ sphenoideum	4·5
Sphenoideum to ovalion	12·5
Length of palate	9·1
Breadth of „	4·8
Length of nasals	8·1
Greatest breadth of nasals	1·4
Breadth of brain-case	5·7
„ zygomata	9·6
Length of $\underline{P.\,1}$	0·6
„ $\underline{P.\,2}$	1·2
„ $\underline{P.\,3}$	1·3
„ $\underline{P.\,4}$	2·0
„ $\underline{M.\,1}$	1·2
„ $\underline{M.\,2}$	0·6
Breadth of $\underline{P.\,4}$	0·8
„ $\underline{M.\,1}$	1·65
„ $\underline{M.\,2}$	1·1
Length of $\overline{P.\,1}$	0·4
„ $\overline{P.\,2}$	1·05
„ $\overline{P.\,3}$	1·20
„ $\overline{P.\,4}$	1·4
„ $\overline{M.\,1}$	2·2
„ $\overline{M.\,2}$	1·0
„ $\overline{M.\,3}$	0·5
Breadth of $\overline{M.\,1}$	0·8
„ $\overline{M.\,2}$	0·7
„ $\overline{M.\,3}$	0·4

THE INDIAN JACKAL.

CANIS AUREUS.

Canis aureus, Linn. Syst. Nat. 12th edit. vol. i. p. 59 (1766); Schreber,
    Säugth. Theil iii. p. 365, pl. 4 ; Cuvier, Règne An. vol. i.
    p. 154; Desmarest, Mammalogic, p. 200; J. A. Wagner's
    Supplem. Abth. ii. p. 383; Pallas, Zoographia, vol. i.
    p. 39, pl. 3 ; Jerdon, Mammals of India, p. 142 ; Hodgson,
    Asiatic Researches, vol. xviii. p. 237 ; Blanford, Fauna
    Brit. India, p. 140.
Canis syriacus, Ehrenberg, Symb. Phys. z. pl. 16 (1832).
Lupus aureus, Kämpfer, Amœnitatum Exoticarum politico - physico -
    medicarum, p. 403 (1712) ; Gray, Catalogue of Car-
    nivorous Mammalia, p. 188.
Sacalius aureus, Hamilton Smith, Jardine's Naturalist's Library, vol. ix.
    p. 214, pl. 15 (1839).
Oxygöus indicus, Hodgson, Journal Asiatic Soc. Bengal, vol. x. p. 908
    (1841).
Le Chacal, Buffon, Hist. Nat. vol. xiii. p. 255; F. Cuvier, Hist. Nat.
    des Mammifères, vol. ii. ; Isid. Geoffroy St.-Hilaire, Expé-
    dition de Morée, pp. 15 and 19–27 (1833).

The Indian Jackal has obtained a much wider range than the Indian Wolf. It is found not only throughout the peninsula of Hindostan, but also in Ceylon, Burmah, and Pegu. It is also to be met with both in forests and open plains, and both in the low lands and at considerable altitudes—that is, at an elevation of 3000 to 4000 feet. It even makes its appearance in populous cities, where its almost omnivorous habits cause it to be a useful scavenger ; although it not only clears off garbage, but will occasionally seize a fowl or other small domestic animal. Outside the towns, Jackals will eat any animal they can manage to subdue, and though they may be met with singly or in pairs they sometimes hunt in troops, especially at night, when they may make a great howling. Sickly sheep and goats readily fall a prey to them, as well as any antelopes which have been lamed or wounded. In default of animal food, they will readily eat fruit or sugar-canes, of which they are said to be fond, as well as of the bêr fruit (*Zizyphus jujuba*) and ripe coffee-berries. According to Dr. Jerdon, the Jackal is easily pulled down by greyhounds, but gives an excellent run with foxhounds. He adds that they are very tenacious of life, and "sham dead" so well as to deceive even experienced sportsmen. On one occasion a Jackal came to the aid of another individual—possibly its mate—which had been seized by greyhounds, attacking them furiously although Dr. Jerdon was close by on horseback.

The cry of the Jackal is described by Mr. Blanford as consisting of two parts—" a long wailing howl three or four times repeated, each repetition in a note a little higher than the preceding, and then a succession of usually three quick yelps, also repeated two or three times. The common Anglo-Indian version of '*Dead Hindoo ; where, where, where,*' gives some idea of the call."

Besides its ordinary cry, it will utter another, very distinguishable one when it finds itself in the vicinity of a tiger or leopard. It is doubtless a cry of terror and warning, as the leopard preys on jackals, and there can be little doubt but that a hungry tiger would make short work of one. It appears to have been this habit which has given rise to the fable of the Jackal being the "lion's provider," and which is current in India [*].

The Jackal breeds in burrows much as does a fox, and produces about four at a birth. It breeds freely with the domestic dog.

The Indian Jackal varies much in size and somewhat in coloration, and it is a nice question whether the Common Jackal of North Africa should or should not be regarded as of the same species. If they are united, then the European Jackal must also belong to that one species.

---

[*] See H. Torrens on "Native Impressions regarding the Natural History of certain Animals" (Journal of the Asiatic Soc. of Bengal, vol. xviii. part ii. p. 788).

If they be separated, then another question arises as to whether the European Jackal is altogether distinct, or, if not distinct, whether it is to be classed with the Indian or with the North-African Jackal.

The specimen represented by our artist (Plate X.) came from Northern India to the British Museum through Colonel Cobbe.

Certainly the differences of coloration which exist between these forms is not nearly so great as those which are to be found to occur between the different local varieties of *C. lupus*.

We are nevertheless inclined, for reasons which will be stated shortly, to keep the North-African and Indian Jackals distinct; but we only do so provisionally, and freely recognize the full right of other naturalists to take the opposite view. It is a mere question of probability, and a very obscure one. The reasons why we prefer to keep them provisionally distinct is that though the difference between the two forms (African and Indian) is slight as regards coloration, yet it appears to be a very constant one. Out of seventeen skins of the Indian form, we have only found one which is wanting in the main characteristic as to difference of hue. The ears also are relatively shorter than in the North-African form.

But there is another character to which we attach greater weight. However much the different races of Wolves differ in size, we have not succeeded in finding any constant distinctive characters in the form of the skull or the proportions of the lobes of any of the teeth. So far as we have been able to observe, such differences do exist between the Indian and the North-African Jackals. Should further observations do away with this distinction—as may very probably turn out to be the case—then, of course, the North-African form must be united in one species with the Indian one, as we have already united the Indian and American Wolves in one species with the European Wolf.

Having so determined, the next question is, in which category shall we rank the European Jackal?

The European form is found in Greece and Turkey, and as far west as Dalmatia, nor can we doubt but that the Jackal of the Caucasus and of Asia Minor is of the same species as that of European Turkey.

Unfortunately we have had but little opportunity of examining specimens from these localities, but in our National Collection there is a skin * and skull of one from Anatolia, presented by Sir Charles Fellowes. If we may judge from this example, then this local variety agrees both as to coloration and dental characters, not with the North-African Jackal, but with that of India.

In 1833 there was published an account of the French exploration of the Morea, the Mammals being described by M. Isidore Geoffroy St.-Hilaire. That illustrious naturalist was disposed to regard the Jackals of the Morea, of India, and of North Africa as forming together but a single species, which, we have already admitted, may well be the case. Nevertheless, according to his description, the colour of the limbs and head of the Crimean Jackal agrees with what we find in the Indian Jackal, and not in the North-African one He lays much stress on the greater amount of black upon the back of the Crimean form; but this is just one of those characters in which we have found a considerable amount of variation in skins all derived from the same locality.

He describes the Jackal as being very common in the Morea, hunting in packs, uttering cries like the wail of an infant, and suddenly surprising a traveller by their proximity, when the pack is itself invisible. They not only, as usual, feed on carrion, but he found they had the habit of disinterring dead bodies. During the war of liberation they would also enter an encampment at night and eat any boots and shoes they could find. They were camp-followers, and the scientific expedition found regions to be free of them where they abounded during the war; they had left with the troops.

The general colour is a pale dirty yellow, with more or less of a reddish tinge mixed with a variable amount of black on the upper part of the body, and a brown underfur. The limbs are decidedly rufous, as also between and behind the ears and on the muzzle; the backs of the ears are tawny. The underparts of the body are always paler and sometimes almost white. The tail is reddish brown, except the tip, which is black, but the hairs on the lower portion of the tail are also

* No. 44. 7. 13. 3.

black towards their apices. There is generally a tendency to develop two black lines over the haunches, the two lines converging towards the tail. Examples of melanism and albinism have been met with, and the colour may be intensified to bright rufous. We have also seen a specimen from Nepal, and another from the Deccan, of a dusky tint.

Habitat. India, Ceylon, Burmah, and southwards to south of Pegu. South-western Asia to Caucasus, Asia Minor, Turkey, Greece, and Dalmatia.

	Centimeters.
Length from snout to root of tail	80·0
,, of tail	19·5
,, from heel to end of longest digit	14·4
,, of ear	5·0

Sometimes the ear is longer. The maximum we have found is 6·5.

Skeletal and Dental Characters.

When the skull is viewed in profile, and compared with that of the Wolf, the elevation between the orbits and the antero-posterior concavity of the dorsum of the muzzle are both very slight; the two tubercles behind the principal cusp of the third upper molar are very small.

	Centimeters.
Basion to ovalion	2·6
,, sphenoideum	3·9
Sphenoideum to gnathion	9·3
Length of palate	6·6
Breadth ,,	4·2
Length of nasals	5·1
Breadth of ,,	1·3
,, brain-case	4·7
,, zygomata	7·6
Length of P. 1	0·45
,, P. 2	0·7
,, P. 3	0·9
,, P. 4	1·6

THE INDIAN JACKAL.

	Centimeters.
Length of $\overline{M.1}$	1·1
,, $\overline{M.2}$	0·7
Breadth of $\overline{P.4}$	0·6
,, $\overline{M.1}$	1·3
,, $\overline{M.2}$	0·9
Length of $\overline{P.1}$	0·45
,, $\overline{P.2}$	0·7
,, $\overline{P.3}$	0·8
,, $\overline{P.4}$	1·0
,, $\overline{M.1}$	1·8
,, $\overline{M.2}$	0·9
,, $\overline{M.3}$	0·3
Breadth of $\overline{M.1}$	0·7
,, $\overline{M.2}$	0·5
,, $\overline{M.3}$	0·3

41

THE NORTH-AFRICAN JACKAL.

CANIS ANTHUS.

Canis anthus, F. Cuvier, Hist.' Nat. des Mammifères, vol. ii. (1824);
   Rüppell, Atlas, Zool. p. 44, pl. 17 (1826).
Canis variegatus, Rüppell, Atlas, Zool. p. 31, pl. 10 (1826).
Canis lupaster, Ehrenberg, Symb. Phys. ff. (1832).
Lupus anthus, Gray, Proc. Zool. Soc. 1868, p. 502.
Dieba anthus, Gray, Catalogue of Carnivorous Mammalia, p. 189.
Satalius barbarus, Hamilton Smith, Jardine's Naturalist's Library,
   vol. ix. p. 218 (1839).
Chacal d'Alger, Isid. Geoffroy St.-Hilaire, Expédition de Morée, vol. iii.
   Zoologie, p. 22.

As we observed in treating of the last described species, it is only with much doubt and hesitation that we provisionally separate the North-African Jackal from its Indian analogue. The specimens which we have had the opportunity of examining, and which came from Abyssinia as well as from Egypt and Tunis, all agreed, however, in having a distinct tone of coloration from that which we found to prevail in Indian Jackals, as well as in possessing a different form of skull and somewhat differently shaped premolar teeth.

It is a question whether or not the *C. variegatus* of Rüppell is a variety of this species: such is the opinion of Mr. Blanford. We will consider the question when treating of the species next described.

The habits and mode of life of the African Jackal are similar to those of its Asiatic and European congeners. Though the African kind seems to be generally larger than the Indian one, a considerable variation occurs in the size of individual specimens. There is also much variation as to the length of the fur and the amount of black hair to be found amongst it.

G

The ears of *C. anthus* are somewhat longer relatively than those of *C. aureus*.

The specimen we have selected for our illustration (Plate XI.) is one which was brought from Abyssinia by Captain Harris, and is in our National Collection.

We identify this species with the *C. variegatus* of Rüppell, mainly on the authority of Mr. Blanford, who has had so large an opportunity of becoming acquainted with this species and with that next to be described, in their native country. Indeed the specific distinctness of *C. variegatus* has been given up by its first describer, Rüppell himself. Mr. Blanford met with numerous individuals of the form he identifies with *C. variegatus* in the highlands of Abyssinia, at an elevation of 5000 feet. Rüppell's figure represents the ears as somewhat longer than those of *C. anthus*, a character in which it agrees with the form next to be described; but the ears of *C. anthus* are long compared with those of *C. aureus*, and they may have been either stretched, or may be somewhat exaggerated in the drawing.

The coloration of this species is similar to that of *C. aureus*, except that the sides of the body are greyer and the limbs somewhat less rufous. The backs of the ears are fawn-coloured. The amount of black on the back varies as to extent and disposition of the markings, for they tend to produce rather an irregularly-shaped blotch of black, than a stripe, over each haunch. The underparts may or may not be whitish in tint. The end of the tail we have found black, but F. Cuvier does not so represent it; whereas more than half the tail is black in Rüppell's figure.

Habitat. Africa north of the Sahara, Egypt and Abyssinia.

	Centimeters.
Length from snout to root of tail	81·0
,, of tail	29·0
,, from heel to end of longest digit	16·5
,, of ear	8·0

CANIS ANTHUS. 43

Cranial and Dental Characters.

The skull of *C. anthus* differs from that of *C. aureus* in its greater elevation between the orbits, and in the consequent greater antero-posterior concavity of the dorsum of the muzzle in front of that elevation.

Fig. 20.

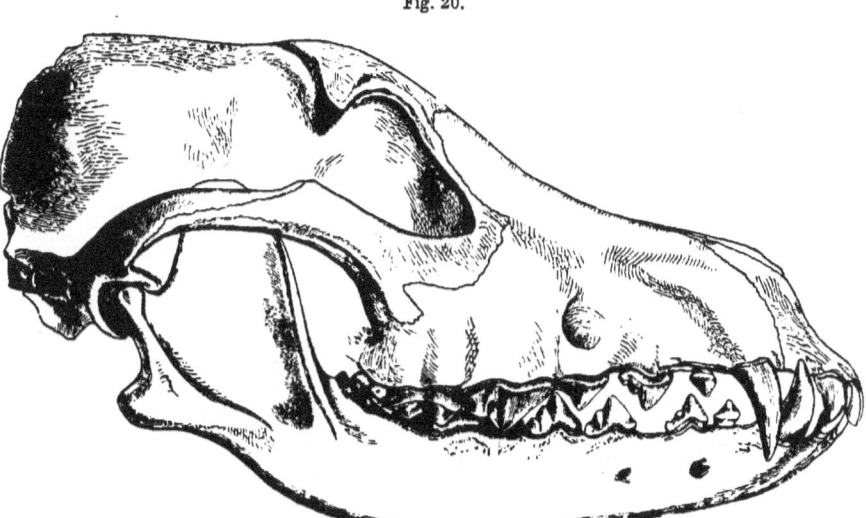

CANIS ANTHUS.

The anterior palatine foramina are also larger, and the small posterior tubercles of the third upper premolar are more developed.

	Centimeters.
Basion to ovalion	2·8
,, sphenoideum	4·0
Sphenoideum to gnathion	10·9
Length of palate	7·8
Breadth ,,	4·6

THE NORTH-AFRICAN JACKAL.

	Centimeters.
Length of nasals	6·1
Breadth ,,	1·5
Width of brain-case	5·2
,, zygomata	8·9
Length of $\underline{P.1}$	0·5
,, $\underline{P.2}$	0·9
,, $\underline{P.3}$	1·0
,, $\underline{P.4}$	1·6
,, $\underline{M.1}$	1·2
,, $\underline{M.2}$	0·7
Breadth of $\underline{P.4}$	0·65
,, $\underline{M.1}$	1·50
,, $\underline{M.2}$	0·90
Length of $\overline{P.1}$	0·45
,, $\overline{P.2}$	0·80
,, $\overline{P.3}$	0·95
,, $\overline{P.4}$	1·05
,, $\overline{M.1}$	1·90
,, $\overline{M.2}$	0·90
,, $\overline{M.3}$	0·40
Breadth of $\overline{M.1}$	0·70
,, $\overline{M.2}$	0·60
,, $\overline{M.3}$	0·30

THE BLACK-BACKED JACKAL.

CANIS MESOMELAS.

Canis mesomelas, Schreber, Säugthiere, Theil iii. p. 370, pl. 95 (1778);
  Desmarest, Mammalogie, p. 201 (1820); Smith, S. African
  Quart. Journal, vol. ii. p. 85 (1825); Rüppell, Neue
  Wirbelthiere, p. 39 (1835–40); J. A. Wagner, Supplement
  to Schreber's Säugth., Abth. ii. p. 396 (1840); Blanford, Observations on Geol. and Zool. of Abyssinia, p. 237 (1870).
Vulpes mesomelas, Gray, Proc. Zool. Soc. 1868, p. 150; id. Cat. of
  Carnivorous Mammalia, p. 203.
Thous mesomelas, Hamilton Smith, Jardine's Nat. Library, vol. ix.
  p. 193, pl. 12.

This very handsome and strongly marked form of Jackal is well represented in our National Museum, where there are seven skins of it from South Africa, and two from Abyssinia. It is a most conspicuous animal, from the very red colour of the side of its body and its very black back, the two diversely coloured spaces being sharply marked off along a definite line, as shown in our Plate XII., which represents an adult male, and is one of the most distinctly marked individuals we have ever seen. It was brought from the Anseba by Mr. Blanford, F.R.S. This species appears to be widely spread over South Africa, and its earliest designation was "Jackal of the Cape of Good Hope."

The form of Jackal which Rüppell found in Abyssinia was named by him *Canis variegatus*. Its specific distinctness is extremely doubtful, and has, as already said [*], been given up as a species by its describer himself. Mr. W. T. Blanford, in his expedition to Abyssinia in

---

[*] See above, p. 42.

1867–68, occasionally met with examples of *C. mesomelas* in the pass between Komayli and Senafé, and much more frequently about the base of the hills west of Massowa, and on the Anseba. He also tells us * that at least on one occasion Jackals of this species were met with in the immediate vicinity of a lion, attention having been called to the place where that formidable beast lay hidden by the peculiar motions of the Jackals. As they walked slowly and warily away from his vicinity, they constantly directed their glances towards the bush which concealed him.

Mr. Blanford did not find the Black-backed Jackal in the highlands of Abyssinia (that is, at an elevation above 5000 feet); but met with numerous individuals of the common Jackal of the country, which, as before said, he regards as being *C. variegatus* of Rüppell.

The colour of the young is a uniform dusky brown. The adult is always brightly coloured, but the sharpness of the distinction between the back and the sides, and the extent and intensity of the black colour of the back vary considerably. The hairs of the body are all, or almost all, annulated, and each is white a considerable part of its extent, as well as black and yellow. Thus the superficial aspect of different parts of the body is apt to differ, and present sometimes nearly black, sometimes nearly white, patches of colour. The black patch on the back is widest over the shoulders, then narrowing backwards. The sides of the body are red. The limbs and proximal part of the tail are reddish yellow or yellowish red; the end of the tail is black. The underpart of the lower jaw, chest, belly, and inner side of the limbs are white or whitish. The back of the ears are light yellowish brown, well clothed with hair without and within.

It seems to me most probable that the Jackal noticed by Dr. T. Noack † under the name *C. hagenbeckii* is a form of *C. mesomelas* in which the hairs of the back are somewhat longer than usual. Species have been proposed by Hemprich and Ehrenberg under the names *lupaster*, *sacer*, and *riparius*, but they are so slightly characterized

---

* *Op. cit.* p. 238.
† See Zoologische Garten, xxvii. Jahrgang (1886), p. 233.

that our experience of the variability of the Jackals convinces us that further notice of them would occasion mere waste of time.

Habitat. Southern Africa and Abyssinia.

	Centimeters.
Length from snout to root of tail	91·0
,, of tail	31·0
,, from heel to end of longest digit	16·0
,, of ear	10·0

Cranial and Dental Characters.

The skull is not so elevated between the orbits as in *C. anthus*, though more so than in *C. aureus*, but, as in the latter, the anterior palatine foramina are small. The shape of the third upper premolar agrees with that of *C. aureus* (*i. e.* the tubercles behind the principal cusp are very small), and differs from that of *C. anthus*.

	Centimeters.
Basion to ovalion	2·56
Ovalion to sphenoideum	3·75
Sphenoideum to gnathion	9·9
Length of palate	7·4
Breadth ,,	4·1
Length of nasals	5·2
Breadth of ,,	1·4
,, brain-case	5·1
,, zygomata	8·4
Length of $\underline{P.1}$	0·45
,, $\underline{P.2}$	0·80
,, $\underline{P.3}$	0·90
,, $\underline{P.4}$	1·60
,, $\underline{M.1}$	1·10
,, $\underline{M.2}$	0·60
Breadth of $\underline{P.4}$	0·50
,, $\underline{M.1}$	1·40
,, $\underline{M.2}$	1·00

THE BLACK-BACKED JACKAL.

	Centimeters.
Length of $\overline{P.1}$	0·35
,, $\overline{P.2}$	0·70
,, $\overline{P.3}$	0·80
,, $\overline{P.4}$	1·00
,, $\overline{M.1}$	1·70
,, $\overline{M.2}$	0·90
,, $\overline{M.3}$	0·50
Breadth of $\overline{M.1}$	0·60
,, $\overline{M.2}$	0·60
,, $\overline{M.3}$	0·40

THE SIDE-STRIPED JACKAL.

CANIS ADUSTUS.

Canis adustus, Sundevall, Öfversigt af Kongl. Vetenskaps-Akademiens
　　Förhandlingar, Tredje Årgången, p. 121 (1846); Peters,
　　Reise nach Mossambique, Zool. Säugeth. p. 125.
Canis lateralis, Sclater, Proc. Zool. Soc. 1870, p. 279, pl. 23.
Vulpes adusta, Gray, P. Z. S. 1868, p. 515; id. Cat. of Carnivorous
　　Mammalia, p. 203.

THIS elegant species had its most marked character, its light-coloured lateral stripe, first adequately called attention to by Dr. Sclater, who proposed for it the new name of *C. lateralis.* It is, however, we think the same kind of animal as that which was described by Sundevall and named *Canis adustus.* Not only do the skins preserved in the British Museum show that there are great individual differences as to the distinctness of the lateral stripe, but the very skin of the type of the species, which, when it was figured, had the stripe very plain and distinct, has since come almost entirely to lose it. This typical skin is preserved in our National Collection; but we have not thought well to have it represented on our Plate XIII., because of its present defective condition. We have preferred to figure the skin of a fine male brought by Mr. H. H. Johnston from Kilimanjaro, which well shows the typical character of the species in its most perfect form. The individuals described by Sundevall and Peters were doubtless examples in which the lateral stripe was as little noticeable as that of the type of the species has now become. The character by which *C. adustus* most differs from all the other Jackals is the dark colour of the hinder surface of the ears, and this character also exists in the striped specimens, which cannot be doubted to be examples of the form called *C. lateralis* by Sclater.

H

This animal was met with by M. Du Chaillu in the Gorilla region of Africa. He says *:—" Before we got to town again I shot a *mboyo*, a very shy animal, of the wolf kind, with long yellowish hair and straight ears. I have often watched these beasts surrounding and chasing small game for themselves. The drove runs very well together; and as their policy is to run round and round they soon bewilder, tire out, and capture any animal of moderate endurance."

Mr. H. H. Johnston found the species to be very common near a village on Kilimanjaro, to which it was attracted by the chance of stealing refuse or other food. He did not find it elsewhere much above 3000 feet, but the locality where he found it was 5000 feet high.

The snout is long and slender; and the ear is not quite so long relatively as in *C. mesomelas*, but is longer than in the other Jackals.

The colour of *C. adustus* is yellowish brown, paler beneath; the backs of the ears dark brown. On each side in the typical specimen a light-coloured line runs from behind the shoulder-blade, upwards and backwards to the side of the root of the tail; this light-coloured stripe is bordered by black at its lower margin.

The greater part of the tail is black, but the apical portion is white, although in two specimens in the British Museum there are but a few white hairs at the tip of the tail.

Habitat. Central to Southern Africa.

	Centimeters.
Length from snout to root of tail	86·0
,, of tail	33·0
,, from elbow to end of longest digit	17·2
,, of ear	7·0

Cranial and Dental Characters.

The skull of this animal is remarkable for the length of the palate, which extends backwards beyond a line joining the posterior margin of the hinder true molars.

* 'Explorations in Equatorial Africa' (1861), p. 243.

One skull * we found to present the singular anomaly of having five premolars on the right side above, an extra one being introduced between the normal first and second premolars. That such is the case is shown by the presence of a corresponding diastema between the first and second upper premolars on the left side of the skull.

		Centimeters.
Basion to ovalion		2·9
Ovalion to sphenoideum		4·0
Sphenoideum to gnathion		10·6
Length of palate		8·1
Breadth ,,		4·1
Length of nasals		6·4
Breadth of ,,		1·4
,, brain-case		4·7
,, zygomata		8·0
Length of $\underline{P.1}$		0·4
,, $\underline{P.2}$		0·7
,, $\underline{P.3}$		0·85
,, $\underline{P.4}$		1·5
,, $\underline{M.1}$		1·1
,, $\underline{M.2}$		0·7
Breadth of $\underline{P.4}$		0·6
,, $\underline{M.1}$		1·3
,, $\underline{M.2}$		0·9
Length of $\overline{P.1}$		0·2
,, $\overline{P.2}$		0·7
,, $\overline{P.3}$		0·85
,, $\overline{P.4}$		1·0
,, $\overline{M.1}$		1·7
,, $\overline{M.2}$		0·9
,, $\overline{M.3}$		0·5
Breadth of $\overline{M.1}$		0·6
,, $\overline{M.2}$		0·6
,, $\overline{M.3}$		0·4

* No. 71. 5. 27. 8 in the British Museum Collection.

THE MAGELLANIC DOG OR COLPEO.

CANIS MAGELLANICUS.

Canis magellanicus, Gray, Proc. Zool. Soc. 1836, p. 88; id. Mag.
   Nat. Hist. 1837, p. 578; Waterhouse, Zoology H.M.S.
   'Beagle,' Mammalia, p. 10, plate 5 (1839); J. A. Wagner,
   Suppl. to Schreber's Säugth., Abth. ii. p. 431; Gay, Hist.
   de Chile, Zool. vol. i. p. 59.
Canis (Pseudalopex) magellanicus, Burmeister, Fauna Brasiliens, pp. 24
   and 51 (1856); id. République Argentine, vol. iii.
   p. 146.
Pseudalopex magellanicus, Gray, Proc. Zool. Soc. 1868, p. 512; id.
   Cat. Carnivorous Mammalia, p. 199.
Cerdocyon magellanicus, Hamilton Smith, Jardine's Nat. Library, vol. ix.
   p. 266, pl. 30 (1839).
Canis culpaeus, Molina, Compendio d. l. hist. nat. del Regno de Chili,
   p. 330; id. Essai sur l'hist. nat. du Chili (Paris, 1789),
   p. 274.

THIS handsome animal is represented in our National Collection by two skins from Tierra del Fuego, and two other skins from Chile, with several skulls and skeletons. Like so many other species of the Canidæ, it is evidently subject to individual variations, probably due to habitually different climates or the change of the seasons. The fur of both the specimens from the extreme south is much longer than that of those from Chile, although the skulls of specimens from both localities are alike.

The species was first made known by the Abbé Molina, who, however, believed it to be the same species as that described by us under the name of *C. antarcticus*. In some respects its habits appear to be similar, for the Abbé tells us that he often met with it in the woods, and that each time he did so, if he stood still, it would come towards him, stopping every now and then and staring at him, and then turned and went away. It was an animal not at all feared, and with rather a weak voice, and had the habit of burrowing like a fox.

The first specimen brought to this country was obtained by Captain P. P. King, during his survey of the coast of South America, at Port Famine in Tierra del Fuego. It was this individual which was named *C. magellanicus* by Dr. Gray, and is the type of the species. It is preserved in the British Museum and is represented on our Plate XIV.

Mr. Darwin brought back in the 'Beagle' another individual, which he had found in the Valley of Copiapó, in the northern part of Chile. It thus, as Mr. Darwin observes *, has a range of the western coast of South America from the humid and entangled forests of Tierra del Fuego to the almost absolutely desert country of Northern Chile—a distance of fully 1600 miles. He neither found it, nor did he believe it was to be found, on the Atlantic side of the continent. The inhabitants told him that the creature still has the curious habit of approaching near to a man to stare at him, which Molina described, and this in spite of so strange a habit having been the occasion of great numbers being killed. Though not feared, it is very much disliked by the inhabitants on account of its craft and destructiveness. Two of these animals are said to have destroyed nearly two hundred fowls at a farmhouse in the Copiapó valley.

Though apparently nocturnal, it also wanders about by day, and is very strong and fleet. " When riding one day," Mr. Darwin tells us, " accompanied by a half-bred greyhound, I happened to come across one of these " animals, " and although the ground was, in the first part of the chase, level, it soon entirely distanced its pursuer. Whilst running it barked so like a dog, that until it had run some way ahead of the greyhound, I could not tell from which animal the noise proceeded. After the Colpeo had reached the mountains, it made a sudden bend from its course, and returned in a nearly parallel line, but at the base of a steep cliff of rocks it seated itself on its

* Zool. of H.M.S. 'Beagle,' Mammalia, p. 11.

haunches, and seemed to listen with much satisfaction to the dog, which was running the scent on the mountain side above its head."

The Colpeo is often spoken of as the Magellanic "Fox," but it has no marked similarity to that animal, and it is a considerably larger and stouter animal than is the European fox. As we have said, it was confounded by Molina with *C. antarcticus*, but it is a greyer and less red animal, and the end of the tail is not white but black. It is also a decidedly smaller animal.

It may have a long, thick, and loose coat with abundant woolly underfur, with long hair under the feet beneath the pads; or it may have short hair and more scanty underfur, with no long hair under the feet.

The hairs are much annulated, and the disposition of the apparently resulting general coloration is thus irregular and varied. The back, however, is dark, with more or less black. The sides of the body are brownish grey, and the limbs are more or less rufous externally, and of a lighter tint internally. The under surface of the lower jaw, the throat, and the underparts are of a dirty yellowish white, as also are the cheeks. The ears are dark-coloured externally, but have long yellowish-white hairs within. The tail, which is bushy, is a light reddish grey, save towards its tip and on the dorsum towards its root, where it is black.

Habitat. Tierra del Fuego and Chile.

	Centimeters.
Length from snout to root of tail	88·5
,, of tail	41·0
,, from heel to end of longest digit	16·0
,, of ear	6·5

Cranial and Dental Characters.

The skull has a much elongated facial portion. The interorbital region appears very little elevated when the skull is viewed in profile; behind it is a distinct sagittal ridge. The nasals extend a little further backwards than do the nasal processes of the maxillæ. The suture between the palatines and the maxillæ does not extend forwards beyond a line joining the anterior margins of the two fourth upper premolars. The posterior extension of the bony palate varies

Fig. 21.

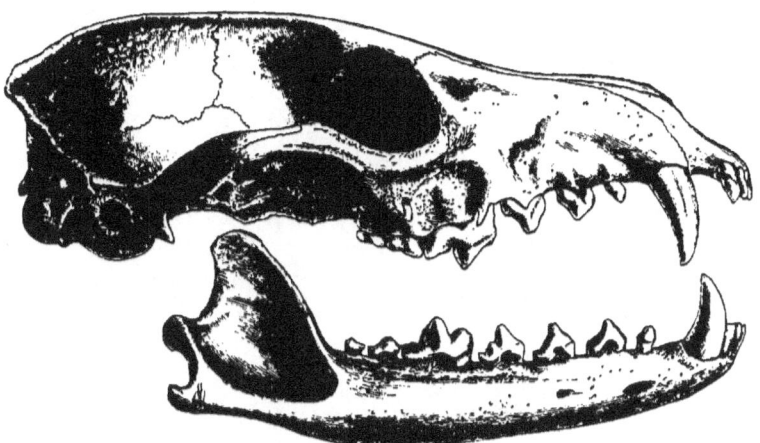

Skull of the type of CANIS MAGELLANICUS.

considerably; it may extend backwards to a line joining the hinder margins of the two hinder upper molars, or a little further backwards, or not backwards beyond the middle of those molars.

	Centimeters.
Basion to ovalion	2·7
,, sphenoideum	4·4
Sphenoideum to gnathion	11·2
Length of palate	8·2
Breadth ,,	4·2
Length of nasals	6·2
Breadth of ,,	1·3
,, brain-case	5·1
,, zygomata	9·1

THE MAGELLANIC DOG.

		Centimeters.
Length of	$\underline{P.1}$	0·4
,,	$\underline{P.2}$	0·8
,,	$\underline{P.3}$	1·0
,,	$\underline{P.4}$	1·5
,,	$\underline{M.1}$	1·0
,,	$\underline{M.2}$	0·55
Breadth of	$\underline{P.4}$	0·7
,,	$\underline{M.1}$	1·4
,,	$\underline{M.2}$	0·65
Length of	$\overline{P.1}$	0·4
,,	$\overline{P.2}$	0·8
,,	$\overline{P.3}$	1·0
,,	$\overline{P.4}$	1·1
,,	$\overline{M.1}$	1·6
,,	$\overline{M.2}$	0·8
,,	$\overline{M.3}$	0·3
Breadth of	$\overline{M.1}$	0·7
,,	$\overline{M.2}$	0·4
,,	$\overline{M.3}$	0·3

THE CARASISSI OR CRAB-EATING DOG.

CANIS CANCRIVORUS.

Canis cancrivorus, Desmarest, Mammalogie, p. 190 (1820); J. A.
 Wagner, Supplem. to Schreber's Säugth., Abth. ii. p. 403;
 Schomburgk, Ann. Nat. Hist. vol. iv. p. 431 (1840); Bur-
 meister, Fauna Brasiliens, p. 31, plate 32; id. Archiv f.
 Naturgesch. xlii. Jahrg. Bd. i. p. 120; id. République
 Argentine, vol. iii. p. 143.
Canis brasiliensis, Lund, Blik paa Brasiliens Dyreverden, femte Afhand-
 ling, p. 10, pl. 42. figs. 1–3 (1843).
Canis melampus, Wagner, Archiv f. Naturgesch. ix. Jahrg. Bd. i. pp. 357
 & 358 (1843).
Canis melanostomus, Wagner, Archiv f. Naturgesch. ix. Jahrg. Bd. i. p. 358.
Canis rudis, Günther, Ann. & Mag. Nat. Hist. 5th ser. vol. iv. pp. 316 &
 400 (1879).
Thous cancrivorus, Gray, Proc. Zool. Soc. 1868, p. 514; id. Cat. Car-
 nivorous Mammalia, p. 201.
Viverra cancrivora, Meyer, Zool. Annalen, vol. i. p. 135 (1794).
Chien des bois, Buffon, Suppl. vol. vii. p. 146, pl. 38.
L'Agoura, Azara, Essais, vol. i. p. 307 (1801).

BESIDES *C. antarcticus* and *C. magellanicus* there are an, as yet, uncertain number of different kinds of canine animals inhabiting South
America and the islands immediately adjacent to that continent. The
oldest of these which has received a scientific designation is that
which was called by Desmarest *Canis cancrivorus*. It is an animal
sometimes attaining a considerable size; it has a somewhat obtuse
muzzle, rather short tail, and a powerful frame, so that it is very unlike
the Common Fox, though the South-American *Canidæ* we are about to
describe are very commonly spoken of as "foxes" of different kinds.

The Carasissi appears to be subject not only to considerable variation
as to colour, but also as to size. The British Museum is well off for

skins of this species, which well exemplify its variability; for there are transitional forms which appear to bridge over differences between the darkest and the palest, the greyest and the reddest of the number.

We have selected for illustration (Plate XV.) one from Gozo which well shows the hues of that variety in which the coloration is somewhat intense. It is probable that later researches and more abundant collections will show that variations in colour go either with seasonal or local differences, or both; we have as yet, however, no direct evidence on these points with regard to the Carasissi.

The animal ranges through the forests and bushy plains of America, from the Orinoco down to the La Plata, but does not extend into the Pampas. It feeds on small animals, such as agoutis and pacas, on birds, and also upon crayfish (whence its English name), and it will also partake of vegetable food. Mr. Schomburgk was assured by Indians that packs of these animals would run down deer. In his account of the expedition he made to Guiana he tells us that, when marching early one morning, he frequently observed a number of footprints, like those of a dog, on the sandy path leading to a native village. His Indian companions assured him that they had been made the night before by a pack of Carasissi (the native name of *C. cancrivorus*) in search of fowls; and on entering the village the gestures and exclamations of the squaws proved both the truth of the assurance he had received and the considerable amount of damage the unwelcome visitors had caused. At the time of his visit (1839) they were abundant in the wilder inland parts, though they had grown scarce in the neighbourhood of the sea-coast. They pursue their prey by the eye in the open country, but in the woods follow it readily by scent. Mongrels between this animal and the domestic dog were much prized by the Indians as being excellent hunters. Mr. Schomburgk purchased a young one which he considered to be about three weeks old, and it was darker in colour than the adult individuals he saw. He fed it on boiled yams, plantains, and fish, but it appeared to prefer plantains. It would follow those who fed it, as a dog would. When angry it would growl like a puppy, and emit a harsh grating sound as if in pain.

Amongst what appear to us to be varieties of this species we must reckon that which has been named by Dr. Günther *C. rudis*, as after the most careful investigation we have been unable to find any distinctive characters which some one or other specimen of *C. cancrivorus* does not share. It was sent alive to Dr. Günther from Demerara, and was a domesticated creature, allowed to run about the house like a dog. It was very playful, especially towards evening, but slept at night. It never barked or wagged its tail, but uttered a short, sharp cry when left by itself, or a hiss when an attempt was made to take away its food. During a temporary absence of its master from home it was confined in a cage, a change which it only survived a few weeks.

On dissection its cæcum was found to be straight [*], as is that of the true *C. cancrivorus* [†].

The two forms which Wagner has named *C. melampus* and *C. melanostomus*—the first from Mato Grosso and the river Araguay, and the latter from Ypanema—are too briefly noticed to render their satisfactory determination possible. That on which Lund has bestowed the name *brasiliensis* seems only to be a dark (red and black) variety of *cancrivorus*, although the skull is remarkable for the absence of any anteroposterior concavity dorsally, between the interorbital region and the end of the nasals.

The colour of *C. cancrivorus* varies extremely. Its prevailing tint may be a uniform light reddish grey, or it may be darker and mottled. It may have a black back and bright red legs, or may be a dull grey with very little black on the back, or grey with a very black back. The hue of the underfur may vary as well as that of the longer hairs of the coat, which is of a rather harsh texture. The most normal tint seems to be brownish grey above, with the crown of the head, sides of the body, and outside of the limbs slightly or strongly rufous. The back is generally more or less black, as also more or less of the dorsum of the tail, as well as its distal end. There may or may not be a dark band on either cheek. The underside of the lower jaw is black or dark brown; the latter colour may extend for some distance on the neck, which lower down becomes yellowish or even white. The ears are reddish

---

[*] P. Z. S. 1879, p. 767.   [†] P. Z. S. 1873, p. 743.

brown externally, and have yellowish-white hairs within. The belly and inner side of the thighs are generally of a dirty pale yellow.

Habitat. Guiana and Demerara to the La Plata.

Dimensions of a large and of a small specimen.

	Centimeters.	
Length from end of snout to root of tail.	70·5	86·5
„ of tail	29·5	30·5
„ from heel to end of longest digit	13·0	13·0
„ of ear	6·0	6·4

Cranial and Dental Characters.

We have been unable to detect any remarkable cranial characters as distinctive of this species, but it seems to be subject to remarkable abnormalities of dentition. An additional $\underline{M.3}$ is occasionally present, and we have found in one instance * an additional lower molar ($\overline{M.4}$) on both sides. The most singular anomaly we have found, however, is, as mentioned in our Introduction, the existence on one side of a group of five small denticles, placed close together, in lieu of the third lower molar †.

As we have said, the outline of the skull of the variety *brasiliensis*, as represented by Lund, is somewhat aberrant.

The average dimensions of $\underline{P.4}$ to that of $\underline{M.1+M.2}$ we have found to be 1·27 and 1·57 respectively, or as 100 to 123. That of the same teeth in the figure of Lund's *brasiliensis* is as 100 to 122.

	Centimeters.
Basion to ovalion	2·6
„ sphenoideum	3·8
Sphenoideum to gnathion	8·8
Length of palate	6·5
Breadth „	3·7
Length of nasals	4·7
Breadth of „	1·1
„ brain-case	4·2
„ zygomata	7·1

* No. 1033 *b* in the British Museum. † See *ante*, p. xxiv.

CANIS CANCRIVORUS.

	Centimeters.
Length of $\underline{P.1}$	0·4
,, $\underline{P.2}$	0·7
,, $\underline{P.3}$	0·75
,, $\underline{P.4}$	1·2
,, $\underline{M.1}$	0·95
,, $\underline{M.2}$	0·6
Breadth of $\underline{P.4}$	0·5
,, $\underline{M.1}$	1·2
,, $\underline{M.2}$	0·95
Length of $\overline{P.1}$	0·3
,, $\overline{P.2}$	0·65
,, $\overline{P.3}$	0·8
,, $\overline{P.4}$	0·9
,, $\overline{M.1}$	1·4
,, $\overline{M.2}$	0·8
,, $\overline{M.3}$	0·4
Breadth of $\overline{M.1}$	0·65
,, $\overline{M.2}$	0·5
,, $\overline{M.3}$	0·4

THE SMALL-EARED DOG.

CANIS MICROTIS.

Canis microtis, Sclater, Proc. Zool. Soc. 1882, p. 631, pl. 47.

This interesting and seemingly peculiar species of *Canidæ* was made known to science through a living individual which came to the Gardens of the Zoological Society from the Amazons, in September 1882, and was described, named, and figured in the 'Proceedings' of the Society by Dr. Sclater, F.R.S.

After its death it was deposited in the British Museum, and the skin of this unique specimen and type of the species we have had represented (Plate XVI.), as well as its skull.

When alive the animal stood about fourteen inches high over the shoulders. The nose is rather elongated and pointed, but the ears, as its names implies, are remarkably short.

The fur is short and close, and generally of a dark iron-grey; the hairs, which are black at their tips, being white towards their base. The limbs and tail are nearly black. The ears are of a rufous colour both internally and externally, but there are some whitish hairs within. The snout is also of a rufous colour. The tail is bushy, and there is a curious round patch of white underneath it, near its root.

Habitat. Banks of the Amazons.

	Centimeters.
Length from snout to root of tail	78·0
„ of tail	27·0
„ from heel to tip of longest digit	13·0
„ of ear	3·4

CANIS MICROTIS.

Fig. 22.

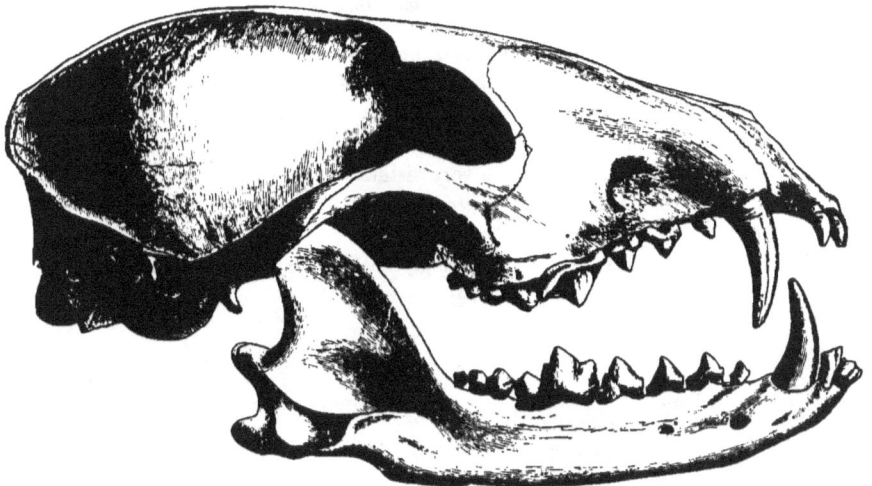

Side view of skull of CANIS MICROTIS. (Size of nature.)

Fig. 23. Fig. 24.

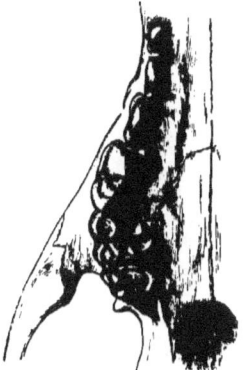 

Surfaces of molar teeth of upper jaw (right side). Surfaces of molar teeth (lower jaw).

Cranial and Dental Characters.

The cranial structure of this animal will be best understood on reference to figs. 22–24 (p. 63), which are of the size of life.

Frontal sinuses are present. It may be well here to note that the nasals do not extend so far backwards as do the nasal processes of the maxillæ. The mandible has a very distinct subangular process, much more marked than in *C. cancrivorus*, or in the variety described by Lund as *C. brasiliensis*.

The third lower molar is exceedingly small. The proportion borne by $\frac{P.4}{}$ to $\frac{M.1+M.2}{}$ is as 100 to 126.

	Centimeters.
Basion to ovalion	3·1
,, sphenoideum	4·2
Sphenoideum to gnathion	9·8
Length of palate	7·1
Breadth ,,	3·8
Length of nasals	4·8
Breadth of ,,	1·1
,, brain-case	4·9
,, zygomata	8·5
Length of $\underline{P.1}$	0·45
,, $\underline{P.2}$	0·65
,, $\underline{P.3}$	0·90
,, $\underline{P.4}$	1·30
,, $\underline{M.1}$	1·00
,, $\underline{M.2}$	0·65
Breadth of $\underline{P.4}$	0·65
,, $\underline{M.1}$	1·15
,, $\underline{M.2}$	0·95
Length of $\overline{P.1}$	0·30
,, $\overline{P.2}$	0·65
,, $\overline{P.3}$	0·80
,, $\overline{P.4}$	0·90

		Centimeters.
Length of $\overline{M.1}$		1·50
,, $\overline{M.2}$		0·80
,, $\overline{M.3}$ . . .		0·30
Breadth of $\overline{M.1}$		0·60
,, $\overline{M.2}$		0·50
,, $\overline{M.3}$		0·25

AZARA'S DOG.

CANIS AZARÆ.

Canis azaræ, Prinz Max. zu Wied, Beiträge zur Naturgesch. von Brasilien, vol. ii. p. 338 (1826); Rengger, Naturgesch. v. Paraguay, p. 143 (1830); J. A. Wagner, Supplement to Schreber, Abth. ii. p. 434; id. Archiv f. Naturgesch. ix. Jahrg. Bd. i. p. 356 (1843); Waterhouse, Zool. H.M.S. 'Beagle,' Mammalia, p. 14, pl. 7; Tschudi, Fauna Peruana, p. 121 (1846); Gay, Hist. de Chile, Zool. vol. i. p. 61 (1847); Burmeister, Uebersicht Thiere Brasil. Th. i. p. 96 (1854); id. Fauna Brasiliens, p. 44, pls. 28 & 29 (1856); id. Reise d. d. La Plata, vol. ii. p. 405 (1861); id. République Argentine, vol. iii. p. 147; Philippi, Archiv f. Naturg. xxxv. Jahrg. Bd. i. p. 50 (1869); Burmeister, Archiv f. Naturg. xlii. Jahrg. Bd. i. p. 118 (1876); Mivart, Proc. Zool. Soc. 1890, p. 99.

Canis fulvipes, Martin, Proc. Zool. Soc. 1837, p. 11; Waterhouse, Zool. H.M.S. 'Beagle,' p. 12, pl. 6; Gay, Hist. de Chile, vol. i. p. 58; Philippi, Arch. f. Naturg. xxxv. Jahrg. Bd. i. p. 45.

Vulpes griseus, Gray, P. Z. S. 1836, p. 88; id. Mag. Nat. Hist. vol. i. p. 578.

Canis griseus, Burmeister, Fauna Brasiliens, p. 43, pls. 25, 28, 29; id. Reise d. d. La Plata, p. 407; id. République Argentine, vol. iii. p. 151.

Canis gracilis, Burmeister, Reise d. d. La Plata, vol. ii. p. 406 (1861); id. République Argentine, vol. iii. p. 150; id. Archiv f. Naturgesch. xlii. Jahrg. Bd. i. p. 116.

Canis entrerianus, Burmeister, Reise d. d. La Plata, vol. ii. p. 400 (1861).

Canis patagonicus, Philippi, Archiv f. Naturgesch. xxxii. Jahrg. Bd. i. p. 116 (1866).

Canis vetulus, Lund, Blik paa Brasiliens Dyreverden, femte Afhandling, p. 21, pl. 40 (1843).

Canis fulvicaudus?, Lund, Blik paa Brasiliens Dyreverden, femte Afhandling, p. 20 (1843).
Pseudalopex azaræ, Gray, Proc. Zool. Soc. 1868, p. 512; id. Cat. Carnivorous Mammalia, p. 199.
Cerdocyon azaræ, Hamilton Smith, Jardine's Nat. Library, vol. ix. p. 264, pl. 29.
L'Agouarachay, Azara, Essais, vol. i. p. 317 (1801).

AMONGST the South-American *Canidæ* there are a variety of forms to which different specific names have been assigned, but which, at present, we can only regard as so many, more or less local, varieties of that kind which was first described by Prince Wied under the name *Canis azaræ*.

Intermediate varieties of coloration are to be found amongst all of those here referred to as most distinct, while it has been well ascertained that the abundance and texture of the furry coat, as well as its hue, vary with the seasons of the year.

The characters which can be best relied on as distinctive are those presented by the structure of the teeth; and in this respect all the forms which we have grouped together in the above list remarkably agree, while, as we shall hereafter see, other forms upon which the same names have been bestowed have teeth of a very different type.

Further researches may very likely show that two or more of the forms we have here associated together are really distinct, but evidence of their distinctness is not yet before us.

It is greatly to be desired that a numerous collection should be made of all the kinds of South-American dogs, the locality and sex of each individual being noted, as well as the time of year when it was obtained, the skull not being extracted from the skin, save at the Museum in which it may be deposited.

The type of this species, named *C. azaræ*, is the individual specimen, or specimens, described by Wied and preserved in his collection. Mr. Ogilby examined the collection, and, through his aid, Mr. G. Waterhouse identified that type with the specimen brought back by Mr. Darwin, and now deposited in the British Museum. This individual we have had figured in our Plate XVII.

The *Canis azaræ* is described by Rengger as occurring over the greater part of South America east of the Andes; but we know now that it occurs on both sides of that mountain-chain. Rengger tells us that in Paraguay it dwells in bushy districts, whence it makes excursions into the great forest on the one hand, and into the open country on the other, seeking its prey in the twilight and at night. Its food consists of small quadrupeds and birds; but it does not refuse frogs and lizards, while it occasions great damage amongst the sugar-canes by the quantity it bites through and wastes, only eating that part which it finds to be the sweetest. This careful observer sometimes, when camping out at night, was able in bright moonlight to study the animal, and, when in a locality where ducks were kept, noticed its cautious approach always against the wind, by which means it would be the better warned of danger, and its own, often disagreeable, odour be less perceived. After thus approaching its prey with great care and circumspection, it would suddenly spring on a duck, seizing it by the neck so that it could not cry out. It would then make off, holding up its victim as much as it could, that obstacles might the less impede its retreat. If alarmed, during its approach, by the smell of man or dog, it would quickly retreat to the bush, and later make another approach by a different route, repeating the attempt four or five times. On one occasion, after Rengger had been thus robbed of a duck, he had the animal watched for several nights: nothing was seen of it, although its footprints were visible in the morning. The first night this watch was relaxed, a fatal visit was made to the hen-roost.

When hunting its prey the creature runs with its nose to the earth like a hound, but every now and then raises its head to the wind.

In summer and autumn these animals go about in a solitary manner; but in winter the sexes associate, and then at night and in the evening their loud cries are to be heard. But they are also to be heard at other seasons, especially when a change in the weather begins.

The male and female inhabit the same nest, which is sometimes made in the densest scrub, sometimes under the roots of trees, and sometimes in the abandoned burrow of an armadillo; but they do not make an earth for themselves, as European foxes do. In the spring the female brings forth from three to five young, rarely leaving her nest during the first week, when she is fed by the male. As soon, however, as the young are able to eat, both parents go off on the hunt, and bring back food for their offspring. Towards the end of December the male leaves his family, and the young follow their mother about for a time till she leaves them also.

When taken young, they are very readily tamed, know their master, will come when called, or even seek him themselves, and lick his hand, but they are not otherwise very obedient without the aid of a stick. They can be left free to run about, and they often go off at night, but return home in the morning. They will be friendly enough and play with the dogs of the house in which they live; but if a strange dog approaches, their hair bristles up and they will growl or bark.

The greater part of the day they pass in sleep, waking up towards evening to look after their food and play with their master.

They will readily hunt with hunting-dogs, even joining in the pursuit of the terrible jaguar; but if the hunt lasts several hours, they get tired and go home.

They have a curious habit of carrying away in their teeth to the bush or into long grass any portable objects, such as pieces of leather or cloth, or indeed the most various objects novel to them. This is not with a wish to eat them, and indeed they are simply left in the place to which they are thus oddly carried away. Travellers have to be on their guard against this strange habit.

Rengger found that this animal was never eaten by the natives of Paraguay (on account of its strong taste and odour), and that even its skin was in but little request. They, however, waged war against it vigorously, on account of its mischievous habits—trapping it or hunting it with dogs. In the latter case it would at first run with such speed that horsemen could with difficulty keep it in sight. After a quarter of an hour, however, it would generally begin to show fatigue, after which it would soon be taken.

A skin which was brought from the island of Chiloe was described by Mr. Martin as a distinct species, under the name of *C. fulvipes*. This skin, which is the type of the species, is deposited in the British Museum, and it is the skull extracted from it which we here figure.

Fig. 25.

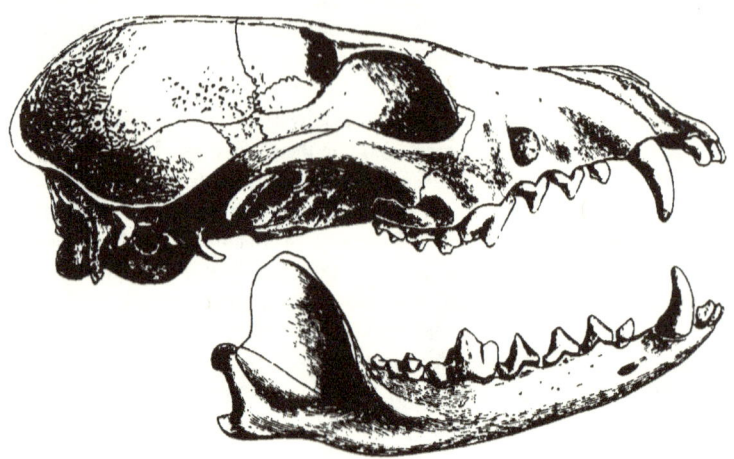

Side view of skull of CANIS AZARÆ (var. *fulvipes*). (Size of nature.)

Fig. 26. Fig. 27.

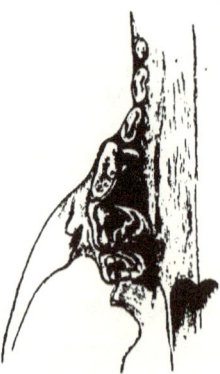 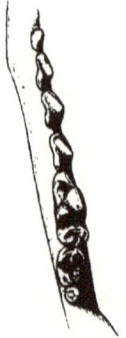

Upper molars (right side). Lower molars (right side).

We do not perceive that it differs from *C. azaræ* by any important character, though the fourth upper premolar is somewhat smaller compared with the length of the two upper molars. Bearing in mind the variability we have found to exist in other species, we cannot bring ourselves to regard this as more than a dark local variety of *C. azaræ*.

Similarly we regard Burmeister's *C. griseus* and *C. gracilis* as but pale varieties of the same species, the skulls and teeth of these forms being in such full agreement with those of *C. azaræ*. Burmeister himself admits that there is much resemblance between these asserted species, his *C. gracilis* being intermediate between his *C. griseus* and his *C. azaræ*. It may be that these are distinct species, but as yet we have no material evidence which, we think, entitles us to assert them so to be [*]. The name *C. griseus*, which was given by Gray to a skin in the British Museum, cannot be seriously regarded, as it was applied to an immature animal.

Dr. Burmeister found between the rivers Parana and Uruguay specimens of a form for which he proposed the name *C. entrerianus*—specimens of different sexes, ages, and seasons. He describes his species as being of "a reddish yellow-brown, with hairs on the back which were black, tipped with white annulations. Face and limbs redbrown, like the back. Front of the neck, breast, and inner side of the limbs whitish or pale yellowish red; end of the tail black."

The young (which he found sucking in January) were of a yellowish brown, except the face, limbs, and tail-end, which were blackish brown.

A female (which was in milk on the 27th of October) was reddish brown, with white and black bristly hairs interspersed. An old male was of a much lighter yellow colour.

These differences of hue show how little distinctions of the kind can

---

[*] He says of *C. gracilis*:—" Le renard de cette espèce ressemble beaucoup à la précédente, mais il est plus petit, plus élégant de forme." Of *C. griseus* he tells us:—" C'est un renard extrêmement élégant et sans doute la plus jolie espèce du groupe, se distinguant des autres par le pelage assez long, fort épais, plus doux, d'apparence presque soyeuse et de couleur plus harmonique, avec une teinte générale tirant plus sur le roux que chez les autres."—Description physique de la République Argentine; vol. iii. (1879), pp. 150 & 151.

be depended on for characterizing species, when, as in this case, not accompanied by some weighty differences as to the skulls and teeth. We therefore cannot feel justified in regarding this form as more than a somewhat strongly coloured local variety of *C. azaræ*.

Another variety from the shores of the Straits of Magellan has been distinguished by Philippi by the designation of *C. patagonicus*. He makes its distinctness depend on its having a paler, thicker coat, with a shorter tail marked with black and white rings. But it is in no way surprising that an individual from so cold a region should have a thicker, paler coat. We have found that specimens of *C. azaræ* from the south have longer hair than specimens from Chile. As to the caudal annulations, we have found two such to exist towards the root of the tail of a specimen of *C. azaræ* from Patagonia.

Philippi's species depends only on a single skin, without any skull. It is therefore impossible for us to treat it as more than a local variety.

Two species have been described by Lund under the names *vetulus* and *fulvicaudus*, but they appear to us to be very imperfectly distinguished. The former, he tells us, has the body and limbs "slender;" the latter has them "somewhat slender." The former, is said to be above "light ashy grey;" the latter, "whitish grey." The former is said to have the limbs below "isabel yellow;" the latter "brownish yellow." The only marked distinction asserted is in the tail. That of *vetulus* is said to be black at the end and for one fourth of its length; that of *fulvicaudus* is described as having the end and a patch upon its dorsum yellowish, and it is also said that a patch of ochre-yellow exists behind the ear. This distinction does not appear to us to be a satisfactory one, owing to the variations we have found as to the colour of the tail in other species. Burmeister has also remarked *, as a result of his experience, that a ruddy tail-end forms no distinctive character, and he affirms that Lund's two species approximate together strongly. This is also our opinion. The fourth upper premolar of his *C. fulvicaudus* is small, but the dentition figured, has an aberrant appearance. But Burmeister identifies Lund's *C. vetulus* with Wied's *C. azaræ*;

* Fauna Brasiliens, p. 41.

and certainly the coloured plate of the external form given by Lund looks very like a pale individual of *C. azaræ*; but the figure of the skull and teeth seems to us to clinch the matter. His figures seem carefully drawn and are probably accurate; if so, the *C. vetulus* of Lund must, we think, be the *C. azaræ* of Wied, for the proportion borne by the fourth upper premolar to the upper molars is just that which exists in the variety distinguished as *C. fulvipes*.

Burmeister has also described two species under the terms *C. vetulus* and *C. fulvicaudus*, identifying them with the species so named by Lund. In this identification he seems to us to be in error; but we reserve, till our consideration of the next species, any treatment of the problem what these forms thus named by Burmeister may really be.

The reader may think that we have united an excessive number of varieties under one specific name; but we do not consider that many of the characters upon which the authors of these reputed species have dwelt merit any confidence as specifically distinctive marks.

Thus Philippi even ventures to name a species without having seen the skull of the form he thus names, and Burmeister dwells upon such matters as the degree of development of the sagittal ridge and the form of the postorbital processes. But these characters we have found to vary greatly in different specimens undoubtedly belonging to the same species.

The coloration presented in the adult condition, by what appears to us to be a medium average variety of this species, is as follows:—

Burmeister tells us [*] that the hair is much longer and more grey in winter than in summer, also that the back becomes almost black and the face greyish brown instead of yellowish grey, and that the tint of the limbs changes. At birth the young are entirely brown, except that they are slightly greyish on the underparts. Sometimes individuals are met with entirely white.

The dorsal region of the body, which is covered with long hair, is mottled with black and white, with black patches over the shoulders, middle of the body, and rump. The sides of the body are grey. The

[*] See ' Description physique de la République Argentine,' vol. iii. p. 148.

limbs externally are fulvous, pale yellowish internally. The underparts of the body are dirty white, and there is more or less white behind the fore limbs and on the inner side of the thighs. A black patch often traverses the outside of either hind leg a little above the heel. The edge of the upper lip, thorax, and chest are white. The chin is black, and this colour may extend backwards beyond the angle of the mouth. The head is of a yellowish colour above. The ears are lined with whitish hairs, while those outside these organs are yellowish brown tipped with black; the base of the ears and the adjacent parts of the neck are buff colour. The moustaches are long and black. The tail is mottled white and black, and is black at its terminal portion and on the proximal part of its dorsum.

Habitat. Brazil to Tierra del Fuego, Chile, and Chiloe.

	Centimeters.
Length from snout to root of tail	66·5
„ of tail	33·0
„ from heel to end of longest digit	14·0
„ of ear	7·0

Cranial and Dental Characters.

The sagittal ridge variously developed, its anterior portion is wide and flattened, with a curved margin on either side, so that the two together resemble somewhat the outline of a lyre.

The fourth upper premolar is well developed compared with the length of the two upper molars. We have found the average of a number of specimens to be as 100 to 118.

	Centimeters.
Basion to ovalion	2·5
„ sphenoideum	3·8
Sphenoideum to gnathion	8·4
Length of palate	6·3
Breadth „	3·3
Length of nasals	4·6
Breadth „	1·0

CANIS AZARÆ.

	Centimeters.
Breadth of brain-case	4·4
,, zygomata	7·2
Length of $\overline{P.1}$	0·35
,, $\overline{P.2}$	0·7
,, $\overline{P.3}$	0·9
,, $\overline{P.4}$	1·3
,, $\overline{M.1}$	1·0
,, $\overline{M.2}$	0·5
Breadth of $\overline{P.4}$	0·5
,, $\overline{M.1}$	1·3
,, $\overline{M.2}$	1·0
Length of $\underline{P.1}$	0·3
,, $\underline{P.2}$	0·7
,, $\underline{P.3}$	0·8
,, $\underline{P.4}$	0·85
,, $\underline{M.1}$	1·5
,, $\underline{M.2}$	0·8
,, $\underline{M.3}$	0·4
Breadth of $\underline{M.1}$	0·6
,, $\underline{M.2}$	0·5
,, $\underline{M.3}$	0·3

$\overline{P.4}$ to $\underline{M.1+M.2}$ as 100 to 115.

THE SMALL-TOOTHED DOG.

CANIS PARVIDENS.

Canis parvidens, Mivart, Proc. Zool. Soc. 1890, p. 108.
Canis vetulus, Burmeister, Fauna Brasiliens, p. 37, plates 23, 28, & 29 (1843); id. Uebersicht d. Thiere Brasil. p. 99 (1854); id. Reise d. d. La Plata, p. 407 (1861).
Canis fulvicaudus, Burmeister, Fauna Brasiliens, p. 40, plates 24, 28, & 29; id. Reise d. d. La Plata, p. 407.

BURMEISTER, in his work first above cited, describes a specimen in his possession which he regards as identical with the *C. vetulus* of Lund, which species (as we have before observed) he also identifies with the *C. azaræ* of Wied. But his description and his plates show that an important distinction exists between what he calls *C. vetulus* and that of Lund; for its fourth upper premolar is extremely small, while its two upper molars are relatively very large. $\frac{P. 4}{}$ is to $\frac{M. 1 + M. 2}{}$ as 100 is to 155. In Lund's *C. vetulus* the fourth upper premolar is large.

Now although the proportions of the teeth in the *Canidæ* are not perfectly constant, they yet afford the best distinctive characters we have, and much better ones than can be derived from differences in the tints of the furry coat.

Similar reasons render it impossible for the *C. vetulus* of Burmeister to be the *C. azaræ* of Wied, and therefore the species requires a new denomination.

In the British Museum there are two skins and three skulls * from

---

* Nos. 821 A, 821 B, and 821 C. The first skull (here figured) was extracted from the skin No. 44. 3. 7. 3.

Brazil, which show dental characters remarkably distinct from all the forms which we have grouped with our *C. azaræ*, but which remarkably agree with those depicted by Burmeister as pertaining to his *C. vetulus*. The skins also fairly resemble the same form, and therefore we are disposed to regard the specimens in the Museum as belonging to the same species as named *vetulus* by Burmeister. That species of Burmeister, however, was anonymous, and therefore we employed the new name *parvidens* to denote the British-Museum specimen, which must retain that name even if it should turn out that Burmeister's species is different and needs yet another designation, which, however, we are not inclined to believe.

There are no particulars recorded of the specimen which is our type, save that it was brought from Brazil in the year 1844. Burmeister also was unable to give any particulars of the specimen which he obtained from Campos.

The type is represented on our Plate XVIII.

In colour this species is yellowish grey, slightly darker on the back; but the dorsum of the tail is not darker, save a small black spot near the root. The end of the tail is black. The top of the head is grey like the sides of the body. The ears, externally, are of a darker grey, but reddish ochre towards the base and on the dorsum of the head adjoining the roots of the ears. The limbs are rufous on the hinder aspect of each. The underparts of the body are of a yellowish white, the fur of the throat being the whitest. The white throat is separated from the yellowish white of the ventral part of the body by a yellow patch, interposed on the front and under surface of the chest. The under surface of the lower jaw is dark. The lips are not white, and there is no distinct spot between the eye and the nose. There is a paler greyish patch obscurely indicated on either shoulder. The hairs of the sides of the body are yellowish below, white towards the tip. The hairs of the back are yellowish below and then white, but they are black towards the tips. The hairs of the black terminal portion of the tail are rufous-grey towards the root. The hairs of the thighs are yellowish below but with whitish tips. About the heel the hairs are dusky below, but yellowish red towards their tips.

THE SMALL-TOOTHED DOG.

Fig. 28.

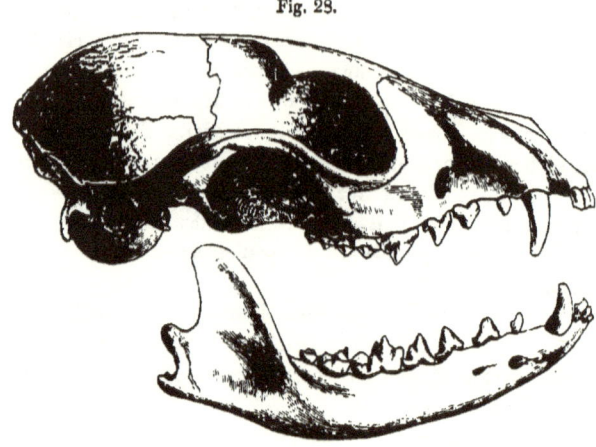

Side view of skull of type of CANIS PARVIDENS.

Fig. 29. Fig. 30.

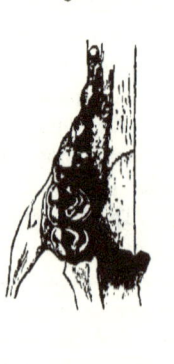 

Surfaces of molar teeth (right side). Lower molars (right side).

This animal appears to stand somewhat lower on its limbs than does *C. azaræ*.

Habitat. Brazil.

	Centimeters.
Length from snout to root of tail	60·0
,, of tail	27·5
,, from heel to end of longest digit	11·0
,, of ear	4·8

Cranial and Dental Characters.

The sagittal ridge may be very strongly marked posteriorly or be obsolete. There is generally a raised flattened tract in front of it, the lateral margins of which have a somewhat lyrate outline.

The relative length of the postorbital processes varies in different individuals, as also does their curvature.

The dentition is remarkable for the very small size of the fourth upper premolar compared with the combined lengths of the first two upper molars, its proportional length to theirs being, on an average, as 100 to 166, three specimens being examined.

	Centimeters.
Basion to ovalion	2·0
,, sphenoideum	3·0
Sphenoideum to gnathion	6·3
Length of palate	4·8
Breadth ,,	2·8
Length of nasals	3·1
Breadth of ,,	0·9
,, brain-case	4·0
,, zygomata	6·3
Length of $\frac{P.1}{}$	0·3
,, $\frac{P.2}{}$	0·5
,, $\frac{P.3}{}$	0·55
,, $\frac{P.4}{}$	0·7
,, $\frac{M.1}{}$	0·7
,, $\frac{M.2}{}$	0·5

		Centimeters.
Breadth of $\underline{P.4}$	. . .	0·4
,, $\underline{M.1}$	.	0·8
,, $\underline{M.2}$	.	0·7
Length of $\overline{P.1}$	.	0·25
,, $\overline{P.2}$		0·5
,, $\overline{P.3}$		0·55
,, $\overline{P.4}$		0·6
,, $\overline{M.1}$		0·9
,, $\overline{M.2}$		0·6
,, $\overline{M.3}$		0·3
Breadth of $\overline{M.1}$		0·4
,, $\overline{M.2}$	. . . . .	0·4
,, $\overline{M.3}$	. .	0·3

THE STRIPED-TAILED DOG.

CANIS UROSTICTUS.

Canis urostictus, Mivart, Proc. Zool. Soc. 1890, p. 112.

In the British Museum there is a skin from Brazil, and also the skull extracted from it*. We deem this form so remarkable from its dentition as to need a distinct notice. It most nearly approaches *C. parvidens*, but not only the hue of its pelage differs greatly from the latter, but it has a very distinct mark in the form of a deep black stripe along the middle two fifths of the dorsum of its tail. Nothing is known about the sex of the specimen or the exact locality where it was derived, but it was obtained in 1844. This type we have had figured in Plate XIX., and its skull † in our woodcuts figs. 31–33.

The general colour is rufous-ochre, washed with black and white. The hairs of the back are dusky at the base, then ochre, and then white, becoming black towards the tips. The sides of the head and the outsides of the ears are more rufous than the back. The limbs, especially towards the heels, are rufous, and there is a dark mark in front of each wrist. The underparts and the inner sides of the thighs are also rufous, but rather lighter, while the throat is whitish, the under surface of the lower jaw being blackish; a darker shade interposes between the whitish throat and the light rufous of the ventral part of the body. The lips are not white, and no distinct mark is visible between the eye and the nose. The inner sides of the fore limbs have a slight rufous tinge. The hairs of the head are like those of the back, but shorter. The hairs of the tail are mostly dusky towards the root, and then of an ochre colour. Towards

* Skin No. 44. 3. 7. 4.   † No. of skull 1033 E.

82 THE STRIPED-TAILED DOG.

Fig. 31.

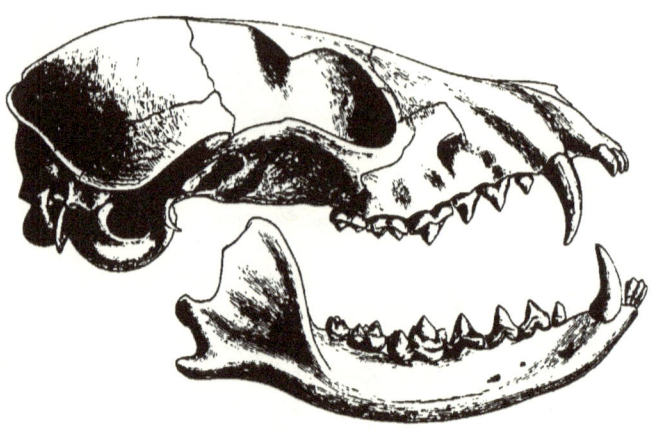

Side view of skull of type of CANIS UROSTICTUS.

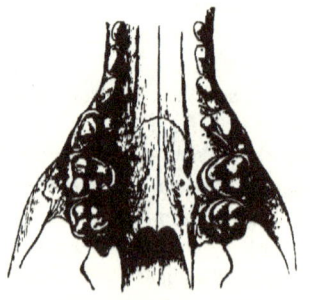

Fig. 32.

Surfaces of upper molars.

Fig. 33.

Surfaces of molar teeth of lower jaw.

the end of the tail and in the region of the black dorsal stripe the hairs of the tail are black towards their tips. Thus the general colour of the tail is grey. It is blackish towards its apex, and very black at the dorsal stripe before mentioned, as shown in our Plate.

Habitat. Brazil.

	Centimeters.
Length from snout to root of tail	67·5
„ of tail	22·0
„ from heel to end of longest digit	13·0
„ of ear	5·2

Cranial and Dental Characters.

The flattened sagittal tract is rather narrow, and ends posteriorly in a short sagittal ridge.

The upper molars are very large, but their combined length differs slightly on the two sides, being 1·5 on one side and 1·4 on the other.

Taking the mean and comparing this with the fourth upper premolar the relative length of the latter to that of the molars is as 100 to 160.

	Centimeters.
Basion to ovalion	2·1
Ovalion to sphenoideum	2·9
Sphenoideum to gnathion	7·2
Length of palate	5·0
Breadth of „	2·8
„ brain-case	4·0
„ zygomata	5·8
Length of P.1	0·3
„ P.2	0·6
„ P.3	0·55
„ P.4	0·9
„ M.1	0·8 or 0·85
„ M.2	0·6 or 0·65
Breadth of P.4	0·5
„ M.1	1·0
„ M.2	0·8

THE STRIPED-TAILED DOG.

		Centimeters.
Length of	$P.\overline{1}$	0·2
,,	$\overline{P.2}$	0·5
,,	$P.\overline{3}$	0·55
,,	$\overline{P.4}$	0·65
,,	$\overline{M.1}$	1·05
,,	$\overline{M.2}$	0·8
,,	$\overline{M.3}$	0·4
Breadth of	$\overline{M.1}$	0·55
,,	$\overline{M.2}$	0·55
,,	$\overline{M.3}$	0·4

THE COLISHÉ.

CANIS VIRGINIANUS.

Canis virginianus, Schreber's Säugthiere, Theil iii. p. 585, plate 92 B;
Erxleben, Syst. Reg. Anim. p. 567 (quoted from Schreber)
(1777); Gmelin, Syst. Nat. i. p. 74 (1788); Desmarest,
Mammalogie, p. 203 (1820); Harlan, Fauna Americana,
p. 89 (1825); Richardson, Fauna Boreali-Amer. p. 96
(1829).

Canis cinereo-argentatus, Erxleben, op. cit. p. 567; Gmelin, op. cit. p. 74;
Harlan, op. cit. p. 90; Hamilton Smith, Jardine's Nat.
Library, vol. x. p. 254, pl. 23.

Canis griseus, Boddaert, Elenchus Anim. i. p. 97 (1784).

Vulpes virginianus, De Kay, Nat. Hist. New York, p. 45, pl. 7. fig. 2
(1842); Audubon and Bachman, Quadrupeds of N. Amer.
p. 162, pl. 21 (1852); Baird, Mammals of N. Amer. p. 138
(1857); id. U.S. Mexican Boundary, ii. p. 16 (1858); Allen,
Bull. Mus. of Comp. Zool. Harvard Coll. vol. i. p. 160 (1863);
Alston, Biologia Centrali-Americana, Mamm. p. 67 (1880).

Vulpes littoralis, Baird, Mamm. of N. Amer. p. 143 (1857).

Urocyon (as a subgenus), Baird, Mamm. of N. Amer. p. 121 (1857).

Urocyon virginianus, Gray, Proc. Zool. Soc. 1868, p. 522; id. Catalogue
of Carnivorous Mammalia, p. 209 (1869); Frantzius, Archiv
f. Naturgesch. Jahrg. xxxv. Bd. i. p. 284 (1869); Allen,
Bulletin U.S. Geolog. Survey, vol. ii. p. 320 (1876).

Urocyon littoralis, Gray, op. cit.

Oztuhua, Hernandez, De Quad. Nov. Hisp. fol. 6, caput xvi. (1651).

Grey Fox, Catesby's Nat. Hist. of Carolina, ii. p. 78 (1731).

Zorro of the Mexicans, Baird, Rep. U.S. Mexican Boundary, p. 17.

Tigrillo of the Costa-Ricans, Frantzius, loc. cit.

Colishé of the Apaches, Baird, U.S. Mexican Boundary, ii. p. 17.

THIS exceedingly distinct species has been commonly spoken of as the
" Grey Fox " or the " Virginian Fox; " but as it is a widely different
animal from the true fox, we have preferred to denote it by a native

name, rather than employ a trivial one which we deem misleading. Indeed, this species appears to us to have affinities rather with the South-American *Canidæ* than with its other Nearctic congeners, all of which latter species and varieties are closely allied to, where they are not specifically identical with, the Common Fox of Europe and Northern Asia. Though spoken of as a "Virginian" animal, it has a very southern range. There are specimens in the British Museum from Guatemala, Honduras, and Costa Rica, and it may thus be an animal which has extended northwards from its original area.

Canis virginianus appears to have been first made known, after Hernandez, by Catesby, who, in his 'Natural History of Carolina,' gives a very bad figure and a few words as to its habits. Its scientific name was bestowed by Schreber, although the work in which it appears is dated a year later than Erxleben's, who nevertheless refers to Schreber's name and to his (for its date) very tolerable figure.

But the first really good representation is the coloured plate of F. Cuvier, although it represents an immature individual. A good figure of an adult animal appears to us still a desideratum, and this we have endeavoured to supply by our Plate XX., which represents an individual obtained from Texas.

Two specimens from Santa Rosa Island appear to represent the small form described as *V. littoralis* by Baird, but which we agree with our late lamented friend, the very accomplished naturalist Mr. Alston, in regarding as a mere variety of *C. virginianus*. The American naturalist, Mr. Allen, came to the same conclusion after comparing a variety of specimens, declaring that the individuals were the smaller in size the more southern their habitat. This species, indeed, seems to vary more in size than in coloration, which, so far as we have observed, remains pretty constant. Allen gives the length of the skull of a specimen from Pennsylvania and of one from Yucatan as 4·77 and 3·74 respectively, or a proportional difference of 127 to 100.

The Colishé is said to be less enterprising and sagacious and more timid than the Common Fox. It is more often caught in steel traps than is the latter animal. It must also be less destructive to the farmer, as Audubon never heard of any well-authenticated account of its entering a farmyard, although it would readily seize upon any poultry that strayed from home into the woods. In Costa Rica, however, according to Frantzius, it lives by preference in the vicinity of human dwellings, on which account it is difficult to protect poultry from its depredations. However this may be, it is always very fond of birds, and Audubon had once an opportunity of seeing the animal spontaneously "point." It was observed in a field of broom-grass, coursing against the wind and hunting in the manner of a pointer. Suddenly it stood still and squatted on its haunches. Then it went on again, but with slow and cautious steps, raising its nose to sniff at intervals. Soon it began to crawl and finally made a dead halt, with its ears drawn back and nose but a few inches from the ground. After remaining in this attitude about half a minute, it made a sudden pounce on its prey, and secured a partridge, as the rest of the covey flew away. The animal feeds on any birds it can obtain and their eggs (notably those of the marsh-hen), also on rabbits and small mammals, such as the cotton-rat, Florida rat, and voles. It will, sometimes at least, also eat insects and vegetable food, especially the ears of maize.

It is often to be seen, Baird tells us, in broad daylight, although it is mainly a nocturnal animal, for the most part only coming forth at twilight from the bushes or tall grass in which it hides by day.

The sounds emitted by it are somewhat like those of the Coyoté (*C. latrans*), but far less abrupt, so that they cannot with any propriety be called a bark.

Catesby asserts that they will climb trees, and so escape pursuit, a statement the truth of which has been denied. But Audubon and Bachman tell us that though they have often seen the Colishé run down and killed by hounds without its having attempted to climb a tree, yet that when its strength begins to fail it will do so if it happens to meet with one the trunk of which slopes sufficiently to enable it to get up. On one occasion a Colishé was observed to leap on a low branch four or five feet from the ground and thence ascend by cautious rather awkward leaps from branch to branch till it got into a lofty fork, where it stopped. It has also been seen to get up a small pine-tree by clasping its stem as a bear would do. When pursued these animals seek the protection of trees more in summer than in winter, probably because in hot weather they become more speedily exhausted.

The animal has not so rank and penetrating an odour as has the European Fox, but it seems to afford good sport to hunters. It does not, however, run far ahead of the hounds, but keeps about seventy to a hundred yards in front of them. A two hours' chase is said to be generally necessary to capture it, but a very fleet pack has been known to run it down in forty minutes. Next to deer-hunting the chase of the Colishé is the favourite sport in the Southern States of the Union.

From three to four young are produced in a litter. This occurs between the middle of March and the middle of April in Carolina, and somewhat later further north. It makes its home in caves or fissures in rocks, or holes in the ground, sometimes even in stone walls. Frantzius found four cubs in a cavity in a wall; they had a woolly coat, blackish grey above and whitish below, with whitish-grey markings on the muzzle and feet. We found the young to be of a dark brown hue, with the tips of the hairs of the back white.

The coloration of the adult a good deal resembles that of a short-haired specimen of *C. magellanicus.* The general colour of the trunk is a grizzled grey, with the sides of the body and legs more or less rufous. The tail is dusky above, light chestnut-coloured below, dark at its termination, with a dark patch on its dorsum, and with a dorsal patch of stiff, bristly hairs, the existence of which has led to its generic separation as "*Urocyon.*" There is a dark mark along the middle of the back extending to this tail-patch. The chin is black, and there is a black spot between the nose and the eye, with a light mark in front and behind it. The backs of the ears are of a rusty tint; within there are whitish hairs. Throat white or whitish, and underparts of the body yellowish white. White on the side of the head, behind the mouth, and beneath the eye.

Habitat. United States and Central America.

		Centimeters.
Length from snout to root of tail		63·5
,, of tail		28·5
,, from heel to end of longest digit		13·5
,, of ear		5·3

CANIS VIRGINIANUS.

Fig. 34.

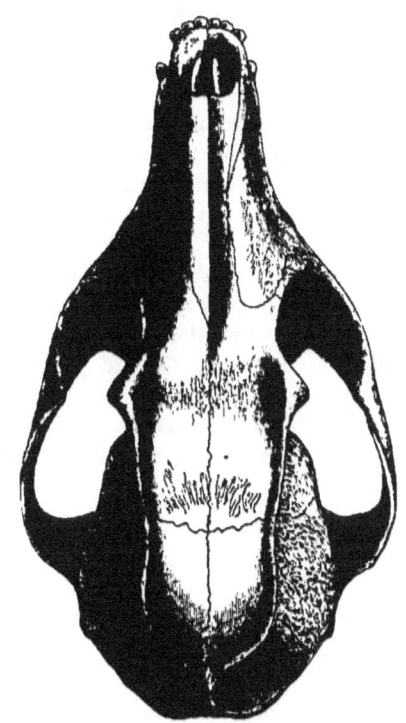

Top view of skull of CANIS VIRGINIANUS.

Fig. 35.

Side view of lower jaw.

THE COLISHÉ.

Cranial and Dental Characters.

As before mentioned the skull of this animal is very distinctly characterized. Instead of the dorsal surface of the skull showing a lyrate sagittal elevation ending in a simple margin on either side, there is a distinct, elevated, cord-like ridge running backwards in an undulating manner from the postorbital process of the frontal to the occipital crest, on either side; these two lateral ridges enclose a lyrate space indeed, but not a uniformly elevated tract.

The mandible also is very differently shaped from that of any of the *Canidæ* as yet here described. It has been said to show a subangular lobe, but it seems to be rather the case that what has been called the "subangular lobe" is an almost normally formed part, and that the abnormality consists in the shape of the angle itself, which is small in size and, as it were, pushed upwards towards the condyle of the jaw.

The length of the fourth upper premolar compared with that of the two upper molars is as 100 to 130.

		Centimeters.
Basion to ovalion		2·3
,, to sphenoideum		3·7
Sphenoideum to gnathion		8·2
Length of palate		6·1
Breadth of ,,		2·9
Length of nasals		4·0
Breadth of ,,		1·0
,, brain-case		4·5
,, zygomata		7·1
Length of P. 1		0·3
,, P. 2		0·5
,, P. 3		0·6
,, P. 4		1·0
,, M. 1		0·8
,, M. 2		0·5
Breadth of P. 4		0·5
,, M. 1		1·0
,, M. 2		0·8

CANIS VIRGINIANUS.

		Centimeters.
Length of	$\overline{P.1}$	0·2
,,	$\overline{P.2}$	0·5
,,	$\overline{P.3}$	0·6
,,	$\overline{P.4}$	0·7
,,	$\overline{M.1}$	1·1
,,	$\overline{M.2}$	0·7
,,	$\overline{M.3}$	0·3
Breadth of	$\overline{M.1}$	0·45
,,	$\overline{M.2}$	0·4
,,	$\overline{M.3}$	0·3

THE COMMON FOX.

CANIS VULPES.

Canis vulpes, Linneus, Syst. Nat. p. 59 (4) (1766); Schreber, Säugthiere, Theil iii. p. 354, pl. 90; Desmarest, Mammalogie, p. 201 (1820); Pallas, Zoographia, vol. i. p. 45 (1831); J. A. Wagner, Supplem. Schreber's Säugth., Abth. ii. p. 405; Blasius, Naturgesch. d. Säugethiere Deutschlands, p. 191 (1857).

Canis alopex, Linneus, Syst. Nat. p. 59 (5).

Canis fulvus, Desmarest, Mammalogie, p. 203; J. A. Wagner, Suppl. to Schreber's Säugth., Abth. ii. p. 413; Richardson, Fauna Boreali-Americana, p. 93 (1829); Harlan, Fauna Americana, p. 89.

Canis argentatus, Shaw, Gen. Zool. vol. i. p. 325 (1800); Desmarest, Mammalogie, p. 203 (1820); Harlan, Fauna Americana, p. 88.

Canis decussatus, Desmarest, Mammalogie, p. 203 (1820); Harlan, Fauna Americana, p. 88 (1825).

Canis himalaicus, Ogilby, Proc. Zool. Soc. 1836, p. 103.

Canis niloticus, Desmarest, Mammalogie, p. 204; Rüppell, Atlas, p. 41 (1826); Ehrenb. Symb. Phys. pl. xix.

Canis vulpes montana, Pearson, Journ. As. Soc. Bengal, vol. v. p. 313 (1836); J. A. Wagner, Suppl. to Schreber's Säugth., Abth. ii. p. 408.

Vulpes vulgaris, Brisson, Règne Animal, p. 239 (1756); Bell, Hist. of Brit. Quadrupeds, 2nd edit. p. 225 (1874); Allen, Bulletin of Mus. at Harvard Coll. vol. i. p. 158.

Vulpes crucigera, Brisson, Règne Animal, p. 240 (1756).

Vulpes alopex, Blanford, Fauna Brit. India, Mamm. p. 153 (1858).

Vulpes montanus, Blyth, Journ. Asiat. Soc. Bengal, xi. p. 589, and xxiii. p. 730; Adams, Proc. Zool. Soc. 1858, p. 516; Jerdon, Mammals Brit. India, p. 152; Blanford, Journ. Asiat. Soc. Bengal, xlvi. 2nd part, p. 323, and xlviii. p. 95; Scully, Proc. Zool. Soc. 1881, p. 202.

Vulpes nipalensis, Gray, Charlesworth's Magazine of Nat. Hist. vol. i.
   p. 578 (1838).
Vulpes flavescens, Gray, Ann. & Mag. Nat. Hist. xi. p. 118 (1843);
   Hutton, Journ. Asiat. Soc. Bengal, xix. p. 344; Adams,
   Proc. Zool. Soc. 1858, p. 516; Blanford, Yarkand Miss.,
   Mammalia, p. 23, plate 2.
Vulpes fulvus, Fischer, Synopsis Mammalium, p. 190 (1829); De Kay,
   Nat. Hist. of New York, p. 44, plate 7. fig. 1 (1842);
   Audubon and Bachman, Quadrupeds of N. Amer. vol. ii.
   p. 263, pl. 87, and vol. iii. p. 70, pl. 116; Baird, Mammals
   of N. Amer. (Reports of Mississippi Railroad), p. 123,
   plate 31.
Vulpes japonica, Gray, Proc. Zool. Soc. 1868, p. 517.
Vulpes hoole, Swinhoe, Proc. Zool. Soc. 1870, p. 631.
Vulpes lineiventer, Swinhoe, Proc. Zool. Soc. 1870, p. 632.
Vulpes melanogaster, Bonaparte, Fauna Italica, plate i. (1832); J. A.
   Wagner, Suppl. to Schreber's Säugth., Abth. ii. p. 409.
Vulpes macrurus, Baird, Stansb. Exploration Great Salt Lake, p. 309
   (1852); id. Mammals of N. Amer. (Reports of Mississippi
   Railroad), p. 130, pl. 33.
Vulpes pennsylvanica, Gray, Proc. Zool. Soc. 1868, p. 518; id. Catalogue
   of Carnivorous Mammalia, p. 205.
Vulpes Utah, Audubon and Bachman, Quadrupeds of N. Amer. vol. iii.
   p. 255, plate 151.
Renard, Buffon, Hist. Nat. vol. vii. pp. 75 & 82, pl. 4; F. Cuvier, Hist.
   Nat. des Mammifères, vol. ii., three plates.

THE great variability which we have already found to be a character of the Wolf, will prevent the reader being surprised on reading that at least an equal degree of variability is to be met with in the Fox.

The Foxes, not only of Europe, but even of England itself, suffice to show this, and also to put us on our guard against the too common tendency which exists to regard vague and very inconstant differences of pelage as sufficient evidence of a difference of kind. Thus English varieties have been distinguished as "Greyhound," "Mountain," "Bush," or "Cur" Foxes upon such characters, together with some variations in absolute size, and small differences in the proportions of different parts of the body. But the total length of the head and body of adult English Foxes may differ so much that if the length of one be represented by 100, that of another will be 170, the length of the tail and ears remaining much more constant. The English Fox may not only vary in general colour, but even the characteristic white end to the "brush" may be absent, the end of the tail being black or dark grey. Bell records that an individual taken in Warwickshire had all the underparts of a greyish-black hue, thus resembling the Italian variety which Bonaparte distinguished by the name *melanogaster*, on account of the black fur existing on the abdomen; and Dr. Edward Hamilton brought with him from the Ardennes * an example of this form, which has also been described by Nilsson as existing in Scandinavia. But a careful and detailed criticism made by Dr. Cæsar Lepori † must, we think, suffice to convince every reader, of the specific identity of these two forms. The differences which are to be found in our own island and in Europe being thus so considerable, it is not wonderful that others should also exist in the Foxes of Northern Asia, Africa, and America. Something more, then, than differences of tint and small variations in markings is needed to justify our acceptance of any form, which is only peculiar in such respects, as the representatives of a distinct species.

The habits of the English Fox are so well known that we feel we might almost be dispensed from saying anything here on so trite a subject. Still to some readers the few following words may not be altogether superfluous.

Like some of the animals we have already described, the Fox will occasionally make use of the burrow of a badger or a rabbit, though commonly excavating its own earth. It will also repose, away from its burrow, in woods or under the shelter of banks or hedges, and has even been known to make its nest in an old straw-rick, a situation which may have been convenient for farmyard depredations.

Foxes with us bring forth in April, and have about from four to six young in a litter. Gestation lasts between sixty and sixty-four days.

As every one knows, the Fox preys upon poultry when it has the chance, and also on partridges, pheasants, hares, rabbits, eggs, rats and

* See Proc. Zool. Soc. 1869, p. 247.
† See 'Atti della Società Italiana di Scienze Naturali,' vol. xxiv. p. 252 (Milan, 1881).

mice, moles, frogs, lizards. It will likewise readily devour any cheese and butter which it may find. Even worms and beetles are eaten by it, as also fish, mollusks, and crabs by Foxes which live near the sea and can find such left on land by the tide. Carrion, moreover, does not come amiss, nor vegetable food, especially fruit, when animal matter is scarce.

The Fox will give forth a variety of different sounds according to circumstances—yelping, barking, screaming, or sometimes when at rest emitting a gentle murmur.

The tricks and wiles practised by Foxes when hunted are so well known in England, that any details on the subject would be here out of place. Col. Hamilton Smith considered that in such matters English Foxes had educated themselves far above their continental fellows; but this might be expected from our persistent fox-hunting having gradually exterminated all the less sagacious and less wily individuals.

The peculiar and penetrating odour of the Fox (due to the secretion formed by its subcaudal gland) and the absence of it in the dog * may be one reason why the fox and dog will not breed together, as we have seen the dog and jackal and the dog and wolf will do.

The Fox becomes adult in a year and a half or soon after, and is said to live thirteen or fourteen years. It seems hardly susceptible of being thoroughly tamed, and certainly is much less capable of attachment than either the jackal or the wolf.

The Fox has, compared with most of the species already here described, a long, sharp, and very specially pointed muzzle and a very long and bushy tail, the "brush" being more or less cylindrical in outline for a great part of its length. The eyes are oblique, and their pupils become nearly linear when exposed to strong light.

The general colour of the English Fox is fulvous on the head, back, and sides, and on the outside of the upper part of the limbs. The cheeks, upper lip, belly, inner side of the limbs, and the end of the tail are white. The throat and chest are greyish or whitish, and the shoulders are mostly reddish grey. There is a black mark between the inner angle of the eye and the mouth. The anterior aspects of the limbs, from a

---

* See Buffon's remark, *op. cit.* p. 81.

little below the elbows and heels, are also more or less black, as is the hinder surface of each ear, except at the base. Great individual variation, however, exists, the pelage being sometimes yellowish rather than reddish, or largely washed with either black or white. The Honourable R. C. Trollope has been so kind as to send us word that a pure white English Fox was killed near Taunton in 1886. The specimen has been stuffed, and is in the possession of C. J. Erdaile, Esq., of Cotheleston House, Taunton, on whose property it was killed.

The length of the head and body may be from about twenty-seven to forty-six inches, and that of the tail from twelve to fifteen inches.

Our figure (Plate XXI.) is drawn from a living specimen of an English Fox.

We have already referred to the Italian variety described by Bonaparte as *Canis melanogaster*, but a considerable number of other forms have been described as distinct species, which forms we cannot but regard as mere varieties of *C. vulpes*. No less than four types of such named forms exist in the British Museum as well as representatives of three other reputed species, which also seem to us to be mere varieties.

One of these is the so-called *C. niloticus*, of which two specimens from Egypt and three from Algiers and Syria are in our National Collection. Our judgment as to the non-distinctness of this form from *C. vulpes* is confirmed by the figures of *C. niloticus* given by Rüppell and Ehrenberg, which differ strikingly from each other, and, indeed, Rüppell admits that a great likeness exists between the Fox of the Nile and that of Europe. The representation of a young female Fox from Algiers given by F. Cuvier, in the second volume of his 'Histoire Naturelle des Mammifères,' further confirms our judgment, and indeed the author only represents it as being a doubtfully distinct kind.

The type of the variety distinguished as *C. montanus* is, with seven other specimens, preserved in the British Museum. As to it, the founder of the species, Mr. Pearson, himself says* that it seems to be intermediate between *C. vulpes* and *C. decussatus*, " which, indeed, may, after all, be probably varieties of the same species." Jerdon also

* *Loc. cit.* p. 314.

speaks of its resemblance to the Common Fox, and Blanford, after having treated it as a distinct species, now considers it but a variety of the Common Fox. As this form has been a subject of so much doubt, we think it well to give a figure of the variety. Our Plate XXII. represents the type of this reputed species. *C. himalaicus* of Ogilby belongs to this variety of *C. vulpes*.

Another variety, as we deem it, is that which was first described by Gray as *Vulpes flavescens*, of which we have seen specimens obtained from Thibet, as well as from Persia. The best account of this form is given by Blanford in his 'Mammalia of the Yarkand Mission,' p. 22, plate ii. Therein he expressed his suspicion, rather than belief, that *C. flavescens* is a really different animal from *C. montanus*. He tells us: "That the two are closely allied is certain, and it is extremely doubtful whether any definite characters can be found to distinguish them." Cranial and dental characters afford better criteria; but here, again, distinctions break down. He observes:—"As a rule, the skulls of *V. montana* are larger," but one skull of *V. montana* scarcely differs in measurement from that of *V. flavescens*. Distinctions in the relative size of the teeth are to be more relied on, but, from his dimensions, the length of the first upper molar of *flavescens* only differs from that of *montana*—the fourth upper premolar being taken as 100—as 69·22 differs from 69·43. He notes, indeed, certain differences as existing between the teeth of *flavescens* and the Common European Fox, but sagaciously and most truly adds:—" There is, however, sufficient variation amongst the teeth of these skulls to render it doubtful how far specific characters can be made to depend upon them alone." These doubts seem to us to be put an end to by this author's 'Fauna of British India,' wherein he identifies both *C. montanus* and *C. flavescens* with the Common Fox. Any doubt which might have lingered in our own mind as to the validity of such an identification is dissipated by the judgment of a naturalist not only so distinguished and able, but one who has enjoyed such exceptional opportunities for arriving at a correct final decision on the subject. We regard, then, the variety *C. montanus* as a Himalayan variety of the Common Fox, and *C. flavescens* as another variety from Central Asia. We represent in our Plate XXIII. the type specimen of *C. flavescens*.

As to habits, Mr. Blanford tells * us:—"The Himalayan Fox lives in brushwood and cultivated land, from an elevation of 5000 or 6000 feet upwards, frequently haunting the neighbourhood of human habitations and feeding upon such birds and small mammals as he can capture. . . . The Central-Asiatic variety lives in open country, hiding in burrows or amongst bushes or rocks by day." The honeycomb of wild bees is eaten by these animals, which are also exceedingly fond of grapes.

There are preserved in the British Museum the individual skins whereon Mr. Swinhoe founded his two proposed species *V. hoole* and *C. lineiventer*. The former of these, he tells† us, is a "Fox of the plains and lower hills of South China, and in form and size very similar to that of Europe; but it is paler, wants the black spot on the sides of the snout, and has the colours of its coat differently arranged." It is common on the bare granitic hills of Amoy, and Mr. Swinhoe saw as many as six together at one time. It also inhabits Hongkong island. When pursued, they spring with great agility from rock to rock, and will soon outrun a greyhound in such a locality.

V. lineiventer was obtained by Mr. Swinhoe at Amoy, from the higher mountains of Fokien. He describes it as very like Bonaparte's *melanogaster*, but is "remarkable for having a fine line of chestnut on each side of the belly. It is very brightly coloured, and so differs conspicuously from" *V. hoole*, "though in form and size very similar."

With Mr. Swinhoe's careful description in hand, we have compared these skins with those of a number of European and other foxes, and cannot consider them to be more than local varieties. The same must be said with regard to a Fox from Japan described by Mr. Adams‡, and Gray's *V. japonica*, which are of a uniform dull brown colour, or nearly so, when adult, while a younger specimen is intermediate between the forms named *hoole* and *linciventer*.

---

* *Loc. cit.* p. 154. † *Op. cit.* p. 631.
‡ See Proc. Zool. Soc. 1860, p. 195.

Our view is supported by that of Professor Martens*, who had such good opportunities of examining Foxes in Japan, and has declared them to be identical with the European Fox. The great variation to which the Fox is subject is further illustrated by four skins brought from Siberia by Seebohm: in them the hair is very long and very light in colour, though the underfur is black.

Skulls of all the varieties of the Fox hitherto described by us have been carefully compared together, and the judgment which we have formed from a consideration of the skins is thereby confirmed. We deem them all to be but varieties, generally local ones, of *Canis vulpes*.

The only form now remaining for consideration is the variety of the Common Fox which inhabits North America.

This animal has been supposed not only to be a species distinct from the Fox of the Old World, but its subvarieties have been regarded as distinct kinds distinguished by the names of the Red Fox (*V. fulvus*), the Cross Fox (*V. decussatus*), and the Silver or Black Fox (*V. argentatus*) respectively. Even now another form, known as *V. macrurus*, is treated as a separate species by Baird—a course, however, in which we cannot follow him, for reasons hereinafter given.

The red variety, *fulvus*, is generally of a reddish-yellow colour, with the hinder part of the back grizzled. The throat and more or less of the belly are white; the ears are black posteriorly, and the ends of the hairs of the tail are black, except, of course, on the white terminal portion of that organ.

The cross variety, *decussatus*, has a dark band crossing the shoulders, as well as a longitudinal band in the middle of the back. The tail is darker than in *fulvus*, and legs, muzzle, and underparts black or blackish.

The silver or black variety, *argentatus*, is generally almost entirely black save the tip of the tail, which is mostly white. On the hinder half of the back the hairs are annulated with grey, as they are also on the top and sides of the head and outside of the thighs. A choice skin of

---

* See 'Die Preussische Expedition nach Ost-Asien,' Zoologischer Theil, p. 152 (Berlin, 1876).

this variety is represented in our Plate XXIV.; but specimens may be met with which are entirely black or entirely grey.

Thus the American Fox varies rather more than the European one; and when we consider how great and how parallel these variations are, and how impossible it is, so far as we can see, to detect any cranial or dental characters to distinguish the American Fox from the Fox of the Old World, we cannot hesitate to unite them under one title, that of *Canis vulpes* *. A statement of Audubon strongly confirms this judgment. He says of the Red Fox:—"The young are covered, for some time after they are born, with a soft woolly fur, quite unlike the coat of the grown animal, and generally of a pale rufous colour. Frequently, however, the cubs in a litter are mixed in colour, there being some red and some black cross Foxes together; when this is the case it is difficult to tell which are the red and which the cross Foxes until they are somewhat grown." F. Cuvier has given a plate of two young 30 days after birth, the offspring of parents of the red variety, clothed in grey down like the underfur of the adult; in them the red colour began first to appear about the head. That estimable American zoologist Mr. J. A. Allen † not only considers the European and American Foxes to be of one species, but declares the three American varieties to differ in nothing save different degrees of melanism.

Audubon is of opinion that the American Fox has gradually extended its range southwards ‡. According to him Pennsylvania was once its southern limit. Next it made a home in the mountains of Virginia. A few years afterwards it appeared in the more elevated portions of North Carolina, and finally in Georgia, where he had observed it about 1850. The species is said to have been first seen in Lincoln county, Georgia, in 1840. A Mr. Beile informed Audubon that "as he was using a

---

* Baird, in his 'Mammals of North America,' p. 130, remarks on the fact that no remains of the Fox have been detected among the fossils derived from the Carlisle and other bone-caves, although *C. virginianus* is abundantly represented. This, as he says, would lend colour to the idea that the Fox, like the existing American horse, is an immigrant from the Old World.

† See 'Bulletin of the Museum at Harvard College,' vol. i. p. 159.

‡ *Op. cit.* vol. ii. p. 267.

call for wild turkeys, a little before sunrise, in the vicinity of Augusta, two Red Foxes came to the call, supposing it to be that of a wild Turkey, and were both killed by one discharge of his gun."

The silver variety is that the skin of which is so valuable an article of commerce. It is a relatively scarce animal, though in 1850 it was sometimes seen in the mountains of Pennsylvania and the wilder northern portions of the State of New York. The skins sold by the American Fur Company came from the head-waters of the Mississippi and the territories north-west of the Missouri.

The variety to which Baird gave the name *macrurus* appears to be one confined to the western side of the Rocky Mountains. It seems to be the western form of the American Fox, as the Silver Fox is the northern variety, and the Red and Cross forms are those of the more eastern parts of the United States.

The American Fox is said to be generally larger than its European representative, but the Western-American form is reported to be a magnificent Fox and the finest variety known. The type of the species is deposited in the American Patent Office. The special characters of this variety are its large size, the length of its fur, and its long tail. It is, however, admitted by Baird to be "very similar in general appearance to the red fox," and to vary like it, its colours "being very similar to those of the corresponding varieties of the red fox."

No cranial or dental characters distinguish it, save that it has an exceedingly long and slender muzzle. This difference, however, is admitted not to be greater than differences which may be observed between the skulls of European specimens and those of the red varieties of the American Fox.

Fossil remains of the Common Fox have been found in the Suffolk Crag, which is an Upper Pliocene deposit.

Habitat. The Fox has the most extensive range of any of the *Canidæ*, since, unlike the Wolf, it is found in Africa north of the Sahara. It extends all over Europe and Asia to some distance south of the Himalaya and to the island of Japan. In America it ranges from as far north as the shores of Hudson's Bay and Labrador, down to the latitude of Northern Mexico.

In a specimen chosen for measurement we found the dimensions to be:—

	Centimeters.
Length from snout to root of tail	71·0
,, of tail	29·0
,, from heel to end of longest digit	15·0
,, of ear	6·8

Skeletal and Dental Characters.

Although if we compare the skull of a fox with that of a wolf or jackal we are struck with the length and slenderness of the muzzle, yet we have found it impossible to detect any constant cranial or dental characters which shall serve to distinguish these species from some of those already noticed or shortly to be noticed. At first it seemed that the backward elongation of the nasals compared with that of the maxillæ might answer such a purpose, but an extended survey showed us that the former might or might not reach further backwards than the latter. The same remark applies to differences as to the form of the postorbital processes, or as to whether those processes are or are not concave dorsally.

The dimensions of the various skeletal parts, in a specimen selected by us as an example, are as follows:—

	Centimeters.
Length of cervical vertebræ	11·0
,, dorsal ,,	14·5
,, lumbar ,,	12·2
,, sacral ,,	2·3
,, caudal ,,	3·4
Length from front of atlas to hinder end of sacrum	40·0
Length of whole pectoral limb	30·0
,, whole pelvic ,,	35·0
,, humerus	10·3
,, radius	9·5
,, femur	10·5
,, tibia	11·6
,, index metacarpal	3·4

CANIS VULPES.

	Centimeters.
Length of metacarpal of pollex	1·2
„ whole pollex	2·7
„ last phalanx of third digit (manus)	1·2
„ index metatarsal	4·6
„ metatarsal of hallux	0·7
„ whole hallux	1·25
„ last phalanx of third digit (pes)	1·20
Basion to ovalion	2·5
„ sphenoideum	3·3
Sphenoideum to ovalion	8·5
Length of palate	6·3
Breadth of „	3·7
Length of nasals	5·0
Breadth of „	1·2
„ brain-case	4·5
„ zygomata	6·5
Length of $\underline{P.\,1}$	0·25
„ $\underline{P.\,2}$	0·50
„ $\underline{P.\,3}$	0·55
„ $\underline{P.\,4}$	0·90
„ $\underline{M.\,1}$	0·60
„ $\underline{M.\,2}$	0·45
Breadth of $\underline{P.\,4}$	0·30
„ $\underline{M.\,1}$	0·70
„ $\underline{M.\,2}$	0·60
Length of $\overline{P.\,1}$	0·20
„ $\overline{P.\,2}$	0·50
„ $\overline{P.\,3}$	0·55
„ $\overline{P.\,4}$	0·60
„ $\overline{M.\,1}$	1·0
„ $\overline{M.\,2}$	0·50
„ $\overline{M.\,3}$	0·20
Breadth of $\overline{M.\,1}$	0·30
„ $\overline{M.\,2}$	0·30
„ $\overline{M.\,3}$	0·20

THE KIT FOX.

CANIS VELOX.

Canis velox, Say, in Long's Expedition to Rocky Mountains, vol. i.
p. 487 (1823) ; Harlan, Fauna Americana, p. 91 (1825);
Max. Wied, Reise Nord-Amer. vol. ii. pp. 44 & 256 (1841).
Canis cinereo-argentatus, Sabine in Franklin's Journ. p. 658.
Canis microtus, Reichenbach, Regnum Animale, i. 10, figs. 72 & 73 ; id.
Universum des Thierreichs, vol. i. p. 43 (1846) ; Wagner,
Wiegmann's Archiv, vol. iii. 1837, p. 162.
Canis (Vulpes) cinereo-argentatus, Richardson, Fauna Boreali-Americana,
p. 98.
Vulpes velox, Audubon and Bachman, Quadrupeds of North America,
vol. ii. p. 13, plate 52 (1851) ; Baird, Mammals of North
America, p. 133 (1857) ; Gray, Proc. Zool. Soc. 1868,
p. 519, pl. 34; id. Catalogue of Carnivorous Mammalia,
p. 206.
Kit Fox, Lewes and Clarke's Travels, vol. ii.

The Kit Fox is one of the most elegant and attractive of the whole family of the *Canidæ*, and is also much the smallest of all those found in North America. It was first clearly identified and unequivocally named by Say. Schreber and subsequently J. A. Wagner seem to have confused this animal with *C. virginianus*. The figure given by Schreber (Theil ii. plate 92 A) certainly cannot be taken to represent, and the appellations bestowed by these naturalists cannot be recognized as appertaining to, the present species.

Say was led to apply to it the name *velox* through having been struck with its extraordinary swiftness, when he had opportunities of observing it run with the antelope and comparing their velocities. Its movement has been compared to that of a bird skimming the surface of

J G Keulemans del et lith   THE KIT FOX   Mintern Bros
Canis velox.

the earth. Nevertheless, Audubon relates* that a mounted horseman had no difficulty in keeping up with one and overrunning it. This may, however, have been an exceptionally slow individual. We ourselves have been struck with the rapidity of motion displayed by a specimen in captivity, enclosed in a large cage in our Zoological Gardens.

The Kit Fox was formerly to be found on the open plains between the Saskatchewan and the Missouri, and in the plains of Columbia, burrowing in the earth in a country totally destitute of trees and bushes. It appears, indeed, to be unknown in forest-regions. Audubon brought one back with him to New York, when it was placed in a large cage-box two thirds sunk beneath the surface of the ground and half filled with earth. When thus allowed a comparatively large space and plenty of earth to burrow in, the Fox immediately began to make its way into the loose ground, and soon had dug a hole large enough to conceal itself entirely. It fed regularly, and drank more water than foxes generally do.

Like other foxes, *C. velox* appears to vary in the colour of its pelage. Two skins in the British Museum are remarkable for their beautifully soft, pale, and abundant fur; in these the sides of the muzzle are black.

A living specimen in the Gardens, represented in our Plate XXV., is somewhat darker than the skins in the British Museum, but agrees with them in having the back and tail dark grey (with black and white hairs), a black tip to the tail, rufous cheeks, shoulders, flanks, and outer side of the legs, and the fur underneath the body white.

According to Baird†, its underfur is remarkably full and dense, much more so than in the Common Fox, while the interspersed long hairs exceed the underfur so little in length that the latter can be readily seen. The limbs are rather short but stout, and the feet are shorter and the body lower than in the Red Fox. Long woolly hairs conceal the naked pads of the paws more or less completely from view. The ears are much smaller than in the Common Fox, and are thickly and densely coated with fur. The tail is rather short relatively, being decidedly less than half the length of the head and body, but very bushy.

* *Op. cit.* p. 15. † *Op. cit.* p. 133.

Baird describes the ears as being of a uniform brownish yellow externally, and yellowish white within. He found the hairs of the tail less annulated than those of the trunk and flanks, and blacker at their tips, the blackness augmenting towards the tip of the tail, which appears to be constantly devoid of the white termination almost always to be found in the Common Fox.

Its specific distinctness from the latter animal is unmistakable, and it is constantly very much smaller in size.

Habitat. North-western America.

The skins in the British Museum are imperfect, so that the length of the limbs could not be measured. Baird gives the following dimensions in inches:—

Length from nose to tail	24
Tail to end of vertebræ	9
Height of ear	$1\frac{3}{4}$

In two British-Museum skins I found the dimensions, in centimeters, to be as follows:—

Length of head and body	65	or 75
„ tail	29·5	29

Cranial and Dental Characters.

We have not had an opportunity of examining any skulls of this species, but we learn from Professor Baird[*] what we might expect, namely, "that it exhibits a very close resemblance to that of the Red Fox." He further tells us that the temporal crests do not approach each other so much as in the latter animal. The postorbital processes also appear to be rather shorter relatively and less obtuse, while the distance between the zygomata is wider and the forehead rather flatter.

The dentition is quite like that of the Common Fox.

Baird gives a very good representation of the skull seen laterally, and both above and below; it does not, however, justify his assertion

[*] *Op. cit.* p. 135.

that the temporal crests are more like those of *C. virginianus* than those of *C. vulpes*, for they do not show any appreciable approximation to the very peculiar condition they present in the Colishé.

The dimensions given in Baird's figure are as follows :—

	Centimeters.
Basion to ovalion	2·6
,, sphenoideum	3·1
Sphenoideum to gnathion	7·6

(This last dimension as represented on a plane surface is, of course, somewhat too short.)

Length of palate	5·8
Breadth ,,	3·0
Length of nasals	4·0
Breadth of ,,	0·9
,, brain-case	4·1
,, zygomata	6·2
Length of $\underline{P.1}$	0·5
,, $\underline{P.2}$	0·8
,, $\underline{P.3}$	0·8
,, $\underline{P.4}$	1·1
,, $\underline{M.1}$	0·7
,, $\underline{M.2}$	0·4
Breadth of $\underline{P.4}$	0·6
,, $\underline{M.1}$	0·8
,, $\underline{M.2}$	0·6
Length of $\overline{P.1}$	0·3
,, $\overline{P.2}$	0·7
,, $\overline{P.3}$	0·9
,, $\overline{P.4}$	0·9
,, $\overline{M.1}$	1·4
,, $\overline{M.2}$	0·6
,, $\overline{M.3}$	0·3
Breadth of $\overline{M.1}$	0·5
,, $\overline{M.2}$	0·4
,, $\overline{M.3}$	0·3

THE ARCTIC FOX.

CANIS LAGOPUS.

Canis lagopus, Linnæus, Syst. Nat. 12th edit. vol. i. p. 59 (1766); Schreber, Säugthiere, Theil iii. p. 262, pls. 93 and 93*; Shaw, General Zoology, vol. i. p. 326 (1800); Desmarest, Mammalogie, p. 202 (1820); Tilesius, Nov. Acta Phys.-Med. Acad. Cæsar. Leopold.-Carolinæ, vol. xi. p. 375 (1823); Pallas, Zoographia, vol. i. p. 51 (1831); Sabine, Supplement Parry's First Voyage, p. 187; Harlan, Fauna Americana, p. 92 (1825); Wagner, Supplem. Schreber's Säugth., Abth. iii. p. 426; Middendorff, Reise äussersten Norden u. Osten Sibiriens, Bd. ii. Th. ii. p. 73 (1851).

Canis isatis, Gmelin, Nov. Com. Petrop. vol. v. p. 358.

Canis (Vulpes) lagopus, Richardson, Appendix to Capt. Parry's Journal of his Second Voyage, p. 299 (1825); id. Fauna Boreali-Americana, vol. i. p. 83 (1829).

Vulpes lagopus, Audubon & Bachman, Quadrupeds of N. Amer. vol. iii. p. 89, pl. 121 (1820); Baird, Mammals North America, p. 137 (1857); Fischer & Pelzeln, Internationuale Polarforschung, p. 128 (Vienna, 1886).

Leucocyon lagopus, Gray, Proc. Zool. Soc. 1868, p. 521; id. Cat. Carnivorous Mammalia, p. 208.

Renard blanc, Buffon, Hist. Nat. Supplém. vol. vii. p. 218, pl. 51 (1789).

L'Isatis, F. Cuvier, Hist. Nat. des Mammifères, vol. ii. (two plates).

After the doubts and difficulties we have now so many times encountered in endeavouring to determine whether various forms hereinbefore considered were or were not distinct species, it is refreshing to come upon one which stands out in unmistakable distinctness and, indeed, in marked isolation. Not only in coloration and various details of external form, not only in peculiarities of cranial conformation, not only in habit of body, as evidenced by its odour and the peculiarity of its changing hues, but in its psychical nature also, it is distinct from its congeners, as we may see from its habits and manners, both in a wild state and in captivity. It is also peculiar in its geographical position, since, as its name implies, it ranges through almost all the lands hitherto explored, of both the Old World and the New, which most nearly approximate to the North Pole.

We have already met with various species which we may confidently affirm, or reasonably suppose, to vary with the season in the abundance or in the tints of their furry coat; but the Arctic Fox is much more remarkable in this respect, for in the summer it is of a bluish or sometimes brownish-grey tint, while in the winter it becomes almost entirely white. This change, which is like that met with in the Ermine and the Variable Hare, seems to occur in no other member of the Canine family. The transformation, however, does not, by any means, invariably take place even in this species. Individuals seem often to be met with in their native haunts with their summer dress in winter*, while others appear to remain entirely white the whole year round. This has given rise to the opinion, which F. Cuvier favoured, that there were two species, one changing and the other permanently white. Mr. Bartlett, however, assures us, as the result of his observations on specimens living in our Zoological Gardens, that amongst a number of individuals, otherwise absolutely indistinguishable, the greater number of which undergo their seasonal change, there will be some which do not do so. Schreber also relates, on the authority of trustworthy hunters, that both white and grey cubs are sometimes found in the same litter.

The head of this animal is less pointed than that of the true Fox, the muzzle having a somewhat swollen appearance. The ears also are short and rounded. There are long hairs on the hinder part of the cheek, which, projecting backwards, give the face a peculiar aspect. The soles of the feet are covered, especially in winter, with dense woolly hair;

---

* Messrs. Fischer and Pelzeln met with grey foxes till the 27th of December, although a white one was seen by them on the 21st of November.

this not only protects them from the effects of extreme cold, but aids them in rapid locomotion over slippery ice.

Another most exceptional peculiarity of these animals is their practice, at least in some regions, of a sort of migration—a practice which, so far as we know, exists in no other member of the family of dogs.

Richardson * tells us that when he wrote they were numerous on the shores of Hudson's Bay, and that they do not breed in solitary fashion, like the Red Fox, but, as it were, in little villages of twenty or thirty burrows constructed in close proximity. Towards the middle of winter the Foxes of the far north migrate southwards, keeping as much as possible to the coast, and going much further southward in districts where the coast-line is in the direction of their march. Captain Parry found that they began to leave Melville Peninsula in November, and that by January few remained. Towards the centre of the continent, in latitude 65°, they were only seen in winter, and then not in large numbers. They were very scarce in latitude 61°, and at Carlton House, in latitude 53°, only two were seen in forty years. It is stated by Hearne † that they arrived at Churchill, in latitude 59°, about the middle of October, and afterwards received reinforcements from the north in very great numbers; those that escaped capture, crossed the Churchill river as soon as it was frozen over, and then went on to the Nelson and Severn rivers.

The Arctic Fox is said, as a rule, to be easily tamed. It is less cunning and spiteful, and more gentle and confiding, than the true Fox, and has nothing of the offensive odour of the latter. Captain Lyon, who carefully studied this animal during a residence of two winters in Melville Peninsula, tells us ‡ that it is an extremely cleanly animal, being very careful not to dirt those places where it eats or sleeps.

"Their first impulse on receiving food," he adds, "is to hide it as soon as possible, even though suffering from hunger, and having no

---

* Fauna Bor.-Am. p. 87.
† See his 'Journey from Hudson's Bay to the Northern Ocean,' 1769-72, p. 363.
‡ See his 'Private Journal of the Voyage of H.M.S. 'Hecla,' under Capt. Parry,' pp. 102-105 (London, 1824).

fellow-prisoners of whose honesty they are doubtful. In this case snow is of great assistance, as being easily piled over their stores, and then forcibly pressed down by the nose. I frequently observed my dog-fox, when no snow was obtainable, gather his chain into his mouth, and in that manner carefully coil it so as to hide the meat. On moving away, satisfied with his operation, he of course has drawn it after him again, and sometimes with great patience repeated his labours five or six times, until, in a passion, he has been constrained to eat his food without its having been rendered luxurious by previous concealment."

In 1863 Professor Alfred Newton, F.R.S., joined in an expedition to Spitzbergen, and amongst the interesting notes published by him are the following *, which refer to the animal we are here concerned with:—" The Arctic Fox is pretty numerous along the shores of Ice Sound; and we not only frequently saw examples of it, but in the immediate neighbourhood of the cliffs wherein the *Alcidæ* were nesting one could, by listening almost at any time in the twenty-four hours, hear its yapping bark. It is of course the chief enemy of all the different kinds of birds, and their dread of it appears to influence them greatly in their choice of breeding-quarters. What the Foxes do to get a living in winter when the birds have left the country, is one of the most curious questions that has presented itself to my mind for some time. The greater number of them are said to remain on the land, and to be as active during the long polar night as they are in summer; yet there are no berries by which they might eke out their existence, and there can be no open water, on the margin of which they might find food, within miles of their haunts. The most natural explanation which occurs to one is that they lay up a stock of provisions; but nobody, that I am aware of, has ever found such a store-closet." He adds: " A considerable collection of shells of *Mya truncata*, which I found one day on the moraine of a glacier in Safe Haven, may possibly have been due to the cause suggested." Professor Newton's sagacious anticipation concerning "store-closets" was subsequently abundantly and very interestingly confirmed by H. W. Feilden, F.G.S., who

* See Proc. Zool. Soc. 1864, p. 496.

accompanied the Arctic Expedition undertaken in 1875, under Captain G. S. Nares, R.N. From his account of the Mammalia of North Greenland and Grinnell Land, we learn* that the Arctic Fox was found to decrease in numbers up Smith's Sound. Its footprints were seen in the snow at Floe-berg Beach. From Dumbbell Harbour (some miles further north) an expedition was made to the Uplands after big game. Having ascended eight hundred feet, the party became enveloped in snow and mist. "All of a sudden," he tells us, "we were startled by the sharp bark of a Fox. More than a year had elapsed since we had heard such a sound. It seemed very close to us, and as the fog lifted we saw the animal standing on a little hill of piled-up rocks that rose like an islet from the plateau. Separating, we approached the Fox from opposite directions. Parr fired at it, when it dropped down, and crawled below some heavy rocks: out rushed the female from its lair, and we secured her.". . . . "As we rested there, many little Lemmings popped up from their holes, and undismayed by our presence, commenced feeding on plants. We noticed that many dead Lemmings were scattered around. In every case they had been killed in the same manner, the sharp canine teeth of the Foxes had penetrated the brain." . . . "Then to our surprise we discovered numerous deposits of dead Lemmings. In one out-of-the-way corner, under a rock, we pulled out a heap of over fifty dead Lemmings. We disturbed numerous 'caches' of twenty and thirty, and the ground was honeycombed with holes which each contained several bodies of these little animals, a small quantity of earth being placed over them. In one hole we found the major part of a hare carefully hidden away." It was observed by this author that the flora in the neighbourhood of the spots where he found these animals was wonderfully rich, the soil having thus been fertilized. He adds:—"It is a very beautiful arrangement that the increased flora induced by the presence of the Foxes should be the means of attracting and sustaining the Lemmings in the immediate vicinity of the Foxes' den." The Arctic Fox may be

* See 'The Zoologist' (3rd series), vol. i. p. 318 (1877).

considered somewhat rare on the northern part of Grinnell Land. The northern specimens did not differ in size from those killed further south.

The Esquimaux take this Fox in traps of a very ingenious kind, which have been thus described by Captain Parry:—"They consist of a small circular arched hut, built of stones, having a square aperture at the top, but quite close and secure in every other part. This aperture is closed by some blades of whalebone, which, though in reality only fixed to the stones at one end, appear to form a secure footing, especially when the deception is assisted by a little snow laid on them. The bait is so placed that the animal must come upon this platform to get at it; when the latter, unable to bear the weight, bends downwards, and after precipitating the Fox into the trap, which is made too deep to allow of his escape, returns by its elasticity to its former position, so that several may then be caught successively."

They are said by Audubon * to be so little cunning, that with a simple barrel trap the same individual has been caught several times, "their hunger or want of caution leading them again into the barrel when only a short time released from captivity." Some that had been kept on board an ice-bound vessel several days did not appear anxious to escape, while others which had not been caught would approach it. They did not appear frightened at seeing a man, but would run a little way, and then sit down and stare before retreating finally. They appear to be good eating and fat all the winter, as, in addition to their stores, they have been seen to follow the polar bear and feed on his leavings of seals, fish, &c.

In summer dress, the Arctic Fox may have the back and tail of a brown or dirty rufous tinge, the belly being yellowish white. The head, chin, outside of the limbs, and the external surface of the ears are also brown. White hairs are interspersed and also grey ones; all the hairs are more or less bluish grey towards their roots and the

---

* *Op. cit.* p. 92. He refers to the expedition in search of Sir John Franklin under Mr. Henry Grinnell.

underfur is of that colour. Often by a large development of the bluish-grey parts of the hairs and a less degree of brown, the predominant colour of the animal in summer becomes bluish grey. Sometimes, as in a specimen in the British Museum, the back may be bluish grey, with the sides and underparts nearly white. In another skin the apices of the hairs generally are much darker than lower down, so that the animal looks as if it was white, with a veil of grey thrown over it.

As winter approaches the fur lengthens, the white hairs increase in number, and all the hairs become white towards their tips, but remain for a time grey towards their roots. When the perfectly developed winter dress is put on, the hairs are wholly white, the animal becoming of snowy whiteness, save the tip of the nose, and sometimes the tip of the tail, which is occasionally black.

But this perfectly, or almost perfectly, white condition is by no means constantly to be met with, as before said, even in winter; so many of the hairs may remain grey as to greatly diminish the brilliancy of the white coat, or even to cause it to be predominantly grey.

Richardson [*] tells us that many individuals retain a little duskiness on the nose, and others remain more or less coloured all the year, while a pure white Fox is sometimes to be met with in summer. The duskiness may sometimes be due to the animals being young, for, according to Hearne, the young are of a very dark colour.

Prof. A. Newton [†] informs us that in Iceland all Arctic Foxes are "Blue" Foxes—that is to say, their winter coat is of nearly the same colour as their summer coat.

Our Plate XXVI., drawn from life, represents two individuals which were living at the same time in the Zoological Gardens.

Habitat. The Arctic Fox inhabits almost all hitherto explored lands within the Arctic Circle, and descends southwards in the New World to 50° north latitude, but (according to Pallas) not below 60° N. in the Old World.

---

[*] *Op. cit.* p. 84.   [†] *Loc. cit.* p. 407, note *.

	Centimeters.
Length from snout to root of tail	70·0
„ of tail	31·0
„ from heel to end of longest digit	13·0
„ of ear	4·5

Cranial and Dental Characters.

The skull of the Arctic Fox is remarkable at the first glance from its swollen appearance at the root of the muzzle between and beneath the orbits.

The postfrontal processes are more or less concave dorsally, and

Fig. 36.

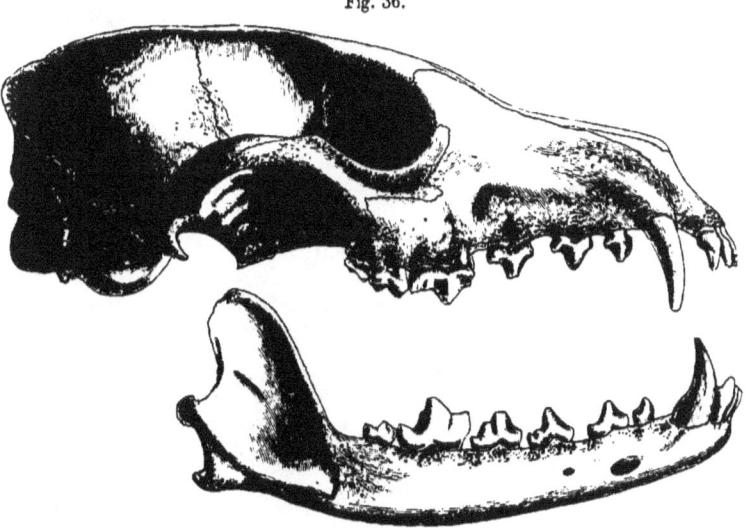

Side view of skull of CANIS LAGOPUS *.

there is a concavity on the dorsum of the skull between them. The nasals do not extend backwards nearly so far as do the frontal processes of the maxillæ.

The dentition exhibits a largely developed first lower molar.

* The last lower molar is accidentally wanting in the skull figured.

	Centimeters.
Basion to ovalion	2·4
„ sphenoideum	3·45
Sphenoideum to gnathion	8·45
Length of palate	6·3
Breadth of „	3·2
Length of nasals	4·3
Breadth of „	1·0
„ brain-case	4·1
„ zygomata	6·6
Length of $\underline{P.\,1}$	0·4
„ $\underline{P.\,2}$	0·7
„ $\underline{P.\,3}$	0·9
„ $\underline{P.\,4}$	1·3
„ $\underline{M.\,1}$	0·9
„ $\underline{M.\,2}$	0·4
Breadth of $\underline{P.\,4}$	0·65
„ $\underline{M.\,1}$	1·2
„ $\underline{M.\,2}$	0·5
Length of $\overline{P.\,1}$	0·4
„ $\overline{P.\,2}$	0·7
„ $\overline{P.\,3}$	0·8
„ $\overline{P.\,4}$	0·9
„ $\overline{M.\,1}$	1·5
„ $\overline{M.\,2}$	0·5
„ $\overline{M.\,3}$	0·3
Breadth of $\overline{M.\,1}$	0·5
„ $\overline{M.\,2}$	0·37
„ $\overline{M.\,3}$	0·2

THE CORSAC FOX.

CANIS CORSAC.

Canis corsac, Linneus, Syst. Nat. 12th edit. vol. iii., Appendix, p. 223
(1768); Erxleben, Syst. Nat. p. 566 (1777); Gmelin, Syst.
Nat. vol. i. p. 74 (1788); Pallas, Reise d. d. Russisch.
Reichs, vol. i. p. 234 (1771); id. Neue Nordische Beyträge,
p. 29 (1781); id. Zoographia, vol. i. p. 41, pl. 4 (1831);
Schreber, Säugthiere, Theil iii. p. 359, pl. 91 B (1778);
J. A. Wagner, Supplement to Schreber, Abth. ii. p. 425;
Tilesius, Nova Acta Phys.-Med. Acad. Cæsar. Leopold.-
Carolinæ Nat. Curiosorum, vol. xi. p. 400 (1823);
Fischer, Syn. Mammalium, p. 185 (1829); Radde, Reisen
im Süden von Ost-Sibirien, vol. i. p. 67, pl. 3 (1862).
Canis karagan, Erxleben, Syst. Nat. p. 566; Schreber, Säugth. Theil iii.
p. 359; Pallas, Reise d. d. Russ. Reichs, vol. i. p. 234.
Canis melanotus, Pallas, Zoographia, vol. i. p. 44.
Vulpes corsac, Gray, Proc. Zool. Soc. 1868, p. 518; id. Catalogue of
Carnivorous Mammalia, p. 205.
Cynalopex corsac, Hamilton Smith, Jardine's Naturalist's Library, vol. ix.
p. 223, pl. 16 (1839).
L'Adive (?), Buffon, Hist. Nat. Suppl. vol. iii. p. 113, pl. 16 (1786).

THE Corsac Fox is a species which has been generally known by description for more than a hundred and twenty years, but naturalists in England have had small opportunity of examining it. Our National Collection possesses three specimens, two of which came from Siberia, and the third from Amoorland.

Whether or not the Corsac Fox is distinct from the kind, or even the two kinds, which will be next described, seems to us to be a matter which cannot be affirmed with certainty. We, however, propose to treat them provisionally as distinct, on account of the very estimable and experienced naturalists who think them so, and who are familiar with one or more of these species or varieties in their native haunts. But since, if they are not distinct, they must assume the name of the Siberian animal we are now concerned with, we begin our enumeration of these problematical forms with the latter—*i. e.* with *Canis corsac.* Its name is derived from its native appellation "Korssuk." Its Russian name is "Kirassu."

This Fox is an inhabitant of the open country of Central Asia, and avoids the forest-clad mountains which are near its range in Eastern Siberia *.

It is seldom seen abroad in the daytime, which it spends sleeping in some deserted burrow of a marmot. Its food, like that of most of its congeners, consists of small mammals and birds, especially of the alpine hare (*Lagomys*) and the vole (*Arvicola*).

It does not make a permanent home, but wanders here and there from one burrow to another. When snow has fallen it is readily traced to its temporary home, and then a snare is set for it. Old Foxes, which understand this, are extremely reluctant to go forth, and will not do so till driven by the hunger of a six, seven, and sometimes a nine days' fast. Sometimes even, Radde tells us, nothing will induce them to venture forth, but they will die of hunger where they are, to be dug out afterwards when advancing spring has thawed the deeply frozen ground.

It is also hunted with dogs, and is soon run down if it cannot secure a safe hiding-place. It is no doubt very easily followed on account of its rank odour, in which it differs altogether from the species that inhabits Siberia north of its northern boundary—we mean the kind last described, *C. lagopus*. Of a very suspicious and savage nature, the Corsac seems to be almost, if not quite, untamable, even when taken young.

It is a small animal, much smaller than the Common Fox, but it has a similarly offensive odour. The pupil of the eye is round. The colour of the coat changes towards summer and winter, but less so than

---

* See Radde, *op. cit.* p. 75.

in the northern Wolf and, of course, very much less indeed than in *C. lagopus*. The freshly developed hairs of the summer coat are of a reddish colour. The winter hairs are said to have each a broad silver-white ring, and are black towards the points, producing a general tint which may be a fawn or mouse colour. Indeed the winter coat, which is very thick, may be quite grey. We have found the hairs of the back to be grey for a considerable distance and then rufous, the terminal portions being white. The head above is coloured like the back. The throat, the underparts, and the lips and chin are white; and the inner sides of the limbs are yellowish white or pale yellow; the moustache is black. There is a dark grey triangular patch in front of the eye on either side of the muzzle, while a yellowish ring surrounds the eye itself. A band across the chest is reddish, and the outsides of the limbs are of a yellower red. The tail is isabel-yellow at the root, then mixed yellow and black above (the hairs being black towards their points), beneath it is much paler. The terminal portion of the tail is black, and there is a black mark on its dorsum near the root. The ears are yellowish grey externally, but lined with white. The coloration, however, is, as so usual in the *Canidæ*, variable. Thus Radde tells us that the fore paws may be yellow or white; the dorsum of the tail, where the caudal gland is situated, seems to be constantly black.

Our Plate XXVII. represents a very fine specimen which came from the country of the Amoor.

On the back the hairs are grey for a considerable distance, then rufous, while their terminations are white.

Habitat. From the banks of the Volga and shores of the Caspian to South-eastern Siberia. It is doubtless found in China, but its southern range is uncertain, as also its northern limit, though it does not inhabit Northern Siberia.

	Centimeters.
Length from snout to root of tail	52·5
,, of tail	25·5
,, from heel to end of longest digit	10·0
,, of ear	5·0

Cranial and Dental Characters.

Radde's figure of the skull shows the nasal bones stopping short, very decidedly, of the hinder terminations of the premaxillæ; and such is also the case with the skull preserved in the British Museum—so much so that it seems as if it must be a very marked character of the species.

The only skull we have been able to examine is a mutilated one (extracted from the skin we have had figured), which presents the following dimensions:—

	Centimeters.
Sphenoideum to gnathion	7·6
Length of palate	5·6
Breadth of ,,	3·4
Length of nasals	3·7
Breadth of ,,	0·8
,, brain-case	4·2
,, zygomata	6·5
Length of $\underline{P.1}$	0·4
,, $\underline{P.2}$	0·72
,, $\underline{P.3}$	0·75
,, $\underline{P.4}$	1·2
,, $\underline{M.1}$	0·8
,, $\underline{M.2}$	0·45
Breadth of $\underline{P.4}$	0·6
,, $\underline{M.1}$	1·0
,, $\underline{M.2}$	0·65
Length of $\overline{P.1}$	0·3
,, $\overline{P.2}$	0·65
,, $\overline{P.3}$	0·8
,, $\overline{P.4}$	0·85
,, $\overline{M.1}$	1·3
,, $\overline{M.2}$	0·5
,, $\overline{M.3}$	0·3
Breadth of $\overline{M.1}$	0·5
,, $\overline{M.2}$	0·4
,, $\overline{M.3}$	0·2

THE THIBET FOX.

CANIS FERRILATUS.

Vulpes ferrilatus, Hodgson, Journal Asiatic Soc. Bengal, vol. xi. pt. i.
p. 278, and plate (1842); Gray, Proc. Zool. Soc. 1868,
p. 516; id. Catalogue of Carnivorous Mammalia, p. 204;
Jerdon, Mammals of India, p. 152; Blanford, Fauna of
British India, Mamm. p. 155; Blyth, Journal Asiatic Soc.
Bengal, vol. xxiii. p. 731 (1854).
Cynalopex ferrilatus, Blyth, Catalogue of Mammalia in Mus. Asiat.
Soc. Bengal, p. 41 (1863).
Canis eckloni (?), Prejevalski, Reisen in Tibet, p. 111 (1884); id.
Third Journey to Thibet, p. 216.

Two specimens, from Thibet, are preserved in our National Collection, and one of them (a type of the species) is figured in our accompanying Plate XXVIII. It is not without some doubt and hesitation that we present this as a really distinct species, thinking it far from impossible that it may be but a local variety of *Canis corsac*.

One distinction consists in the white tip to the tail of *C. ferrilatus*, whereas that of *C. corsac* is black. We have, however, already recorded instances which show that this character cannot be relied on as an absolutely constant one. Much more important is the distinction asserted to exist in the length of the ears; for *C. corsac* is rather a long-eared dog, while *C. ferrilatus* has the ears decidedly short. It is this circumstance, together with the fact that it is a native of Thibet, which leads us strongly to suspect that the newly-described species *C. eckloni* of Prejevalski, which is also a Thibetan animal, may really be nothing but *Vulpes ferrilatus* of Hodgson and of Blanford.

Until the detailed description of the animal appears this question must remain undecided, but the photograph already published plainly shows that it, like *C. ferrilatus*, is a short-eared form. The brush also in both this and *C. eckloni* is well developed, and the fur is long, especially on the legs and feet.

Of the habits of this animal no records are known to us.

The coloration of the back and sides is of a pale or bright yellowish rusty. The face and outside of the ears may be less yellow and more grey, or may be rufous. The sides of the neck, breast, and body, and the greater part of the tail have a mixture of black and white hairs, which produces a general tint of nearly pure grey. The tip of the tail is white, but there may be a circle or dorsal patch of dark colour towards the root; the middle of the tail is for the most part grey. There is a faintly marked dark stripe running backwards from the eye, but no dark mark between the eye and the nose. The limbs are yellowish rufous externally, whitish internally. The lower parts are white, the middle of the breast being strongly marked off by its whiteness from the dark grey sides.

This strong contrast between the grey and the white appears (from the photograph) to be exaggerated in *C. eckloni* by a dark patch at the ventral margin of the grey colour of the sides of the neck.

The hairs of the back are light grey at the base, then rufous, and finally black or white.

The vibrissæ are black.

The fur on the legs and feet is rather long.

Habitat. Thibet *.

	Centimeters.
Length from end of snout to root of tail	65·50
,, of tail	29·50
,, from heel to end of longest digit	10·0
,, of ear	4·6

We have not been able to examine a skull of this species.

* According to Stoliczka (see Journal of the Asiatic Society of Bengal, vol. xxxvii. part ii. p. 5) it is also found in the valley of the Upper Sutlej. It would be interesting to have the statement confirmed.

THE DESERT-FOX.

CANIS LEUCOPUS.

Vulpes leucopus, Blyth, Journal Asiat. Soc. Bengal, vol. xxiii. p. 729 (1854); id. ibid. xxv. p. 443; id. ibid. xxvi. p. 239; Jerdon, Mammals of India, p. 151 (1867); Gray, Proc. Zool. Soc. 1868, p. 316; id. Catalogue of Carnivorous Mammalia, p. 204; Murray, Vertebrate Zoology of Sind, p. 37 (1884); Blanford, Fauna Brit. India, Mamm. p. 151 (1888).

Vulpes griffithii, Blyth, Journ. Asiat. Soc. Bengal, vol. xxiii. p. 730; Scully, Ann. & Mag. Nat. Hist. 5th series, vol. viii. p. 226.

Vulpes pusillus, Blyth, Journ. Asiat. Soc. Bengal, vol. xxiii. pp. 729, 730; Adams, Proc. Zool. Soc. 1858, p. 516; Jerdon, Mammals of India, p. 153; Murray, Vertebrate Zoology of Sind, p. 37.

Vulpes persicus, Blanford, Zoology of Eastern Persia, p. 39, plate 2 (1876).

The Desert-Fox of India inhabits the open country, as does *C. corsac*, which it undoubtedly resembles, so that it may be but a local variety of the latter, especially as the ears are similar in relative length, and not short as in *C. ferrilatus*. The end of the tail, however, is white. Moreover, when its furry coat is fully developed, as in the specimen at the British Museum represented in our Plate XXIX., it is a very handsome animal, with very distinct coloration. The colour, however, varies, and the distinct markings are sometimes hardly, if at all, to be detected. Nevertheless, as in the cases of *C. mesomelas* and *C. lateralis*, we have treated forms as distinct on account of very exceptional peculiarities, not invariably present in all specimens, we propose to do likewise in the present instance.

Mr. Jerdon saw this [*] animal in India, at Umballa, and near Hansi

[*] *Op. cit.* p. 152.

and Hissar, almost always on sand-hills or in the broad sandy beds of nearly dry rivers, and only very rarely in fields, and then in the vicinity of sandy tracts. He was informed, however, that in parts of Cutch and elsewhere, where it is without the presence of a rival species, it was to be found in open cultivated land.

It appears to be more exclusively carnivorous in its habits than some other foxes,—for example, than that next to be described. Its food largely consists of the jerboa-like sand-rat (*Gerbillus*), which is very abundant in the sandy regions this Fox inhabits. It is a rather rapid runner—enough so, according to Jerdon, to give huntsmen a capital run, sometimes even with English dogs.

According to Blanford*, it is common in Scinde on the waste land with scattered bushes that forms so large a portion of the province, a region also inhabited by the species next described. But *C. leucopus* appears to be the only form actually found amongst the sand-hills of the desert.

The author last mentioned is now disposed to think that his *V. persicus* may be identical with *C. leucopus*. In this we are disposed to agree, though it may be that his *V. persicus* is a local variety of *C. vulpes*.

A specimen was sent from Bushire, on the Persian Gulf, to the Zoological Society in 1874, the skull and skin of which we have examined. According to Major St. John, it inhabits the low land. It is said to be very plentiful on the rocky ground close to the shore, where it retreats into cavities between the rocks. These animals are easily captured with the aid of dogs, and Europeans resident in Bushire frequently amuse themselves by hunting them, when they are said often to seek safety by taking to the sea to avoid the dogs.

When the colours of this Fox are fully developed, it is easily distinguishable by a very distinct pale patch on each side of the back behind the shoulder (to which Mr. Blanford has already called attention)†, while a dark transverse stripe over the shoulder passes in front of these light patches, to which it forms a strong contrast.

The back varies from brownish yellow to rusty red, more or less speckled with white, while the sides of the body are whitish or greyish,

* *Op. cit.* p. 152.   † *Op. cit.* p. 151.

and the outside of the limbs iron-grey or rufous. The underparts are of a slaty hue, or even darker in winter though probably white in summer; but the chin and generally also the middle of the breast are white at all seasons. The inner side of the fore limbs and the whole front of the hind limbs to the toes are also whitish, if not white. The face is rufous, markedly so around the eyes, in front of each of which there is generally a dark spot. The ears are black or dark brown externally towards their apices, paler near the base; they are margined externally and lined with white or whitish hairs. The tail is generally of the

Fig. 37.

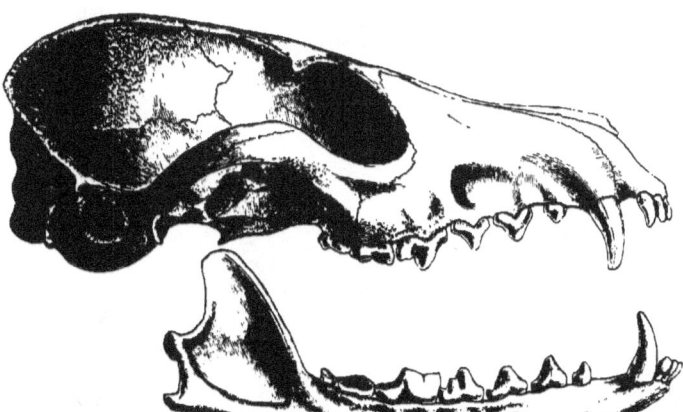

Side view of skull of CANIS LEUCOPUS.

same colour dorsally, as is the back, but less rufous laterally and beneath. Many of the hairs may have black or blackish tips, and there may be a black ring near the end of the tail, or there may be no black at all. The terminal portion of the tail is white.

Habitat. South-western Asia from the Punjaub to Rajpootana, through Afghanistan and Persia to Arabia.

	Centimeters.
Length from end of snout to root of tail	55·0
„ of tail	30·0
„ from heel to end of longest digit	12·3
„ of ear	7·0

Cranial and Dental Characters.

Save the dimensions, we have not observed any skeletal particulars which seemed worthy of note.

	Centimeters.
Basion to ovalion	2·5
„ sphenoideum	3·7
Sphenoideum to gnathion	6·9
Length of palate	5·65
Breadth „	2·8
Length of nasals	3·9
Breadth of „	0·9
„ brain-case	4·15
„ zygomata	5·9
Length of $\underline{P.1}$	0·4
„ $\underline{P.2}$	0·55
„ $\underline{P.3}$	0·7
„ $\underline{P.4}$	1·1
„ $\underline{M.1}$	0·8
„ $\underline{M.2}$	0·54
Breadth of $\underline{P.4}$	0·6
„ $\underline{M.1}$	1·0
„ $\underline{M.2}$	0·8
Length of $\overline{P.1}$	0·3
„ $\overline{P.2}$	0·7
„ $\overline{P.3}$	0·8
„ $\overline{P.4}$	0·85
„ $\overline{M.1}$	1·1
„ $\overline{M.2}$	0·6
„ $\overline{M.3}$	0·3
Breadth of $\overline{M.1}$	0·4
„ $\overline{M.2}$	0·4
„ $\overline{M.3}$	0·3

THE INDIAN FOX.

CANIS BENGALENSIS.

Canis bengalensis, Shaw, Gen. Zoology, vol. i. p. 330 (1800); J. A.
  Wagner, Supplem. to Schreber's Säugth., Abth. ii. p. 423
  (1841).
Canis kokree, Sykes, Proc. Zool. Soc. 1831, p. 101.
Canis chrysurus, Gray, Charlesworth's Mag. of Nat. Hist. vol. i. p. 577
  (1837).
Canis (Vulpes) indicus, Hodgson, Asiat. Researches, vol. xviii. part ii.
  p. 237 (1833).
Canis (Vulpes) bengalensis, Gray, Hardwicke's Illustr. Indian Zool.
  vol. ii. pl. 2.
Canis (Vulpes) rufescens, Gray, tom. cit.
Vulpes bengalensis, Horsfield, Catalogue of Mammalia in Mus. E. India
  Comp. p. 84; Gray, Proc. Zool. Soc. 1868, p. 517; id.
  Catalogue of Carnivorous Mammalia, p. 204; Jerdon,
  Mammals of India, p. 149; Blanford, Fauna of Brit. India,
  Mamm. p. 148.
Vulpes hodgsonii, Gray, Charlesworth's Mag. Nat. Hist. vol. i. p. 578.
Vulpes xanthura, Gray, Proc. Zool. Soc. 1837, p. 68.
Cynalopex bengalensis, Blyth, Cat. Mamm. Mus. Asiat. Soc. p. 41.

THIS little animal is one of the most attractive of the whole family to which it belongs. It is elegant in appearance, with slender limbs, a sharp muzzle, and bushy tail. Its movements are extremely active and it is readily tamed, when its playful, frolicsome nature makes it an agreeable pet—especially as it is a cleanly creature, and has (unlike *C. corsac*) no fox-like smell.

It is a common animal throughout India, save in forest-regions, and is frequently to be seen, as it is not shy, and often enters gardens and other enclosed spaces, though it is said but rarely to molest poultry. Mr. Blanford has seen it on the Maidán in Calcutta, and affirms that its cry may be heard almost nightly in the cold season. Its cry is a sharp yelp, quickly repeated three or four times, and constituting a sort of little chattering bark.

These animals pair from November to January, according to the climate, which is, of course, different in different parts of the vast region over which the species ranges.

It breeds in burrows, when the young, of which there are almost always four in a litter, make their appearance at some time during February, March, or April.

Mr. Jerdon describes the burrow as always having several branches, which radiate from a centre and open separately. With these are other burrows, which end blindly, not opening into the central chamber wherein the animal breeds. The burrow is generally made in a quite open plain, but now and then in some thorny scrub. Advantage is taken of any small rise in the ground to protect the nest from floods, and on this account burrows are often made in artificial mounds. Sometimes, however, it will live for a long time in cavities of old trees.

It is said to feed by preference on lizards, rats, crabs, white-ants, and various other insects, and Blanford cites an instance of its having been watched in the Deccan springing up out of the grass again and again to catch the moths which passed just before dusk. Nevertheless Jerdon saw it hunting quails, and there can be no doubt but that it eats young birds and eggs. But it also habitually takes vegetable food, such as melons, bêr fruit (*Zizyphus*), and pods and shoots of *Cicer arietinum*. Thus altogether it is a much less carnivorous animal than is *C. leucopus*.

It is much coursed in India, and Jerdon tells us that with Arab or country dogs, or half-bred English dogs, it gives a most excellent course. When hunted, it very soon begins to double in a most dexterous manner, and then racing the dogs if it is within a short distance of its earth. It has been known to escape by running in amidst a herd of cattle. If well-bred English dogs are used, the animal has but a poor chance, not being so fleet as the kind last described (*C. leucopus*).

On account of its not having a strong odour, and because of its numerous earths, it is not well suited for fox-hounds. It is believed to be subject to rabies when kept in confinement. Mr. Jerdon knew one or two instances of the occurrence of this malady, but they may have been produced by infection. Certainly nothing of the kind has been experienced in our own Zoological Gardens, where several individuals appear to thrive, and one has sat to our artist for its portrait (Plate XXX.).

This species has been regarded * as "very nearly allied to the Corsac. It is like it in appearance, no doubt, but in addition to its white-tipped tail, the fact of its not possessing a strong odour is against its specific identity with the Corsac of Central Asia.

The colour of this species appears to vary considerably according to locality and season. It is generally reddish grey above, with the sides paler, and the outer surface of the limbs rufous, and the lower parts whitish. There is no dark stripe across the shoulders. The ears are externally dark grey, margined with white, and they are whitish within. The lips and cheeks are whitish, the throat is usually white, and there is a narrow dark line running backwards from the eye, and often a dark spot is interposed between the eye and the nose. In winter the body is of a purer grey, whilst the limbs remain rufous externally. The tail is grey or reddish grey, with a well-defined black tip.

The hairs of the body are each variously coloured, except those of the underparts, which may be entirely white. The hairy coat has on this account that speckled appearance when closely viewed which is so commonly to be met with in the *Canidæ*.

Mr. Blanford † has sometimes found the dorsal fur to be white throughout, except at the tips of the hairs.

The animal, when freshly killed or alive, is said to weigh from 5½ to 8 lbs.

Habitat. South of the Himalayas to Cape Comorin. According to Mr. Blanford, who is so excellent an authority, the animal has not been noticed west of Scinde and the Punjaub, nor east of Assam (where it is rare), and he regards its occurrence in Ceylon as very doubtful, while it is unknown in Burmah.

* Jerdon, *op. cit.* p. 151. † *Op. cit.* p. 149.

THE INDIAN FOX.

	Centimeters.
Length from end of snout to root of tail	56·5
„ of tail	24·0
„ from heel to end of longest digit	10·5
„ of ear	5·6

Fig. 38.

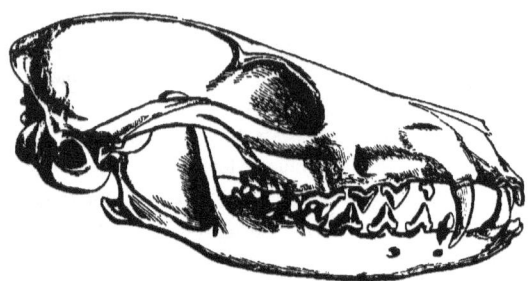

Skull of CANIS BENGALENSIS, side view.

Cranial and Dental Characters.

There is generally a flattened sagittal raised tract between the temporal ridges. The fourth upper premolar is rather small compared with the length of the first and second upper molars.

	Centimeters.
Basion to ovalion	2·15
„ sphenoideum	2·9
Sphenoideum to gnathion	7·3
Length of palate	5·45
Breadth „	2·7
Length of nasals	3·6
Breadth of „	1·1
„ brain-case	4·1
„ zygomata	5·6
Length of P.1	0·3
„ P.2	0·6
„ P.3	0·7

CANIS BENGALENSIS.

		Centimeters.
Length of $\frac{P.\,4}{}$	. . . .	1·0
,, $\frac{M.\,1}{}$	. . . .	0·8
,, $\frac{M.\,2}{}$	. . . .	0·35
Breadth of $\frac{P.\,4}{}$	. . . .	0·5
,, $\frac{M.\,1}{}$	. . . .	1·0
,, $\frac{M.\,2}{}$	. . . .	0·8
Length of $\overline{P.\,1}$	. . . .	0·3
,, $\overline{P.\,2}$	. . . .	0·55
,, $\overline{P.\,3}$	. . . .	0·65
,, $\overline{P.\,4}$	. . . .	0·7
,, $\overline{M.\,1}$	. . . .	1·1
,, $\overline{M.\,2}$	. . . .	0·6
,, $\overline{M.\,3}$	. . . .	0·3
Breadth of $\overline{M.\,1}$	. . . .	0·4
,, $\overline{M.\,2}$	. . . .	0·45
,, $\overline{M.\,3}$	. . . .	0·3

THE HOARY FOX.

CANIS CANUS.

Vulpes canus, Blanford, Journal Asiat. Soc. Bengal, vol. xlvi. part ii.
p. 321 (1877); Sclater, Proc. Zool. Soc. 1878, p. 392;
Blanford, Fauna Brit. India, Mamm. p. 150.

THIS is again a form from South-western Asia. It is a very small species, and is represented in our National Collection by a single skin, which came from Beloochistan. By the kindness of Mr. Blanford, we have had the opportunity of examining two others: one of these and the British-Museum specimen constitute the types of the species. The British-Museum skin is figured in our Plate XXXI. Nothing is known of the habits of this animal.

Blanford gives * the length of the head and body as 18 inches, and that of the tail, without the hair, as $12\frac{1}{2}$ to 13 inches.

His description of the colour is as follows:—" Ashy grey, blackish on the back and sometimes with a rufescent tinge, white below. The basal half of the dorsal fur is dark purplish grey in some skins, the distal half grey or rufescent; in other cases the hairs are light ashy grey almost throughout, the longer and coarser hairs have white rings near the end, and black tips on the back. The long tail-hairs are ashy near the base, white near the ends, the tips black, the black tips being more developed posteriorly so that the tail has a black tip, though less defined than in *V. bengalensis*. Ears grey outside, creamy white on the margin and within; forehead rufous; a dusky or black spot on each side of the muzzle. Outside of the limbs dark rufous or dark ashy, almost black in some cases." All that we would remark in addition is

* *Op. cit.* p. 151.

that it may be the hinder two thirds of the middle of the back which is by far the darkest part.

Habitat. Beloochistan and Southern Afghanistan, possibly extending to Scinde.

	Centimeters.
Length from end of snout to root of tail	53·0
„ of tail	37·0
„ from elbow to end of longest digit	8·0 (?)
„ of ear	6·3

Cranial and Dental Characters.

In the small and delicate skull of this species the auditory bullæ are prominent.

	Centimeters.
Length from basion to ovalion	1·8
„ of palate	4·5
Breadth „	2·4
Length from basion to gnathion	8·4
Breadth of brain-case	3·5
„ zygomata	5·1
Length of nasals	2·9

The individual examined was old and the teeth much worn.

The inner lobe of the upper sectorial tooth was so small as to be almost obsolete; but the breadth from within outwards of the first upper molar was very great.

	Centimeters.
Length of $\overline{P.4}$	1·0
„ $\overline{M.1}$	0·65
„ $\overline{M.2}$	0·3
Breadth of $\overline{P.4}$	0·4
„ $\overline{M.1}$	0·90
„ $\overline{M.2}$	0·65

THE RACCOON-LIKE DOG.

CANIS PROCYONOIDES.

Canis procyonoides, Gray, Illustrations Ind. Zool. vol. ii. plate i. (1834);
id. Charlesworth's Mag. Nat. Hist. vol. i. p. 578 (1837);
J. A. Wagner, Suppl. to Schreber's Säugth., Abth. ii.
p. 430; Schrenck, Reisen im Amur-Lande, vol. i. p. 53,
plates 3 & 4 (1859); Radde, Reisen Süden von Ost-Sibirien,
vol. i. p. 75, plate 3 (1862).

Nyctereutes viverrinus, Temminck, Fauna Japonica, vol. Mammalia, p. 40
plate 8 (1847); Martens, Preussische Expedit. Ost-Asien,
p. 78, plate i. (1876).

Nyctereutes procyonoides, Gray, Proc. Zool. Soc. 1868, p. 522; id.
Cat. Carnivorous Mammalia, p. 210 (1869); Sclater, Proc.
Zool. Soc. 1874, p. 323, plate 50; Garrod, Proc. Zool. Soc.
1878, p. 373.

The external appearance of this Dog (Plate XXXII., from a specimen in the British Museum) is so very peculiar and unlike the aspects of all its congeners, that it is no wonder it should have been placed in a distinct genus, and at first supposed, as it was supposed by Temminck*, to be allied to the raccoon. In reality, however, it is a true dog, as the whole of its anatomy unmistakably proves. At first also it was believed that there were two or more species of Raccoon-like Dogs; but Schrenck, in his careful and exhaustive account of the form and coloration of this animal, has supplied sufficient evidence that it was impossible to distinguish distinct kinds.

The British Museum possesses specimens enough to prove how great is the variation in colour to which the animal is liable, and, indeed, its seasonal changes in this respect were long ago described. But a

* *Op. cit.* p. 40.

specimen which was living in the Zoological Gardens in 1874 presented a coloration different from that of all previously figured individuals *.

The Raccoon-like Dog is an inhabitant of Japan, the valley of the Amoor, and China. Siebold found it to be very common throughout the Japanese islands, where its flesh was considered as good food with an agreeable flavour, and its powdered, calcined bones a valuable medicine. It makes its nest in hollow trunks as well as in burrows which it excavates. It inhabits the woods on mountain-slopes, and is said to climb trees to obtain their fruit. It is sometimes found hidden in the daytime in cavities between rocks, and in winter will now and then make its home beneath the foundations of some country cottage. Its vicinity is in no way dreaded, as it is not deemed destructive to poultry. The natives employ its skin to make bellows, and also to decorate their drums and for winter head-gear.

Radde tells us † that the Raccoon-like Dog is said to hibernate like a badger, if it has had an opportunity of feeding well in the autumn, so that it is in very good condition. If, however, such is not the case, so that as winter approaches it is poor and thin, then it has to remain active and seek its food all through the cold season. This asserted hibernation is very peculiar, as nothing like it is known to occur in any other species of the *Canidæ*. The fat ones which go to sleep, do so in the deserted burrow of some fox, or some other excavation which penetrates below that point to which the frost may extend into the earth during the depth of winter. The creature is only met with most rarely in the mountains during the winter months.

At that season it frequents running streams to feed on fish, sleeping in the daytime concealed behind the tall sedges which extend far and wide in the valleys of the Amoorland. When traversing the ice it progresses with numerous short jumps. It is much less wary than the fox, and extremely greedy, on which account it is easily taken by means of strychnine, although it will sometimes get far away before succumbing to the poison.

* See Proc. Zool. Soc. 1874, pl. 50, p. 323.
† *Op. cit.* p. 85.

In captivity it accustoms itself pretty quickly to the presence of man, remaining rather timid than savage, and it is extremely cleanly in its habits. Its movements are somewhat like those of a civet, and it has a habit of arching its back. After food it takes a long sleep, tightly rolled up, so that head and paws are covered by its long hair, its respiratory movements alone indicating that the round mass is really a living animal.

It is the most omnivorous of dogs, feeding freely and habitually on vegetable substance, and largely on acorns. Fishes are eagerly eaten, especially a kind of carp, of which it will devour eight or ten, always biting them once in the head to make sure of them. In confinement, if given fish and flesh, it will take the former and leave the latter, not eating it, however, at first, save when it feels itself unobserved.

It seldom hunts by day, when it is very timid, but takes the field at night. Its voice is very peculiar. It does not bark like a fox, but rather utters a growl, followed by a long-drawn melancholy whine. When accustomed to confinement it will utter daily a very different kind of sound when hungry, namely, a sort of mewing plaint. It does not run fast, so that a dog easily overtakes it, and it has to resort to peculiar manœuvres to catch the mice which it pursues in summer.

The Raccoon-like Dog has a very pointed muzzle, but short rounded ears and bushy tail. Its coat is always extremely long and thick in winter, but varies in its colouring considerably. Generally the prevailing tint is a dusky yellow. The cheeks and around the eyes are black, and thence forward to near the muzzle, where there is a white spot whence the brown vibrissæ take origin. The sides of the head are yellowish, and the forehead may be so or dusky. The wide rounded ears are white within or in part white externally, but the margin is brown. The chin and front of the neck are brown. A yellowish collar may extend upwards on either side to the shoulder. The whole dorsal region is clothed with long hairs, which are black towards the tip, so that this region is a mixture of black and yellow, and there is much variability as to the amount of black on the back and the degree of its continuity. The ends of the hairs on the flanks are mostly yellowish. The chest and belly are brown, and may be almost black, and the legs are blackish brown. The tail is clothed with long hairs, and is often black distally and dorsally, and may be light yellow on its ventral aspect.

In summer the tint is more rufous and there is more black.

The above description must not be understood as being more than an approximation to what seems the normal condition, the variation being so considerable. The cæcum of this species is almost straight*.

Habitat. Japan, North China, and Amoorland.

	Centimeters.
Length from end of snout to root of tail	53·0
,, of tail	14·0
,, from heel to end of longest digit	9·5
,, of ear	3·2

Fig. 39.

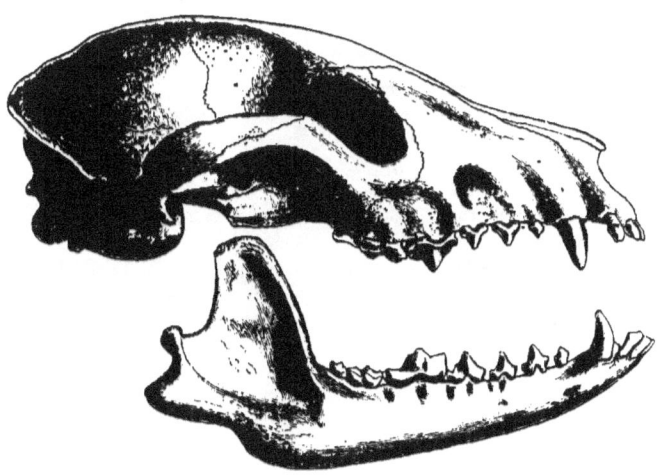

Skull of CANIS PROCYONOIDES.

---

* See Proc. Zool. Soc. 1878, p. 375.

Cranial and Dental Characters.

The skull only presents a really noteworthy character in the form of the mandible, though seen laterally its dorsum is strongly concave antero-posteriorly between the forehead and the end of the nasals.

The mandible is very remarkable for the great development of what has been called the "subangular process." The appearance, however, is rather that of a *supra-angular process*, for the angle of the mandible has the form it has in very many mammals, while above it is a strongly marked, backwardly projecting, distally up-curved process, which is, like the angular process of many other dogs, pushed up towards the condyle.

The second upper molar is well developed, but not much more so than in many others of the *Canidæ*—for instance, in the Common Fox occasionally.

		Centimeters.
Length of cervical vertebræ		10·5
„ dorsal „		14·5
„ lumbar „		11·0
„ sacral „		2·0
„ caudal „		17·0
Length from front of atlas to hinder end of sacrum		38·0
Length of pectoral limb		24·0
„ pelvic „		29·3
„ humerus		8·5
„ radius		7·3
„ femur		9·5
„ tibia		9·8
„ index metacarpal		2·9
„ third „		3·4
„ metacarpal of pollex		1·4
„ whole pollex		2·8
„ last phalanx of third digit (manus)		0·9
„ index metatarsal		3·3
„ metatarsal of hallux		0·7
„ whole hallux		1·15
„ last phalanx of third digit (pes)		1·0

	Centimeters.
Basion to ovalion	2·1
,, sphenoideum	3·5
Sphenoideum to gnathion	6·6
Length of palate	5·3
Breadth ,,	2·9
Length of nasals	3·9
Breadth of ,,	1·2
,, brain-case	4·0
,, zygomata	6·1
Length of $\underline{P.\,1}$	0·3
,, $\underline{P.\,2}$	0·5
,, $\underline{P.\,3}$	0·7
,, $\underline{P.\,4}$	0·9
,, $\underline{M.\,1}$	0·8
,, $\underline{M.\,2}$	0·5
Breadth of $\underline{P.\,4}$	0·4
,, $\underline{M.\,1}$	0·9
,, $\underline{M.\,2}$	0·7
Length of $\overline{P.\,1}$	0·25
,, $\overline{P.\,2}$	0·50
,, $\overline{P.\,3}$	0·55
,, $\overline{P.\,4}$	0·6
,, $\overline{M.\,1}$	1·1
,, $\overline{M.\,2}$	0·7
,, $\overline{M.\,3}$	0·2
Breadth of $\overline{M.\,1}$	0·4
,, $\overline{M.\,2}$	0·4
,, $\overline{M.\,3}$	0·2

THE ASSE FOX.

CANIS CHAMA.

Canis chama, Smith, South-African Quarterly Journal, vol. ii. p. 89
(1835); Sclater, Proc. Zool. Soc. 1875, p. 81, pl. 17.
Fennecus caama, Gray, Catalogue of Carnivorous Mammalia, p. 207.

THIS long-eared South-African Fox leads us towards the true Fennec (*C. zerda*), although it is a much larger animal. Of the specimens in the British Museum one is a type of the species, and it is this which has been selected for representation on our Plate XXXIII.

A living specimen was presented to the Zoological Society in 1875. It came from the diamond-fields in West Griqualand, having been caught near a Dutch Boer's farm there. Other individuals had been seen in the same district. This individual is well figured in the Zoological Society's 'Proceedings.'

The original description of the species given by Sir Andrew Smith is as follows:—

"Muzzle, centre of face, and top of head yellowish brown, variegated by an intermixture of bristly hairs annulated black and white; sides of head a uniform whitish yellow; upper lip, towards angles of mouth, lower lip, and chin blackish brown; whiskers and edges of eyelids black; ears large, outer surfaces yellowish red, inner margined with white hairs, elsewhere bare. Woolly hairs of neck and body abundant; their tips reddish white or yellowish white, elsewhere a dull smoke colour; bristly hairs abundant on back of neck and centre of back; on sides, shoulders, and outsides of thighs, less numerous, all annulated black and white; the tips black. Extremities yellowish white, inclined to white on their anterior surfaces; a large brownish-black blotch on the posterior surface of each hinder extremity about halfway between the feet and the base of the tail. Underparts of neck and body whitish yellow. Tail very bushy, the prevailing colour yellowish white, the upper surface towards base variegated with bristly hairs annulated black and white, the black, about three inches from the root, is so disposed as to give an appearance of one or two waved transverse black stripes; from thence to the point the bristly hairs are all tipped with black, and at the very extremity of the tail they are almost entirely of that colour, so that it appears perfectly black. Length from nose to base of tail 23 inches; length of tail 13 inches; height at shoulder 12 inches, at rump 13 inches."

He adds that it inhabits Namaqualand on both sides of the Orange River.

This animal is evidently subject to variation in colour. In the specimen which lived in our Zoological Gardens, the tail had a black stripe down its dorsum, instead of presenting an appearance of transverse markings.

A British Museum specimen also shows that the general tint may be pale reddish and the underparts pale yellowish, while the tail may be only dark brown at its terminal portion intermixed with a little black. The under jaw may also be very dark-coloured.

Habitat. South Africa, north and south of the Orange River.

	Centimeters.
Length from end of snout to root of tail	63·0
,, of tail	30·5
,, from heel to end of longest digit	13·0
,, of ear	8·0

We have not been able to examine any skull extracted from a skin undoubtedly belonging to this species.

THE PALE FOX.

CANIS PALLIDUS.

Canis pallidus, Rüppell, Zool. Atlas, p. 33, pl. 11 (1826); Cuvier, Règne Anim. 2nd edit. vol. i. p. 152; J. A. Wagner, Supplement to Schreber's Säugth., Abth. ii. p. 422.
Fennecus pallidus, Gray, Proc. Zool. Soc. 1868, p. 520; id. Catalogue of Carnivorous Mammalia, p. 207.
Vulpes edwardsi, Rochebrune, Bulletin d. la Société Philomatique d. Paris, p. 8 (1882); id. Faune de la Sénégambie, Mammifères, p. 93, pl. 5 (1883).

This smaller long-eared Fox approximates still more than the last to the true Fennec. Cuvier deemed that it could hardly be satisfactorily distinguished from *C. corsac*, but in addition to its widely different geographical distribution it is a larger-limbed and higher-standing animal.

The general colour is that of a pale, slightly reddish yellow, the woolly hair of the back being grey towards the roots. There are many white hairs on the head. The ears are coloured like the body externally, and margined with white within.

On the back and neck the hairs are variegated with white, black, and yellow, but black is almost wanting from the hairs on the sides of the body, which are almost entirely yellowish. The cheeks, throat, and underparts are whitish. The tail has a black spot on its dorsum about an inch distant from its roots. There are many black hairs on the tail, which is black towards and at its apex. The inner sides of the feet are white, more or less rusty coloured externally. The specimens in the British Museum, whereof one is the subject of our Plate XXXIV., are covered with close pale hair, and there is a white spot both above and beneath each eye.

We cannot recognize any good specific characters by which to separate the *V. edwardsi* of Rochebrune from the *C. pallidus* of Rüppell. Dr. Rocheburne rests its distinctness on its smaller size, but we have seen again and again how great a difference may exist in this respect between forms of the same species which inhabit different regions. The form distinguished as *V. edwardsi* comes from Senegambia, whereas the other type is an inhabitant of Nubia, Darfur, and Cordofan.

Habitat. Eastern and Western Africa.

	Centimeters.
Length from end of snout to root of tail	40·5
„ of tail	32·0
„ from heel to end of longest digit	10·0
„ of ear	5·5

Another specimen has a larger body and a somewhat shorter tail, but the length of the foot is the same.

Cranial and Dental Characters.

We have only met with an imperfect skull of this species. The muzzle thereof is short, and the nasals do not extend so far backwards as do the nasal processes of the maxillæ. The lower jaw was wanting in the skull examined.

	Centimeters.
Length of $P.1$	0·26
„ $P.2$	0·4
„ $P.3$	0·5
„ $P.4$	0·8
„ $M.1$	0·64
„ $M.2$	0·45
Breadth of $P.4$	0·3
„ $M.1$	0·7
„ $M.2$	0·6

RÜPPELL'S FENNEC.

CANIS FAMELICUS.

Canis famelicus, Rüppell, Zool. Atlas, p. 15, pl. 5 (1826); J. A. Wagner, Suppl. to Schreber's Säugth., Abth. ii. p. 419; Lataste, Actes de la Soc. Linnéenne de Bordeaux, 4ᵉ série, vol. ix. p. 215 (1885).

The still longer ears of this species, first described by Rüppell, cause it to more closely resemble the true Fennec (*C. zerda*) than does any other species of the genus *Canis*, and we therefore distinguish it by the name of Rüppell's Fennec.

He obtained it from the Nubian desert.

There is in the National Collection a skin [*] from Afghanistan, which appears to us, as it has appeared to others, very like Rüppell's *famelicus*, and therefore we have had it represented on our Plate XXXV. The species, however, greatly needs a thorough investigation, which can only be satisfactorily carried out by means of further specimens from the desert of Nubia.

The sides are grey, the back and shoulders reddish, and the underparts whitish. The head is fawn-colour, and also a line along the middle of the back to the tail, but the hairs are only of this light colour towards their tips; for the greater part of their length they are, like the underfur, darker. There is a distinct dark mark (which may be a triangular black spot) between the eye and the nose. The cheeks and lips are white. The ears are dark within margined with white; externally they are fawn-coloured at the base and then black towards the tips, but

---

[*] No. 86. 10. 15. 4.

the tips themselves are lighter. The limbs externally are fawn-coloured like the back. The thighs are whitish within, and the fronts of the hind legs are whitish. The tail is dark above, lighter below, and white at the end; the long hairs on its dorsum are largely black, those below are bright fawn-coloured towards their tips.

If this form is not the *C. famelicus* of Rüppell, it will require distinguishing by a distinct, new appellation. Its eastern origin cannot but suggest doubts as to its identity with the Rüppellian species.

Habitat. Eastern Africa and South-western Asia.

	Centimeters.
Length from end of snout to root of tail	49·0
,, of tail	26·0
,, from heel to end of longest digit	10·0 (?)
,, of ear	8·5

Cranial and Dental Characters.

The skull measured was extracted from the skin figured on Plate XXXV. The auditory bullæ were of moderate size.

	Centimeters.
Basion to ovalion	2·3
,, sphenoideum	3·1
Sphenoideum to gnathion	6·8
Length of palate	5·1
Breadth ,,	2·9
Length of nasals	3·15
Breadth of ,,	0·95
,, brain-case	4·1
,, zygomata	6·0
Length of $\underline{P.1}$	0·3
,, $\underline{P.2}$	0·65
,, $\underline{P.3}$	0·7
,, $\underline{P.4}$	1·1
,, $\underline{M.1}$	0·8
,, $\underline{M.2}$	0·4

	Centimeters.
Breadth of $\underline{P.4}$	0·6
,, $\underline{M.1}$	1·0
,, $\underline{M.2}$	0·8
Length of $\overline{P.1}$	0·2
,, $\overline{P.2}$	0·55
,, $\overline{P.3}$	0·7
,, $\overline{P.4}$	0·8
,, $\overline{M.1}$	1·15
,, $\overline{M.2}$	0·5
,, $\overline{M.3}$	0·2
Breadth of $\overline{M.1}$	0·45
,, $\overline{M.2}$	0·4
,, $\overline{M.3}$	0·2

THE TRUE FENNEC.

CANIS ZERDA.

Canis zerda, Zimmermann, Geograph. Geschichte, vol. ii. p. 247 (1780);
   Rüppell, Zool. Atlas, p. 5, pl. 2; Cuvier, Règne Anim.
   2nd edit. vol. i. p. 153; Smith, S. African Quarterly
   Journal, p. 90 (1835); J. A. Wagner, Supplement to
   Schreber's Säugth., Abth. ii. p. 420.
Canis cerdo, Gmelin, Syst. Nat. vol. i. p. 75 (1788).
Canis fennecus, Lesson, Man. de Mammalogie, p. 168 (1827).
Vulpes minimus zoarensis, Skiöldebrand, Kongl. Vetenskaps-Akademiens
   Handlingar, vol. xxxviii. pp. 265, 267, and plate (1777).
Fennecus brucei, Desmarest, Mammalogie, p. 235 (1820).
Fennecus zoarensis, Gray, Proc. Zool. Soc. 1868, p. 519; id. Cat. of
   Carnivorous Mammalia, p. 207.
Megalotis cerdo, Illiger, Prodrom. p. 131 (1821).
Megalotis zerda, Hamilton Smith, Jardine's Nat. Library, vol. ix. p. 237,
   pl. 30.
The Zerda, Pennant, History of Quadrupeds, vol. i. p. 248, pl. 28
   (1781); Sparrman, Voyage to Cape of Good Hope, vol. ii.
   p. 185 (1786).
Fennec, Bruce, Travels, vol. v. p. 128 and plate (1790).
Animal Anonyme, Buffon, Hist. Nat. Suppl. vol. iii. p. 148, pl. 19
   (1776).

THIS beautiful little animal—at once recognizable by its extremely large ears—was first made known to science by Bruce, inasmuch as he transmitted a written notice and drawing of it to Buffon, who published it in the year 1776, thus preceding a similar publication by Skiöldebrand in the Swedish 'Transactions' for 1777.

Bruce and Skiöldebrand were simultaneously consuls at Algiers, and Sparrman, who in 1786 published the account of his voyage to the Cape, states therein that Bruce had previously seen the animal in

Algiers, and that Skiöldebrand had possessed a figure of the animal many years before, and had been vainly persuaded to publish it in the Swedish Transactions, previously to his paper of 1777, to which he expressly refers. This statement and reference appear to have curiously irritated Bruce, whose remarks may remind us rather of a literary dispute of the sixteenth century than of a scientific discussion of the eighteenth! But, according to the rules of modern science, however long Mr. Skiöldebrand may have possessed a drawing of the animal, such possession, or conversations respecting it, could give him no claim to priority over Bruce, seeing that a figure and notice were first published to the world, in Bruce's name, by Buffon.

But Buffon and Bruce strangely misapprehended the nature of the animal, since Buffon quotes Bruce as saying: "*il paraît* tenir de plus près à l'écureuil."

The true Fennec is perhaps the most attractive in aspect of all the wild *Canidæ*, and it becomes exceedingly tame and gentle in captivity. No less than five individuals have lived in captivity in our Zoological Gardens. Of the specimens in the British Museum, the one we have selected for representation in our Plate XXXVI. is one from which the skull has been extracted, which we have also had drawn.

Bruce strangely represents the Fennec as an arboreal animal, building its nest in a tree, an error which probably arose through information received by him respecting some other animal to which his informant had understood him to refer. As a result of his own observation of a specimen in captivity he says:—"Though his favourite food seemed to be dates or any sweet fruit, yet I observed he was very fond of eggs; pigeons' eggs and small birds' eggs were first brought him, which he devoured with great avidity; but he did not seem to know how to manage the egg of a hen, but when broken for him, he ate it with the same voracity as the others. When he was hungry he would eat bread, especially with honey or sugar. It was very observable that a bird, whether confined in a cage near him or flying across the room, engrossed his whole attention. He followed it with his eyes wherever it went, nor was he at this time to be diverted by placing biscuit before him, and it was obvious, by the great interest he seemed to take in its motions, that he was accustomed to watch for victories over it, either for his pleasure or his food. He seemed very much alarmed at the approach of a cat, and endeavoured to hide himself, but showed no symptom of preparing for any defence. I never heard he had any voice; he suffered himself, not without some difficulty, to be handled in the day when he seemed rather inclined to sleep, but was exceedingly unquiet and restless so soon as night came, and always endeavouring his escape, and though he did not attempt the wire, yet with his sharp teeth he very soon mastered the wood of any common bird-cage."

The Fennec is above of a pale fawn-colour, or a reddish cream-colour, or even a whitish stone-colour, white beneath. The end of the tail is black, and sometimes there are black marks on its dorsum near the root. A portion of the forehead and the parts surrounding the eyes are nearly quite white. The very long, erect and pointed ears are covered externally with short rufous hairs, with long whitish hairs on their inner margins. A longitudinal black mark on the hinder part of the dorsum of the body may be present or absent. In one specimen the hairs on the body were of a light yellowish ochre with the tips white. In another they were rufous ochre with white tips. The presence or absence of the black mark on the back, and the differences which exist as to the length of the ears, may indicate that two species are confounded under the designation *C. zerda*.

Habitat. Northern Africa, certainly from Nubia to Algiers, and throughout the Sahara.

	Centimeters.
Length from end of snout to root of tail	40·0
„ of tail	17·3
„ from heel to end of longest digit	9·0
„ of ear	8·0

In another specimen the ear was 15·0.

150   THE TRUE FENNEC.

Fig. 40.

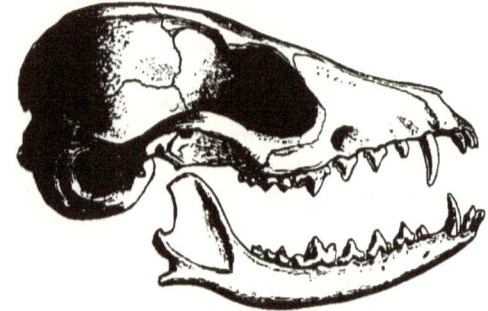

Side view of skull of CANIS ZERDA.

Fig. 41.

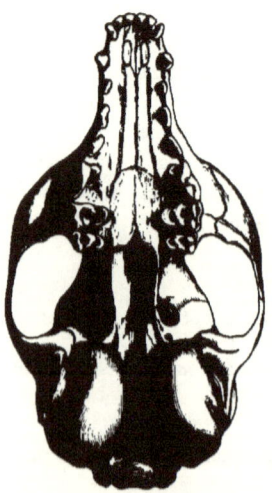

Basis cranii of CANIS ZERDA.

Cranial and Dental Characters.

The most remarkable character of the skull of the Fennec is the very large size of the auditory bullæ and of the external opening of the *meatus auditorius externus*.

The proportion borne by the length of the fourth upper premolar to the length of the two upper molars taken together may be as 100 to 116, or as 100 to 125.

Dimensions of a small specimen.

		Centimeters.
Length of cervical vertebræ		7·2
,, dorsal ,,		11·3
,, lumbar ,,		9·0
,, sacral ,,		1·6
,, caudal ,,		35·0
Length from front of atlas to hinder end of sacrum		29·1
Length of pectoral limb		23·0
,, pelvic limb		27·2
,, humerus		8·0
,, radius		7·9
,, femur		8·1
,, tibia		9·8
,, index metacarpal		2·4
,, third ,,		2·8
,, metacarpal of pollex		0·9
,, whole pollex		1·9
,, last phalanx of third digit (manus)		0·75
,, index metatarsal		3·9
,, metatarsal of hallux		0·4
,, whole hallux		0·7
,, last phalanx of third digit (pes)		0·75

Dimensions of the Skull of the individual figured.

Basion to ovalion	1·8
,, sphenoideum	2·5
Sphenoideum to gnathion	5·8
Length of palate	4·5
Breadth ,,	2·4

THE TRUE FENNEC.

	Centimeters.
Length of nasals . . .	3·2
Breadth of ,, ...	0·7
,, brain-case	3·5
,, zygomata	5·8
Length of $\underline{P.\,1}$	0·25
,, $\underline{P.\,2}$	0·5
,, $\underline{P.\,3}$	0·55
,, $\underline{P.\,4}$.	0·90
,, $\underline{M.\,1}$	0·60
,, $\underline{M.\,2}$.	0·45
Breadth of $\underline{P.\,4}$.	0·3
,, $\underline{M.\,1}$	0·7
,, $\underline{M.\,2}$	0·6
Length of $\overline{P.\,1}$	0·2
,, $\overline{P.\,2}$	0·50
,, $\overline{P.\,3}$	0·55
,, $\overline{P.\,4}$	0·6
,, $\overline{M.\,1}$	1·0
,, $\overline{M.\,2}$	0·5
,, $\overline{M.\,3}$.	0·2
Breadth of $\overline{M.\,1}$	0·3
,, $\overline{M.\,2}$	0·3
,, $\overline{M.\,3}$	0·2

THE DINGO.

CANIS DINGO.

Canis familiaris Dingo, Blumenbach, Handbuch der Naturgeschichte,
p. 103 (1780); id. ibid. p. 85, i.(1830); J. A. Wagner,
Suppl. to Schreber's Säugth., Abth. ii. p. 374 (1840);
Gray, Proc. Zool. Soc. 1868, p. 509; id. Cat. of Carnivorous Mammalia, p. 195; Sclater, Proc. Zool. Soc. 1871,
p. 629.
Canis Dingo, Gould, Mammals of Australia, vol. iii. plates 51 & 52
(1863).
Canis Dingo Australasiæ, Desmarest, Mammalogie, p. 191 (1820); E. T.
Bennett, Gardens and Menagerie, p. 51 (1830); George
Bennett, Wanderings in New S. Wales, vol. i. p. 231 (1834).
Chryseus Australiæ, Hamilton Smith, Jardine's Nat. Library, vol. ix.
p. 188, pl. 10.
Dingo, Shaw, General Zoology, vol. i. p. 277 (1800).
Chien de la Nouvelle Hollande, F. Cuvier, Mammifères, vol. ii. (1824).

WE have now to consider the true dog, the question as to the origin of which has excited such great and continued interest. Has our dog sprung from one source, or from several wild species, and does any wild animal exist which can be supposed to be more nearly related to the domestic dog than are any of the species of *Canidæ* which we have already passed in review?

So far as we have been able to ascertain, there is no animal which has any even apparently valid claim to be regarded as truly wild, and at the same time a true and perfect dog, save the Dingo of Australia. It is for this reason we propose to treat of it before saying the little which it comes within the scope of this work to say concerning the various breeds and races of the domestic dog.

Our Plate, which is taken from a specimen living in the Gardens of the Zoological Society, gives, we think, a fair representation of the most usual aspect of the animal.

So far as we know, the first indication of the existence of the Dingo is given by Capt. William Dampier * in his account of his voyage round the world, speaking of the continent of Australia, as visited by him in 1688 :—" We saw no sort of animal, nor any Track of Beast, but once; and that seemed to be the Tread of a Beast as big as a great Mastiff-Dog."

The creature itself may have been seen by some of his men, for he tells us † :—" My men saw two or three Beasts like hungry Wolves, lean like so many skeletons, being nothing but skin and bones." He adds :—" 'Tis probable that it was the Foot of one of those Beasts that I mentioned as seen by us in N. Holland." In the account of Governor Phillip's voyage in 1788 ‡, however, we have a description and figure of an animal of the kind which is declared to have been then living at Hatfield House, in the possession of the Marchioness of Salisbury.

F. Cuvier has given a good figure of one which was living in the Gardens at Paris in 1806. One of its most remarkable characteristics was its readiness to attack other large and formidable animals without hesitation. It would fly at dogs of much larger size and also at the bars of cages containing lions and bears. It was very exclusive in its affection, only manifesting it to the one who most frequently set it at liberty from time to time.

Mr. George Bennett, who was so many years in Australia, relates various instances of wild Dingoes pretending to be dead when no other means of escape seemed practicable. Mr. Gould believed the Dingo to have been introduced from the north, and had never heard of its being found in Tasmania " in the wild or semi-wild state in which it occurs on the Australian continent." He adds :—" From what I saw of the animal in a state of nature, I could not but regard it in the light of a variety to which the course of ages had given a wildness of air and

---

* See 'A Collection of Voyages,' vol. i. p. 463 (London: James and John Knapton, 1729).

† Vol. iii. p. 106.

‡ See 'The Voyage of Governor Phillip to Botany Bay.'

disposition. . . . I may cite the facility with which the natives bring it under subjection, and the parti-colouring of its hairy coat; for although the normal colouring is red or reddish sand-colour, black or black and white individuals are not unfrequently seen." That this is not a modern result of cross-breeding is shown by the fact (also referred to by Gould) that before 1798 they were observed as of two colours, red or black *. Mr. Gilbert is also referred to by Mr. Gould as reporting the varied colours of the Dingoes of Western Australia.

That, nevertheless, the animal has been for a very long time an inhabitant of the Australian continent is shown by the fact that its remains have been found in a fossil state, as we mention in detail below.

The Dingo is a most destructive animal to sheep, biting and destroying in savage fury to a degree far exceeding its requirements with respect to food. It is also extremely destructive to poultry, and has often shown itself, when more or less domesticated, incorrigible in that matter.

Naturally it never barks, but like wolves and jackals learns to do so in confinement from hearing other dogs bark.

In 1861 the Dingo was to be met with in all the thick forests, deeply-scrubbed gullies, in belts of timber bordering on the large plains throughout the country †. Shy and retired in its habits, it is rarely seen by day.

The most recent account of this animal we have met with gives us ‡ the following information :—" I at once set out to find a Dingo suitable for my next expedition; this was a very difficult matter, for the Dingoes are much more rare here § than farther south in Australia, where natives can be seen followed by ten or twelve dogs, which are of different breeds, for the Dingoes of the natives quickly mix with the shepherd-dogs,

---

* See 'An Account of the English Colony of New South Wales,' by David Collins, p. 567 (1798).

† 'Bush-Wanderings of a Naturalist,' p. 35 (London: Routledge, Warne, and Routledge, 1861).

‡ See ' Among Cannibals,' by Carl Lumholtz, p. 178 (1889).

§ *I. e.* in Queensland, having been so greatly destroyed by Europeans.

greyhounds, and terriers of the colonists. On Herbert river there are rarely more than one or two Dingoes in each tribe, and as a rule they are of pure blood. The natives find them as puppies in the hollow trunks of trees, and rear them with greater care than they bestow on their own children. The Dingo is an important member of the family; it sleeps in the huts, and gets plenty to eat, not only of meat, but also of fruit. Its master never strikes but merely threatens it. He caresses it like a child, eats the fleas off it, and then kisses it on the snout. Though the Dingo is treated so well it often runs away, especially in the pairing-season, and at such times it never returns. Thus it never becomes perfectly domesticated, still is very useful to the natives, for it has a keen scent, and traces every kind of game; it never barks, and hunts less wildly than our dogs, but very rapidly, frequently capturing the game on the run. Sometimes it refuses to go any further, and its owner has then to carry it on his shoulders, a luxury of which it is very fond. The Dingo will follow nobody else but its owner; this materially increased my difficulty in finding a dog, for it was useless unless the owner could be persuaded to go with me; besides, but few of the Dingoes understand hunting the boongary *, for which they have to be specially trained from the beginning."

As to the question of the antiquity and distinctness of the Dingo, it may be well to quote the remarks and opinions of Frederick McCoy, F.R.S., who has done so much for science. He tells us †:—" The origin of the domestic dog is a question of great difficulty and interest, which it has been suggested could be best investigated by a study of the Dog known to the lowest types of the human race; and the aboriginal inhabitants of Australia were thought to afford these conditions. On the other hand, the remarkable absence of the higher orders of Mammalian Quadrupeds in Australia was supposed to render it highly probable that the Dingo was not really a native of the place, but was

---

* A tree-kangaroo (*Dendrolagus*) discovered by Mr. Lumholtz in Australia, and named *D. lumholtzii*.

† See the 'Geological Survey of Victoria. Prodromus of the Palæontology of Victoria,' decade vii. pp. 7–10 (1882).

brought at some remote period from some other country by human savage races arriving to constitute the population of Australia. Taking the case of the Dingo, it was certain that the native dogs of continental Asia were not clearly related, to the extent of specific identity, with the Australian one, nor could any near analogues be found elsewhere; while on the other hand the facts are beyond dispute: (1st) that the Dingo is singularly averse to domestication and man's society when compared with other dogs; (2nd) that it is extremely abundant, with little or no variation, over the whole of Australia; and (3rd) that the further you go from human haunts, near the coast, into the desert interior, the more numerous do the Dingoes appear, indicating that the species was a really indigenous one.

"The announcement, many years ago, of my recognition of bones and teeth of the Dingo in the Pliocene Tertiary strata of Colac and other Victorian localities, in company with similarly mineralized remains of *Thylacoleo*, *Diprotodon*, *Nototherium*, *Procoptodon*, and other extinct genera, therefore excited great interest, as proving that the Dingo was really one of the most ancient of the indigenous mammals of the country, and abounded as now most probably before man himself appeared. . . . . Our present species, although still living in great numbers, I have no doubt dates from the Pliocene Tertiary time, and I find, on the most minute comparison and measurements, no difference between the fossil and recent individuals, either of the adult age, or of the younger periods before the milk-teeth were shed to give place to the permanent molar teeth."

As to the bearing of these facts, concerning the antiquity of the Dingo, on the question as to its origin, we would remark that while they show that the animal existed in Australia at an extremely remote period, they are not decisive as to whether it was introduced by man, or (if it was introduced by him) as to whether it is a race formed in Australia from domesticated breeds, such as now exist in adjacent regions, or whether such latter breeds are themselves derived from the Dingo on its march towards the Australian continent. A recent explorer, Mr. Charles Morris Woodford, expresses * his own judgment as follows :—

* See 'A Naturalist among the Head-hunters' (1890), p. 54.

"The Solomon-Island dog, now, of course, rapidly becoming absorbed and crossed with the mangy curs brought down for the sake of their teeth from Sydney by every trading-vessel, is assuredly a descendant of the Dingo. I have seen individuals that in colour, shape of ears, general expression, and other characteristics were hardly, except in size, to be distinguished from that animal. I have noticed a similar but smaller breed in Fiji among the natives, and I think that probably the Dingo is the progenitor of the domestic dog of all the Pacific Islanders."

It seems almost incredible that the Dingo can have entered Australia without human aid, but nevertheless some conditions may have existed that enabled it to do so, of which conditions we can now discover no trace, and which we are unable to imagine.

As before said, the Dingo varies in its coloration from red to black. There is a greyish underfur, but, save in the black variety, the long hairs are generally yellow or whitish. The top of the head and dorsal region generally are of a darker reddish yellow, often intermixed with black. The underparts are paler, and may be whitish. The end of the tail is very often white, as are frequently the feet and sometimes the muzzle, though this is also sometimes black.

The animal may be of a uniformly light reddish or yellowish brown, save that it is paler beneath, on the outside of the fore legs, below the elbow, as well as on the inner side of the limbs and on the cheeks.

Habitat. The continent of Australia.

	Centimeters.
Length from end of snout to root of tail	103
,, of tail	27
,, from heel to end of longest digit	17
,, of ear	8

Skeletal Characters.

No noticeable and constant characters were found by us to distinguish the cranium and dentition of the Dingo from the skulls and teeth of the other larger species of the genus *Canis*, such as the wolf and the jackal.

CANIS DINGO.

	Centimeters.
Length of cervical vertebræ	16·0
„ dorsal „	24·0
„ lumbar „	18·5
„ sacral „	5·0
„ caudal „	37·5
Length from atlas to hinder end of sacrum	63·5
Length of pectoral limb	47·0
„ pelvic „	54·0
„ humerus	16·5
„ radius	16·0
„ femur	18·0
„ tibia	17·6
„ index metacarpal	5·7
„ third „	6·4
„ metacarpal of pollex	2·0
„ whole pollex	4·3
„ last phalanx of third digit (manus)	1·7
„ index metatarsal	6·3
„ metatarsal of hallux	1·2
„ whole hallux	1·8
„ last phalanx of third digit (pes)	1·7
Length from basion to ovalion	2·9
„ „ sphenoideum	5·1
„ from sphenoideum to gnathion	13·2

Dimensions (in centimeters) of five individuals.

Basion to ovalion	3·0	3·2	3·3	3·5	3·4
„ sphenoideum	5·1	4·9	4·8	4·8	4·9
Sphenoideum to gnathion	13·2	12·5	11·7	12·9	11·6
Length of palate	9·9	9·3	9·0	9·8	8·9
Breadth „	6·1	5·3	5·5	5·6	5·5
Length of nasals	7·5	7·3	7·8	6·9	6·6
Breadth of „	1·3	2·0	1·9	1·9	1·6
„ brain-case	6·1	5·6	5·9	5·6	5·6
„ zygomata	11·9	10·3	11·8	11·5	10·5
Length of $\underline{P.1}$	0·6	0·6	0·6	0·5	0·5
„ $\underline{P.2}$	1·2	1·1	1·1	1·0	1·0
„ $\underline{P.3}$	1·3	1·3	1·2	1·2	1·1
„ $\underline{P.4}$	2·1	2·1	2·0	2·0	1·8

Dimensions of five individuals (continued).

Length of $\underline{M.1}$	1·5	1·4	1·3	1·2	1·2
,, $\underline{M.2}$	0·8	0·8	0·8	0·7	0·7
Breadth of $\underline{P.4}$	1·1	1·1	1·1	1·1	1·0
,, $\underline{M.1}$	1·6	1·6	1·6	1·6	1·6
,, $\underline{M.2}$	1·1	1·1	1·1	1·1	1·0
Length of $\overline{P.1}$	0·5	0·4	0·35	0·4	0·4
,, $\overline{P.2}$	1·0	0·9	0·9	0·8	0·8
,, $\overline{P.3}$	1·1	1·1	1·1	0·95	1·0
,, $\overline{P.4}$	1·2	1·2	1·2	1·1	1·1
,, $\overline{M.1}$	2·3	2·3	2·0	2·0	2·0
,, $\overline{M.2}$	1·0	1·0	1·0	0·9	0·9
,, $\overline{M.3}$	0·5	0·5	0·5	0·5	0·5
Breadth of $\overline{M.1}$	0·9	0·9	0·8	0·8	0·8

THE DOMESTIC DOG.

CANIS FAMILIARIS.

As was declared in our Preface, it is by no means the object of this work to describe the varieties of form and faculty which exist amongst the now multitudinous breeds of the Domestic Dog. Nevertheless, the companion of man must not be passed over altogether in silence; for, whatever may have been its origin, the Domestic Dog has every appearance of constituting, together with the Dingo, one species now. Although it may be true that certain breeds of dogs unite more readily with their own variety than with other forms, it is none the less abundantly evident that dogs of very different races breed freely together, and that their offspring are perfectly fertile. But apart from this matter, no attentive observer of the ways of animals can have failed to note how, when dogs happen to meet, even though of the most diverse breeds—some toy lap-dog and some huge mastiff—each at once makes manifest its feeling that the other is a dog and a brother. Nor will the spontaneous judgment of the ordinary observer fail to accord with that indicated by the animals themselves.

Assuming then, at least provisionally, that the dog, as we know it, is to be considered as a distinct species, it is absolutely the most wonderful species of animal known to us as regards the number and diversity of the races which compose it. We have but to think of the Pug-dog and the Greyhound, the Toy Spaniel and the Bloodhound, the Turnspit and the St. Bernard's Dog, to recognize diversities of bodily conformation exceeding those of any other species of Beast or Bird known to us.

As to the number of breeds, Professor Fitzinger * recognizes no less

* See ' Der Hund und seine Racen.' 1876.

than one hundred and eighty-five varieties, nor do we think his enumeration excessive. He groups these varieties in seven categories, as follows :—(1) House Dogs, 48 varieties; (2) Spaniels, 30 varieties; (3) Terriers, 12 varieties; (4) Hounds, 35 varieties; (5) Mastiffs, 19 varieties; (6) Greyhounds, 35 varieties, and (7) Hairless Dogs, 6 varieties.

With the ancient Romans, dogs seem to have been classed as either *Canes villatici* (House Dogs), *Canes pastorales* (Shepherd Dogs), or *Canes venatici* (Sporting Dogs); the last category being subdivided into A, *pugnaces* (probably like our Bull-dogs and Terriers), B, *nare sagaces* (hunting by scent), and C, *pedibus celeres* (like our Greyhounds).

Lieut.-Col. C. Hamilton Smith * grouped the breeds thus :—

(1) Wolf-Dogs (such *e. g.* as the Esquimaux, Newfoundland, St. Bernard, and Pomeranian Dogs, with the Shepherd's Dog and great Wolf-dog); (2) Watch-dogs (such as the German Boar-hound, the Danish Dog, &c.); (3) Greyhounds (including the Lurchers and the Egyptian street-dog); (4) Hounds (including the Bloodhound, Dalmatian Coach-dog, Turnspit, Spaniel, and Maltese Dog); (5) Cur-dogs (including with the Terrier the Pariah dog of India and the dogs of the natives of Tierra del Fuego), and (6) Mastiffs (including that of Thibet with the Bull-dog, the Pug-dog, and the little Danish Dog).

Mr. Edmund Harting, F.L.S., a naturalist who has paid so much attention to the birds and beasts of our Islands, has proposed † to arrange the breeds in six groups (founded to a certain extent on the form and development of the ears), which he regards as perhaps affording an approximation to a natural classification. These groups are :— I. Wolf-like dogs; II. Greyhounds; III. Spaniels; IV. Hounds; V. Mastiffs; VI. Terriers.

By a judicious crossing of these half-dozen types, he believes it possible to produce every one of the present existing races of domestic dog.

* In Jardine's Naturalist's Library, vol. x. (1840).
† See his article "Dogs: Ancient and Modern," in 'The Zoologist,' vol. viii. (1884), p. 393.

One of the most interesting breeds, from its possible relation to another species, is the Esquimaux Dog, which so closely resembles the wolf that a pack of them were once mistaken for wolves even by so experienced an Arctic traveller as Sir John Richardson. Our Plate XXXVIII. represents a fine specimen of this breed living in the Gardens of the Zoological Society.

The Domestic Dog attains sometimes a larger size than does any wild species of the *Canidæ*, the largest of which is the Wolf. Through the kindness of Dr. Sidney Turner, I have received the dimensions of several very large Mount St. Bernard's Dogs. The largest of these, known as "Young Plinlimmon," is an inmate of the kennels at Leeds belonging to Mr. Sydney W. Smith, who gives the total length of the animal, from "the tip of the nose to the set on of the tail," as $68\frac{1}{2}$ inches, or more than 173 centimeters. Other of his dogs thus measure 60 and 64 inches. A St. Bernard, known as "Cadwallader," belonging to Dr. Russell, measures 63 inches. But the Domestic Dog may not only be thus larger than the wolf, it may also be much smaller than any wild Canine species. One of the smallest of all breeds is the Mexican Lap-dog with its soft curly hair. A specimen of this breed we have had represented (from one in the British Museum) in our Plate XXXIX. Though apparently adult, from the condition of its claws, it measures no more than 18·0 centims. from the apex of the snout to the root of the tail. This breed has most probably been formed from dogs of European origin *.

Everyone knows that Domestic Dogs of different breeds differ hardly less in configuration than in size—configuration of muzzle, ears, length, quality, and even absence of hair, and length and form of tail.

Amongst characters which have been found to differ in different races is the extent of skin between the toes, which in Newfoundland Dogs, and more or less in Otter-hounds, produces a sort of webbed-footedness.

The peculiarities of conformation obviously concern not only external characters, but cranial and dental structures also.

The skull of the Bull-dog is one singularly distorted through the

* Such is the opinion of Fitzinger, as expressed in his 'Der Hund und seine Racen.'

164   THE DOMESTIC DOG.

shortening of the facial portion of the skull, entailing, as it does, a variety of other modifications to afford adequate space and attachment for the vigorous muscles which give the animal its prodigious power of grip.

Fig. 42.

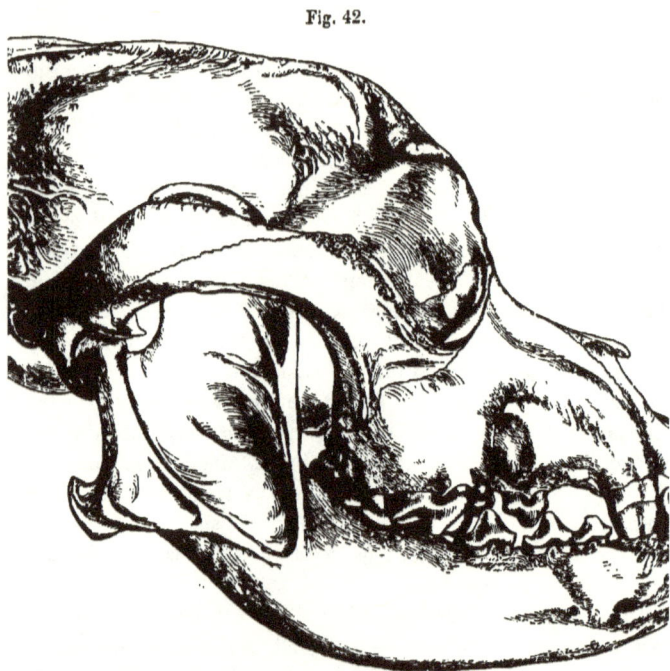

Skull of a Bull-dog.

The cranial and dental conditions which are commonly found in different breeds are subject to much variation. Dr. Windle and Mr. John Humphreys, who have gone, with exceeding care, into this question, tell us * :—" The range of variation (as to skull and teeth) in any breed is much greater, in almost every case, than that existing between

* Proc. Zool. Soc. 1890, pp. 24 & 26.

any two breeds." They also add :—" It becomes apparently a hopeless task to look for evidence as to the proximate or ultimate derivation of the breeds of domestic dogs in their skulls or teeth."

They have also observed a dozen cases of an additional molar on one or on both sides of the upper jaw in Domestic Dogs.

Nehring has noted [*] a Domestic Dog with an additional molar both above and below, and another (a Terrier) in which an inferior molar was deficient, as also a Dingo with five premolars both above and below.

A deficiency of teeth seems to often accompany hairlessness. This was observed by Mr. Yarrell [†] in two hairless dogs living in the Zoological Society's Gardens, neither of which had any premolars, or the full number of incisors, while one was destitute of canines, and he possessed the skull of a hairless Terrier which had no premolars. In another hairless Dog, which died in the Gardens, all the teeth were wanting save one molar on either side of either jaw.

When the muzzle has become shortened in a breed, the teeth, if not deficient in number, become distorted in position [‡].

Most remarkable of all these forms is the Japanese Pug-dog, the skull of which, as here given, was originally figured by Dr. Gray [§], who received it from Dr. W. Lockhart. This degraded type has been erected by Cope [||] into a new genus and species named "*Dysodes pravus*," but we can only regard it as a domestic monstrosity worthy of notice.

The individual, which was living in England, had slender legs, very long hair, and carried its tail, which was rather bushy, closely curled up over its back. It was mainly fed on vegetable food, being particularly fond of cucumbers.

[*] Sitzungsb. d. Ges. naturf. Freunde Berlin (1882), p. 65.

[†] Proc. Zool. Soc. 1833, p. 113. Mr. Yarrell exhibited the specimen referred to "with the view of illustrating the apparent connexion between the hair and the teeth."

[‡] Darwin, 'Animals and Plants under Domestication,' vol. ii. p. 345; and Windle and Humphreys, *op. cit.* p. 28.

[§] Proc. Zool. Soc. 1867, p. 40.

[||] See Proc. Acad. Nat. Sci. Philadelphia, 1879, pp. 188 & 189, and 'American Naturalist,' vol. xiii. (1879), p. 655.

166 THE DOMESTIC DOG.

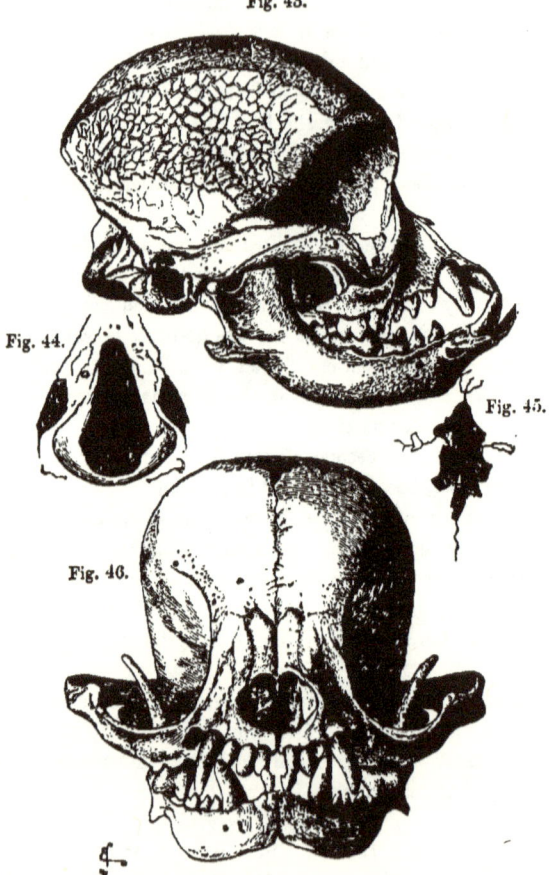

Fig. 43.

Fig. 44.

Fig. 45.

Fig. 46.

Skull of Japanese Dog.

Fig. 44.—Parts around the occipital foramen.
Fig. 45.—Form of fontanelle (defect of ossification) on the crown of the skull, the front portion of which is shown in Fig. 46.

Dr. W. Lockhart wrote to Dr. Gray as follows:—" The Pug-nosed Dog, the skull of which I sent you, probably originated in Pekin and North China, and was taken thence to Japan, whence it was brought to Europe; and thus this breed is called Japanese. . . . . There are two kinds of Pug in China:—one a small black-and-white, long-legged, pug-nosed, prominent-eyed dog; the other long-backed, short-legged, long-haired, tawny-coloured, with pug-nose and prominent eyes. Sometimes in these dogs the eyes are so prominent that I have known a dog have one of his eyes snapped off by another dog at play. The preference for vegetable food is a fact; but I think it is a result of education, as most of them will take animal food; this is usually kept from them so that their growth and organization may be kept down. The sleeve-dog is a degenerated long-legged variety of pug rigidly kept on low diet, and never allowed to run about on the ground; they are kept very much on the top of a kang or stove bed-place, and not allowed to run about on the ground, as it is supposed . . . they will derive strength from the ground and be able to grow large. Their food is much restricted, and consists chiefly of boiled rice. They are very subject to corneitis and ulceration of the cornea from deficient nutrition."

The various breeds of Dogs being so extraordinarily diverse, a question which forces itself on our minds is, " What has been the origin of an animal thus exceptionally polymorphic?" The problem may be exhaustively expressed as follows :—

Did all domestic races spring,

(1) from one species of true dog still existing?
(2) from more than one species of true dog still existing?
(3) from one species of true dog now extinct?
(4) from more than one species of true dog now extinct?
(5) from one species, not a true dog, now existing?
(6) from several species, not true dogs, now existing?
(7) from one species, not a true dog, now extinct?
(8) from several species, not true dogs, now extinct?

At first it might seem reasonable to suppose that animals so diverse as are the Spaniel, the Deerhound, and the Pug-dog have descended from distinct species, each of which possessed the characteristics of one of those breeds, in, as it were, an as yet undeveloped condition. But no such races exist in nature. They can hardly all have once existed and become extinct, for two reasons. In the first place, palæontology affords us no evidence that such has been the case; and, in the second place, what we know of the life-history of existing wild Canines does not favour the supposition. The Dog family is not one the species of which tend readily to disappear, as is shown by the long persistent efforts needed to exterminate the Wolf, even in the most civilized parts of the habitable globe. Therefore the Domestic Dog cannot well be the product of a variety of wild true Dog, once widely diffused but now entirely extinct. That the various breeds known to us may nevertheless have originated from one form must be admitted to be possible, when we consider the changes which have taken place in old breeds, and the new forms which have been called forth in the historical period. The Egyptian and Assyrian monuments show this, and our King Charles' Spaniels have been modified and had their characteristics exaggerated since the days of the Merry Monarch. Darwin, in his admirable work 'Animals and Plants under Domestication,' has collected and published amply sufficient evidence * as to this matter.

Can, then, all the breeds of the Domestic Dog have descended from one wild true dog now existing or extinct? We have not, so far as is known to us, any evidence of an extinct dog for which such a distinction can be claimed, nor has such a claim, to our knowledge, been made. As to an existing Wild Dog, there is but one species—the Dingo—which we think can possibly be supposed to have played such a part. Of course, if the Dingo was always, as now, an Australian animal, then it cannot have played such a part. But the dogs of the Pacific Islands, including the Solomon Islands †, are probably of the same race as the Dingo. Professor Huxley has thrown out the suggestion that not only some of the tribes of Hindostan, but even the ancient Egyptians, were of the same race as the inhabitants of Australia, so that the Australians might thus be regarded as the survivors—degraded

* See vol. i. pp. 40-43. † See above, p. 159.

survivors—of the early parents of such Egyptians and Indians. If we could believe this, we could also believe that with such a more primitive human race (which, on this view, would have survived in Australia) the more primitive domestic canine race may have survived there also and become feral.

The doctrine now generally accepted amongst men of science is that all existing races of mankind sprang from one primitive race and varied locally—radiating from a single geographical centre. We cannot see any impossibility in all existing races of Dogs having also sprang from a single kind and varied locally; also radiating from a single geographical centre. We know that the Dog existed in company with man in prehistoric times, and the fact that different prehistoric races of Dog succeeded one another, and that the earliest historical monuments show that various breeds, more or less like existing breeds, had then arisen, by no means proves that the Dog had not for ages existed in man's company, as little differentiated as was the Dingo when Europeans first visited Australia. That such a primitive dog would tend to vary when exposed to very different climatic conditions, is shown both by the change of coat, according to the seasons, which we have seen so often takes place in other canine species, and also by the fact that the Domestic Dog of to-day does undergo much modification from climatic change. It is also probable that sudden modifications of form might have excited interest, and so been preserved by selection.

Dönitz has described [*] a Fox's skull shaped like a Bull-dog's, with a shortened snout and " underhung," the mandible being upturned in front of the premaxillæ. This is a very interesting and noteworthy instance of a wild and very distinct species with an abnormality like that existing in one of the most peculiar of our races of the Domestic Dog. Darwin cites evidence [†] of the degeneration of Greyhounds, Setters, and Pointers in India, as also of Bull-dogs, after two or three generations, not only losing their pluck and skill, but also their peculiar shape, including the underhung jaw.

[*] Sitzungsb. d. Gesellsch. naturf. Freunde Berlin, 1868, p. 21.
[†] Op. cit. vol. i. pp. 37–39.

We are, however, far from asserting that all our Domestic Dogs have sprung from a dog like the Dingo, which may have arisen as naturally and as altogether apart from human action as the Wolf has arisen; all we would affirm is that such an origin is a possible one. But, as we shall see, it is also possible that the Domestic Dog may have arisen from one or more of the wild kinds of *Canidæ* which we now regard as differing specifically from the Dog. There is much to be said for this view, which is the one that commended itself to Pallas, Ehrenberg, and De Blainville, also to Hamilton Smith, and subsequently to Darwin, as it has since done to various naturalists of distinction. Others, amongst them the English naturalist Bell, have held that all true Dogs are the modified descendants of the Wolf. The general resemblance of some Domestic Dogs to the Wolf is unquestionable—notably the Esquimaux Dog, which is often made to unite with the Wolf to increase the strength and courage of the breed.

The Wolf and the Dog were successfully bred together for four generations by Buffon; and there are many instances of the production of such hybrids *. We are not aware, however, of any recent evidence that such hybrids are fertile *inter se*. The evidence appears to be conflicting †.

On the other hand, Dr. Julius Kühn‡ has recently noted the fertility of hybrids between a Jackal and a Dog, and this not only with the parent species, but *inter se*.

Professor Jeitteles contends that whatever otherwise may have been the origin of the Dog, the Jackal and the Wolf (the variety *Canis pallipes*) have been the parents respectively of the Domestic Dogs of the Neolithic and Stone periods of Human existence in Europe, a view which Mr. Blanford is disposed to accept §. Prof. Jeitteles, of course, grounds his opinion on a consideration of the skull and teeth. Such evidence is to us profoundly unsatisfactory; and therefore, while we

---

* See Dr. Th. Noacke's article, Zoologische Garten, xxviii. Jahrgang (1887), p. 106.
† See Darwin, *op. cit.* vol. i. p. 32.
‡ 'Die Stammväter unserer Hunde-Rassen:' Vienna, 1877.
§ Proc. Asiat. Soc. of Bengal (1877), p. 114.

have no reason or disposition to dispute the truth of his view, we can only regard it as conjectural.

The opinions of naturalists differ much as to this matter. Professor Dr. John N. Woldrich thinks * that the Domestic Dog of Europe can no more be traced to existing wild European species of Jackal, Wolf, or Fox, than the existing European races of man can be traced to existing wild tribes. He thinks that the ancestors of the European Dog no longer exist in Europe, though they may do so in Asia or Africa. He suggests the probability of their derivation from Diluvial predecessors of *C. simensis* and *C. zerda*.

As to the Domestic Dogs of America, as Rengger remarks †, it is certain that at the time of its discovery the natives had already a race of domestic dog. Such were found by Alonso Herera in New Granada and by Garcilasso in Peru. The Mexicans also had dogs which they used as food. It seems to us, however, impossible to determine whether such races really originated from the wild species of the New Continent, or were brought by man from Asia in very ancient times.

This doubt, however, does not exist in the minds of some very able naturalists. Thus Dr. Elliott Coues observes ‡ :—" We have . . . . unquestionable evidence of relationship by direct descent of some Indian Dogs from the Coyoté " (*C. latrans*). And, as we have before stated, the Indians habitually cross their dogs with this species.

As to the race of Dogs which belonged to the Incas of Peru (the *Canis Ingæ* of Tschudi) and were preserved as mummies, Nehring §, who has eighteen specimens, thinks that the animal was derived from the North-American Wolf, and certainly not from any South-American species.

The opinion at which Darwin arrived, after considering the mass of evidence he had accumulated, was that the Domestic Dog had a multiple origin,—that it arose from several races of Wolves and Jackals, and from at least one or two South-American species. With this view

* See Anzeiger d. kaiser. Akad. d. Wissenschaften, xxiii. Jahrgang, 1886, pp. 12–16.
† Naturgeschichte der Säugethiere von Paraguay, p. 151.
‡ American Naturalist, vol. vii. 1873, p. 388.
§ Zoologische Jahrbücher, Biologie, vol. iii. (1888), p. 51.

Mr. Edmund Harting entirely concurs, and we do not think that any one can affirm with confidence that the Dog may not have had such an origin, even if he does not go so far as to consider the view a probably true one. For our part we think that the evidence is as yet insufficient for us to enunciate any judgment in the matter. We have endeavoured to point out that it is possible that the origin of the Dog may have been single or multiple, but we refrain from declaring that we regard either the one or the other as preponderatingly evident.

Nevertheless our judgment inclines to the view that the Domestic Dog is a form which has been evolved by human effort from at least two, probably more, wild species, though it is possible it may be but a modification of one which has long become extinct save in its domestic and feral progeny.

We, however, heartily agree with Professor Nehring that many experiments are needed, not only concerning the fertility of hybrids, but also as to what variations can be induced in pure-bred Wolves and Foxes by long domestication carried on through a considerable number of successive generations.

Before dismissing the problem, we think it well to reproduce the remarks of Mr. A. D. Bartlett, who has been for so many years Superintendent of the Gardens of the Zoological Society. He has had most exceptional opportunity for making valuable observations, and of such opportunities he has again and again made exceptionally good use. He says * :—

"The extraordinary and wonderful number of well-marked breeds of the Domestic Dog, and their variations of size, form, and colour, render any attempt to account for their origin a task of some difficulty; but as many wild dogs appear to be descendants of domestic dogs, it is necessary to endeavour to account for the origin of the domestic race. There can be no doubt, for example, that the Esquimaux Dogs are reclaimed or domesticated Wolves.

"All Wolves, if taken young and reared by man, are tame, playful, and exhibit a fondness for those who feed and attend to them. The

* Proc. Zool. Soc. 1890, p. 47.

same may be said of all the species of Jackals. This being so, it is highly probable that both Wolves and Jackals were for many ages found in the company of man, and that owing to this association the different species of these animals may have bred together and become mixed.

"A mixed breed would at once develop a new variety. A variety once commenced would in all probability, in a few generations, undergo many changes, especially if any well-marked variety should occur. Nothing would be more natural than to suppose that the owners of this variety would endeavour to increase its number, especially if it was found to possess useful qualities.

"The fashion of hunting led in all probability to the separation of Domestic Dogs into two well-known breeds, viz., those that hunt by sight, as distinguished from those that hunt by scent; for there can be no doubt that at a very early period dogs were used in the chase of wild animals. There are plenty of ancient monuments on which there is unmistakable evidence of this fact. The usefulness of dogs being established at a very early period would naturally lead to great care being bestowed upon them, and doubtless to the breeding of them in a domestic state. This would lead to the production of the many breeds and varieties that have been developed, and thus varieties may have been perpetuated by the mixing and crossing of breeds originally obtained from distinct wild animals.

"I have found no difficulty in crossing Wolves and Jackals with Domestic Dogs, when suitably matched. It is a well-known fact that the Esquimaux frequently allows his dogs to breed with wolves, in order to keep up the strength, the power of endurance, and the courage of the race. But as regards Foxes, so far as my experience goes, I have never met with a well-authenticated instance of a hybrid between a fox and a dog, notwithstanding numerous specimens of supposed hybrids of this sort which from time to time have been brought to my notice. The habits of Wolves and Jackals are so much alike that I am unable to point out any marked differences between them.

"Domestic Dogs exhibit many of the habits of Wolves and Jackals, such as the scratching up of earth with the front feet, and the pushing back of it with the hind feet, in order to cover up the droppings.

Again, when about to rest, the turning round two or three times with the object of forming a hole in which to rest may be noticed in pet dogs about to lie down upon the hearth-rug, a habit evidently acquired by inheritance from their wild ancestors.

"The whining, growling, and howling of Wolves, Jackals, and Dogs are so much alike as to be indistinguishable; but the barking of Dogs is undoubtedly an acquired habit, and doubtless due to domestication.

"Wolves and Jackals in a wild state never bark, nor do Esquimaux Dogs nor Dingos, but if kept associated with barking dogs, these and other wild dogs in many instances acquire the habit of barking.

"A well-known instance of this occurred under my notice. A wild Antarctic Wolf, after a few months, hearing the barking of dogs in the immediate neighbourhood, began to bark, and succeeded admirably. The same thing has happened to my knowledge in the case of pure-bred Esquimaux Dogs and Dingos."

This practical naturalist thus strongly declares himself in favour of the view that the Dog is derived from the Wolf* and the Jackal†.

It now but remains for us briefly to notice certain breeds of Dogs which exist in a feral condition—which have run wild—or are domesticated amongst certain more or less savage tribes of mankind, other than the Australians.

The Pacific Islanders, when first discovered, already possessed a

---

* It has been remarked with respect to the Dog and the Wolf, by Dr. H. Landois (Morphologisches Jahrbuch, vol. ix. (1884), p. 163), that the intestines of the former are much longer compared with the length of the body than those of the latter—5 or 6 to 1 instead of 4 to 1; but there is much individual variation in this matter, and, besides, domestication and change of food seem to lengthen the intestine in other animals, and therefore probably in the Dog (see Darwin's 'Variation of Animals and Plants,' vol. i. p. 73).

† The reader desirous of considering other expressions of opinion not already cited may refer to three other papers by Woldrich. One of those is in the Denkschr. Akad. Wien, xxxix. Abth. ii. pp. 97–148; another is in the Mitth. anthrop. Gesellschaft in Wien, xi. p. 8; and the third in the last-named periodical, vol. xii. pp. 27 and 153. We may mention yet another by Studer on "Dogs in relation to ancient Lake-dwellings," in Mitth. naturf. Gesellschaft in Bern (1884), i. p. 3.

domesticated Dog, which was then used as food in Otaheite *, as it is in various islands to the present day. The Domestic Dog which was also found existing in New Zealand, and which is now extinct, was much like that which existed amongst the Pacific Islanders. It was a much smaller animal than the Dingo, with a pointed nose, long hair of different colours, and a short bushy tail. It is described as having had little power of smell, with only a howl and no proper bark, and of a lazy, sullen disposition †. It was trained to catch the Apteryx and was generally much petted by its owners.

Feral Dogs exist in Cuba, of a mouse-colour, with short ears and light blue eyes ‡ ; and Mr. Darwin tells us, on the authority of Mr. C. Clarke, concerning Feral Dogs of Juan de Nova in the Indian Ocean, that " they had entirely lost the faculty of barking; had no inclination for the company of other dogs," but that " they congregate in vast packs, and catch sea-birds with as much address as Foxes could display."

Feral Dogs exist on the continent of South America and in Africa, and one such in Senegambia has been described under the name *C. laoketianus* §.

The Pariah Dogs of India are very numerous and breed in the towns and villages unmolested. Amongst these Colonel Sykes found one with crooked legs and a long back, like a Turnspit Dog ||. It has the appearance of a mongrel form of the Domestic Dog.

To the breeds which now exist, and which are much more numerous than in the earliest days of human history, it is probable that others will be added by variation and careful selection. Nevertheless, when we consider the resemblance which exists between the most ancient breeds (as represented by sculpture and painting) and those of our

* Captain Cook's Voyages, 4to (1873), vol. ii. p. 152.
† See an article, " On the Ancient Dog of the New Zealanders," in the Trans. of the N. Zealand Institute, vol. x. (1877), pp. 135-155.
‡ See Poeppig, ' Reise in Chile,' vol. i. p. 290. Quoted by Darwin, ' Animals and Plants under Domestication,' vol. i. p. 27.
§ G. A. T. Rochebrune, Bull. Soc. Philom. (6) vol. vii. p. 9.
|| See Proc. Zool. Soc. 1831, p. 100.

own day, it seems unlikely that any very profound and startling modification will be produced.

The space which we can afford for the consideration of the Domestic Dog being now exhausted, we must, as we have purposely reserved its consideration for the last of the true Dogs, now proceed to describe the second genus of the family *Canidæ*.

Genus CYON, Hodgson (1838).

Cuon, Hodgson, Ann. & Mag. Nat. Hist. vol. i. p. 152 (1838).
Cyon, Blanford, Fauna Brit. India, Mamm. p. 142 (1888); Mivart, Proc. Zool. Soc. 1890, p. 88.

Generic Characters.

Digits 5—4. Pm. $\frac{4}{4}$, M. $\frac{2}{3}$.

Nasals extending backwards much beyond the adjacent portions of the maxillæ; the external margin of each nasal, distad of the nasal process of the frontal, strongly concave, so that the outer margin of the whole length of each nasal has a subsigmoid outline; face relatively short; dorsal surface of interorbital region but little concave transversely; skull, viewed in profile, showing very little vertical elevation in the interorbital region, the concavity thus apparent between it and the distal end of the nasals being very slight both in degree and in antero-posterior extent; postorbital processes of the frontals projecting outwards but slightly; postorbital processes of the malars rather marked; zygomata not strongly arched outwards; anterior palatine foramina very large and much elongated; first upper premolar approaching the second in size more nearly than in *Canis*; fourth upper premolar with a smaller internal lobe than generally in *Canis*; inner portion of first upper molar small, its inner tubercles having more or less completely coalesced with the cingulum; first lower molar small, especially its inner ridge; tail decidedly less than half the length of the body.

Habitat. Asia, from Siberia to Java.

These animals are generally called "Wild Dogs," and the southern species is commonly termed "The Indian Wild Dog." But the term is unfortunate, as they are generically distinct from the true Dogs, and to call them "Dogs" would therefore lead to confusion and be inconvenient. We therefore propose to designate them by the term "Dhole." This is a term which has been made use of*, and will serve very conveniently for our purpose, whatever may be its origin or present use in the East. Since it is said to be "an antique Asiatic root" signifying recklessness and daring, it will be so far the more appropriate to denote an animal which has hitherto been distinguished, in English parlance, by the term "wild."

* By Captain Williamson and Colonel C. Hamilton Smith. See Jardine's 'Naturalist's Library,' vol. ix. p. 179. There we read that "Dhole" is "an antique Asiatic root, implying daring, recklessness; in Turkish, *Deli*; in Teutonic, *Dol*, mad; in Belgic, *Dulle*, outrageous."

THE SOUTHERN DHOLE.

CYON JAVANICUS.

Canis javanicus, Desmarest, Mammalogie, p. 198 (1820); F. Cuvier, Dict. des Sc. Nat. vol. viii. p. 557.
Canis familiaris, var. *sumatrensis*, Hardwicke, Trans. Linn. Soc. vol. xiii. p. 235, pl. xxiii. (1822).
Canis dukhunensis, Sykes, Proc. Zool. Soc. 1831, p. 100; Blyth, Journ. As. Soc. Bengal, vol. xi. p. 591.
Canis primævus, Hodgson, Asiatic Res. xviii. pt. 2, p. 221 (1833), with a figure.
Canis rutilans, S. Müller, Verhandelingen Zool. Zoogd. pp. 27, 51 (1839); Blyth, Catalogue of Mammals and Birds of Burmah, p. 24; J. A. Wagner, Suppl. to Schreber's Säugthiere, Abth. ii. p. 379.
Cuon primævus, Hodgson, Ann. & Mag. Nat. Hist. vol. i. p. 152 (1838); id. Calcutta Journal Nat. Hist. vol. ii. pp. 208, 412; Adams, Proc. Zool. Soc. 1858, p. 514; Cantor, Journ. Asiat. Soc. Bengal, vol. xv. p. 196; Gray, Proc. Zool. Soc. 1868, p. 498; id. Cat. Carnivorous Mammalia, p. 184; Murie, Proc. Zool. Soc. 1872, p. 715.
Cuon rutilans, Blyth, Catalogue of Mammals and Birds of Burmah, p. 37; Jerdon's Mammals of India, p. 145.
Cuon sumatrensis and *dukhunensis*, Gray, Proc. Zool. Soc. 1868, pp. 498 and 500.
Cyon dukhunensis, Blanford, Fauna of British India, Mamm. p. 143.
Cyon rutilans, Blanford, ibid. p. 147.
Cyon primævus, Scully, Proc. Zool. Soc. 1881, p. 202.
Cyon javanicus, Mivart, Proc. Zool. Soc. 1890, p. 89.

WHETHER there are or are not two distinct species of *Cyon* south of the Himalayas is a question as to which some distinguished naturalists differ. We have carefully examined a very large number of skins —with the several skulls belonging to them—coming from stations ranging from Sumatra and Malacca to Thibet, and have been quite unable to detect what appears to us to be a valid specific distinction. There are, indeed, great differences between different specimens, but intermediate conditions connect together the most divergent forms. The colour, however, is always more or less red, except in specimens which come from the lofty region of Thibet. These latter have a long soft furry coat of a pale colour, while specimens from hot regions have a close and rather harsh coat.

It is not so surprising that this species should vary greatly, seeing that it ranges over so enormous a space—namely, not only over all Hindostan and Eastern Thibet, but also over the Malay Peninsula and its Archipelago as far as Borneo.

The animal is generally, when fully grown, larger than the Jackal, though it varies in size as well as in colour; it has a moderately long tail, which may or may not be bushy. It is an inhabitant of the forests, though not exclusively so. Diurnal, for the most part, and gregarious in its habits, it hunts in packs of from six to twenty in number. Mr. Blanford informs us that in India they live principally upon wild pigs and various kinds of deer, many sámbar and spotted deer, Indian antelopes, and even the nilgai being occasionally killed and devoured by them. In Thibet they feed on wild sheep. They will sometimes attack the Himalayan black bear*, and Elliot has known a tiger leaving a jungle to have been killed by a pack of these creatures. There is also more evidence to the same effect, though such accounts are no doubt sometimes mistaken or exaggerated. According to Blanford they avoid the neighbourhood of man, and, in consequence, rarely attack domestic animals, though they occasionally pull down a tame buffalo. One instance of this has been observed both by Jerdon and McMaster, and Blanford came across a third case in the jungles east of Baroda : "I was curious," he tells us, "to see how so large an animal had been destroyed. There were but a few tooth-marks about the nose and throat, and some of the pack had evidently attacked the buffalo in front, whilst others tore it open. This is probably their usual way

---

* See Captain Baldwin's ' Large and Small Game of Bengal,' p. 19.

of killing large animals." They have been seen to snap at the flank of a running deer.

Although they are thus ferocious and predatory, there is no evidence of their attacking man; and they appear sometimes to feed not only upon carrion but on vegetable food also. McMaster found that an animal of this species kept in confinement would greedily devour herbs, grass, and leaves of various kinds, "not as dogs do when ill, but with a keen relish."

They appear to be very untamable animals. Hodgson, after keeping some ten months in confinement, found them as wild* and shy at the end of that time as at its commencement. They had a peculiarly rank and fetid odour, and were very silent animals, never uttering a sound except when they would snarl at each other in a subdued tone, though they never fought.

One young specimen he found more amenable to kindness, as it would allow itself to be caressed by its master and would play with dogs. In a wild state these animals will howl at night; but it appears they remain quite silent while hunting their prey.

They breed during the winter, producing two, four, six, or even more in a litter between the beginning of January and the end of March. The female makes her nest in caves or hollow spaces amongst rocks; and several females are said† to have been found, near Simla, apparently breeding together.

The colour of this animal is, as we have said, always more or less red, with the lower parts whitish. Part of the tail, generally the terminal portion, is black, though occasionally the extreme end is whitish. There may or may not be underfur. The variety which has been named *rutilans* has no woolly underfur, with hair short and harsh, and a small brush. It may also have much black on the back, as we have seen in a specimen from Moulmein. Our Plate XL. represents a specimen obtained from Sumatra. The type (preserved in the British Museum) of the variety named *dukhunensis* (Plate XLI.) is very red, with longish hair and some underfur. Specimens from

---

* See Jerdon, *op. cit.* p. 148. † Blanford, *op. cit.* p. 146.

182 THE SOUTHERN DHOLE.

Fig. 47.

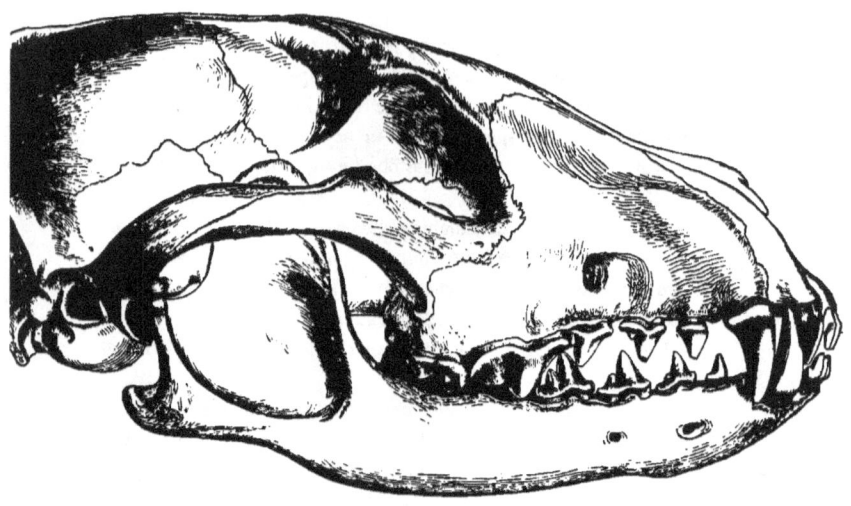

Side view of skull of CYON JAVANICUS.

Fig. 48. Fig. 49.

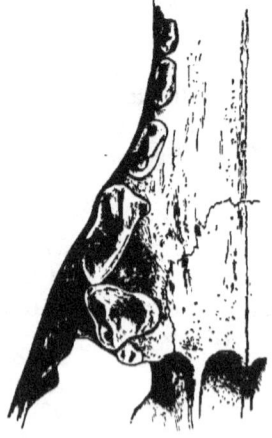 

Molars of upper jaw (right side).   Molars of lower jaw (right side).
(All of the natural size.)

CYON JAVANICUS. 183

Cashmere are paler, and one we have examined from Nepal was quite light-coloured and covered with long woolly fur.

Habitat. South-eastern Asia, from the Himalaya to Borneo, but apparently not in Ceylon.

The dark short-haired variety, called *rutilans*, is found in the Malay Peninsula, Sumatra, Java, and probably in Borneo; it also inhabits Moulmein and possibly Northern Burmah.

The variety distinguished as *dukhunensis* is stated by Blanford[*] to be found in Gilgit, Ladák, and other parts of the upper valley of the Indus, as well as in the Himalayan forests, from Cashmere to Assam. Hodgson obtained it from Eastern Thibet, and it is undoubtedly present in all the larger forests of Hindostan.

	Centimeters.
Length from end of snout to root of tail	92·0
„ of tail	28·0
„ from heel to tip of longest digit	19·0
„ of ear	7·5

Skeletal and Dental Characters.

The main cranial and dental characters have been already noted in describing those common to the genus.

The second upper molar is always small, but we have found a considerable difference as regards its relative size in two skulls extracted from skins which closely resemble each other.

			Centimeters.
Length of cervical region			16·5
„	dorsal	„	24·0
„	lumbar	„	19·0
„	sacral	„	4·0

* *Op. cit.* p. 144.

THE SOUTHERN DHOLE.

	Centimeters.
Atlas to end of sacrum	63·5
Pectoral limb	37·0
Pelvic limb	47·5
Humerus	13·5
Radius to root of styloid process	12·0
Femur	15·5
Tibia to root of malleolus	14·3
Index metacarpal	4·5
Third ,,	5·5
Metacarpal of pollex	1·7
Whole pollex	3·4
Index metatarsal	5·5
Third ,,	6·7
Metatarsal of hallux	1·1
Whole hallux	1·6
Basion to ovalion	3·1
,, sphenoideum	4·4
Sphenoideum to gnathion	10·8
Basion to gnathion	15·0
Length of palate	7·5
Breadth ,,	5·1
Greatest length of nasals	6·3
Breadth of nasals	1·9
Interorbital breadth	3·2
Between postorbital processes	4·4
Breadth of cranium	6·2
,, zygomata	9·7
Longest incisor	1·2
Shortest ,,	0·8
Length of $\underline{P.1}$	0·6
,, $\underline{P.2}$	0·8
,, $\underline{P.3}$	1·0
,, $\underline{P.4}$	1·9
,, $\underline{M.1}$	1·1
,, $\underline{M.2}$	0·6
Breadth of $\underline{P.4}$	1·0
,, $\underline{M.1}$	1·5
,, $\underline{M.2}$	0·8
Length of $\overline{P.1}$	0·45

		Centimeters.
Length of	$\overline{P.2}$	0·8
,,	$\overline{P.3}$	0·9
,,	$\overline{P.4}$	1·1
,,	$\overline{M.1}$	2·0
,,	$\overline{M.2}$	0·8
Breadth of	$\overline{M.1}$	0·7
,,	$\overline{M.2}$	0·5

THE NORTHERN DHOLE.

CYON ALPINUS.

Canis alpinus, Pallas, Zoographia Rosso-Asiatica, vol. i. p. 34 (1831);
J. A. Wagner, Suppl. to Schreber's Säugth., Abth. ii. p. 372;
Middendorff, Reise äussersten Norden u. Osten Sibiriens,
vol. ii. part ii. p. 71 (1851); Schrenck, Reisen in Amur-
Lande, vol. i. p. 48, pl. ii. (1859); Radde, Reisen im
Süden von Ost-Sibirien, vol. i. p. 60 (1862).

Cuon alpinus, Gray, Proc. Zool. Soc. 1868, p. 498; id. Cat. Carnivorous
Mammalia, p. 184.

Cyon alpinus, Mivart, Proc. Zool. Soc. 1890, p. 90.

THIS large, fine species of Northern Asia can only be separated from *C. javanicus* on account of the larger size of its second upper molar, and also of its second or ultimate lower molar.

The two specimens preserved in the British Museum are covered with very long and woolly hair, which is white in one specimen, and whitish with a yellow tinge in the other. The former came from Siberia and is the subject of our Plate XLII.; the other specimen came from the Altai Mountains, and our figure representing its dentition was drawn from the skull which was extracted from it.

We presume that both these specimens display the winter coat of the animal more or less perfectly developed; for it is described by Pallas and Schrenck as being at other times generally red like a fox, with the back somewhat darker—the hairs being partly white, partly black, and partly red—with the lips, belly, and inner side of the limbs white.

This species is subject, like its more southern congener, to great variations in colour, according to season, locality, and possibly somewhat according to sex.

CYON ALPINUS.

Radde has given careful details as to the exact localities in which he ascertained that this animal was to be met with. He believes that it lives by preference in such parts of the mountains as are most densely covered with forest, and that it only exceptionally frequents the open steppes. It appears indeed to be very local. It often goes in troops of from ten to fifteen or even more individuals, led by strong, fully adult male animals, but is sometimes found solitary—in either case eagerly hunting the deer, which it will sometimes entirely banish from

Fig. 50.   Fig. 51.

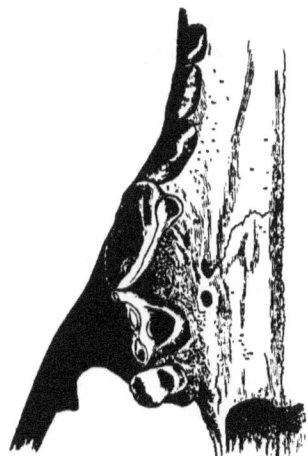 

Upper molar teeth of right side.   Lower molar teeth of right side.
(Natural size.)

one region to another. It is represented to be a creature both cunning and swift, and is feared by the hunters, who sometimes seek safety from it in a tree. The dogs also appear to dread this Dhole, and turn back from its traces, as if they were those of the tiger. The natives do not eat its flesh, nor is its fur of any considerable value.

THE NORTHERN DHOLE.

Habitat. Northern Asia, from Siberia southwards at least to the Altai Mountains, and probably much further south. It is said to frequent the sources of the Yenisei and the tributaries of the Amur.

	Centimeters.
Length from end of snout to root of tail	103·3
,, of tail	48·0
,, from heel to end of longest digit	22·0
,, of ear	8·0

Cranial and Dental Characters.

We have noticed no special cranial character other than that the angle of the mandible is of less massive form than in *C. javanicus*, and that the hindmost teeth are relatively larger.

	Centimeters.
Length of $\frac{P.4}{}$	2·1
,, $\frac{M.1}{}$	1·5
,, $\frac{M.2}{}$	0·7
Breadth of $\frac{M.1}{}$	1·5
,, $\frac{M.2}{}$	1·0
Length of $\overline{M.1}$	2·3
,, $\overline{M.2}$	0·9

Genus ICTICYON, Lund (1845).

Icticyon, Lund, K. Danske Videnskabernes Selskabs, vol. xi. p. 61 (1845).
Cynalicus, Gray, Ann. & Mag. Nat. Hist. vol. xvii. p. 293 (1846).

Generic Characters.

Digits 5—4. Pm. $\frac{4}{4}$, M. $\frac{1}{2}$. Rarely M. $\frac{2}{2}$ or $\frac{1}{1}$.

Nasals extending backwards about as far as the adjacent portions of maxillæ; external margin of each rather sigmoid in outline; face short; mandible with a subangular process; postorbital processes of both frontals and malars small; anterior palatine foramina not very large; first upper premolar small; first upper molar subtriangular; no second upper molar, or only a minute one; second lower molar minute or absent; limbs short; tail and ears very short; cæcum straight.

THE BUSH-DOG.

ICTICYON VENATICUS.

Cynogale venatica, Lund, Blik paa Brasiliens Dyreverden, 4th Afhandling, Kongel. Danske Videnskab. Selskabs, vol. ix. p. 201 (1842).
Icticyon venaticus, Lund, ibid. vol. xi. p. 62, pl. 41 (1845); Wagner, Wiegmann's Archiv, ix. Jahrgang, Bd. i. p. 355; Van der Hoeven, Verhandelingen d. Kon. Akad. van Wetenschappen, Derde Deel, Amsterdam, 1856; Burmeister, Fauna Brasiliens, p. 1, pls. 17–20 (1856); id. Thiere Brasiliens, Theil i. p. 103 (1854); Gray, Proc. Zool. Soc. 1868, p. 498; id. Cat. Carnivorous Mammalia, p. 183; Sclater, Proc. Zool. Soc. 1879, p. 664; Flower, Proc. Zool. Soc. 1880, p. 70, pl. 10.
Cynalicus melanogaster, Gray, Ann. & Mag. Nat. Hist. vol. xvii. p. 293 (1846).

This curious and aberrant canine animal was first described by Lund under a name which was already appropriated to denote an aquatic member of the Civet family *, so that it must receive the second generic name imposed on it by the same author. It is an animal of very considerable antiquity, since remains of the same species have been obtained from caverns and pleistocene deposits of Brazil; and yet it would seem, from its teeth, to be rather a modification of the normal type of the family than a representative of an ancestral form.

In external appearance it is at once remarkable from its short limbs, heel, and ears, its very short tail, its shortened muzzle, and relatively long body and long and thick neck.

A living specimen in Burmeister's possession was omnivorous, but,

* By Dr. Gray in 1836. For further information about *Cynogale*, see our paper on the Æluroidea, Proc. Zool. Soc. 1882, p. 171.

THE BUSH DOG.
Icticyon venaticus.

as might be expected, preferred raw flesh to vegetable substances, and drank milk with avidity. It was a bold and determined animal, which disliked confinement, and gave out a peevish, yelping sound, uttered at different times in different tones.

Mr. Tinné, who sent a living example to the Zoological Gardens in 1879, has stated his belief that these animals hunt in packs by scent and are exceedingly savage. They are, he further tells us, rarely seen, and though taking readily to water, never frequent the low lands on the coast.

An interesting account of the anatomy of this animal has been given by Professor Flower *. It is remarkable for its straight cæcum †, and for a slight modification in the subdivision of the cerebral convolutions.

Our Plate XLIII. is taken from a specimen in the British Museum.

The colour of this species is generally of a dark brown, but the neck, shoulders, head, and ears are rusty red. The hind quarters, belly, and tail are nearly black; the inner side of the thighs and the hindermost part of the belly, in the British Museum specimens, are also dark, with a few whitish hairs on the belly. The insides of the ears are lighter. The fore limbs are brownish black both within and without. Burmeister represents the hinder part of the belly and the inner side of the thighs of a lighter colour.

Habitat. Brazil and British Guiana.

	Centimeters.
Length from end of snout to root of tail	65·0
„ of tail	14·0
„ from heel to end of longest digit	10·8
„ of ear	2·4

Cranial and Dental Characters.

The most noteworthy character of the skull of this species is the shortness of the muzzle, which has a much swollen appearance between anterior margins of the orbits.

---

* See *op. cit.*

† See *ante*, pp. xxviii & xxx, figs. 14, 15, & 16.

192   THE BUSH-DOG.

Fig. 52.

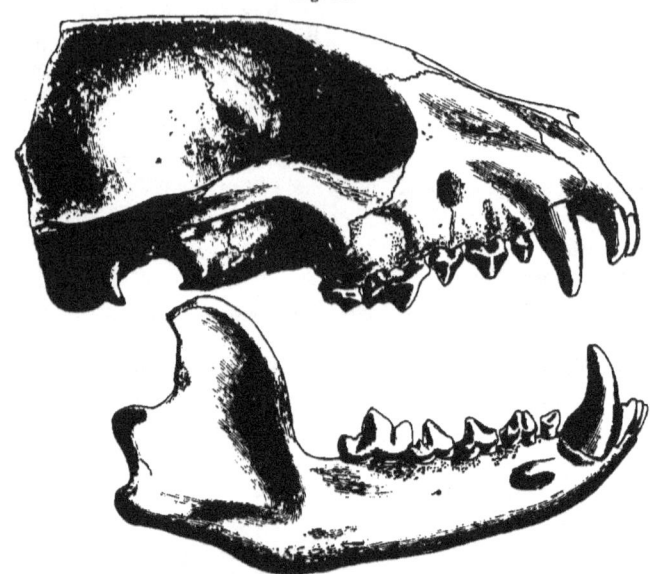

Side view of skull of ICTICYON VENATICUS.

Fig. 53.   Fig. 54.

Upper molars (right side).   Lower molars (right side).
(All of natural size.)

The nasals extend backwards about as far as do the nasal processes of the maxillæ, and the outer margin of each nasal is somewhat sigmoid.

The mandible has a small, subangular process. The teeth are remarkable for the absence or minute size of the second upper molar, both above and below. The third upper premolar has its transverse diameter remarkably large relatively to its antero-posterior extent. In the skull preserved in the College of Surgeons the second upper molar is very exceptionally present; in the skull here figured, which is in the British Museum, the second lower molar is exceptionally absent. The two halves of the mandible are anchylosed together.

	Centimeters.
Length of cervical vertebræ	10·5
„ dorsal „	15·5
„ lumbar „	11·5
„ sacral „	2·5
„ caudal „	12·8
Length from atlas to end of sacrum	40·0
Length of humerus	8·1
„ radius	6·7
„ femur	9·2
„ tibia	8·2
„ index metacarpal	2·6
„ third „	3·1
„ metacarpal of pollex	1·2
„ whole pollex	2·6
„ last phalanx of third digit (manus)	1·0
„ index metatarsal	2·8
„ third „	3·3
„ metatarsal of hallux	0·6
„ whole hallux *.	0·6
„ last phalanx of third digit (pes)	0·9
Basion to ovalion	2·6
„ sphenoideum	3·9
Sphenoideum to gnathion	7·2
Length of palate	5·5
Breadth of „	3·6

* The hallux in the specimen examined had no phalanx.

THE BUSH-DOG.

	Centimeters.
Length of nasals	3·0
Breadth of ,,	1·1
,, brain-case	4·5
,, zygomata	6·9
Length of $\underline{\text{P. 1}}$	0·38
,, $\underline{\text{P. 2}}$	0·6
,, $\underline{\text{P. 3}}$	0·7
,, $\underline{\text{P. 4}}$	1·1
,, $\underline{\text{M. 1}}$	0·6
,, $\underline{\text{M. 2}}$	0·3
Breadth of $\underline{\text{P. 4}}$	0·6
,, $\underline{\text{M. 1}}$	0·7
,, $\underline{\text{M. 2}}$	0·3
Length of $\overline{\text{P. 1}}$	0·3
,, $\overline{\text{P. 2}}$	0·6
,, $\overline{\text{P. 3}}$	0·7
,, $\overline{\text{P. 4}}$	0·7
,, $\overline{\text{M. 1}}$	1·2
,, $\overline{\text{M. 2}}$	0·3
Breadth of $\overline{\text{P. 4}}$	0·40
,, $\overline{\text{M. 1}}$	0·45
,, $\overline{\text{M. 2}}$	0·3

Genus LYCAON, Brookes (1828).

Lycaon, Brookes, Prodromus Animalium (Brookesian Museum), p. 10 (1828).

Generic Characters.

Digits 4—4. Pm. $\frac{4}{4}$, M. $\frac{2}{3}$.

Nasals extending backwards about as far as do the orbital processes of the maxillæ; external margin of each strongly sigmoid in outline; face rather short; palate very broad; no subangular process; post-orbital processes well developed; anterior palatine foramina very large; limbs long; muzzle short; coloration very varied; ears long; cæcum coiled; tongue without a lytta.

THE HYÆNA DOG.

LYCAON PICTUS.

Hyæna pictus, Temminck, Ann. Gén. Sc. physiques, vol. iii. p. 54, plate 35 (1820).
Hyæna picta, Kuhl, Beiträge, p. 73.
Hyæna venatica, Burchell's Travels, vol. i. p. 456, and vol. ii. pp. 99 and 229 (1822).
Canis pictus, Desmarest, Mammalogie, Supplément, p. 538 (1822); Rüppell, Atlas, p. 35, plate 12 (1826); J. A. Wagner, Supplement to Schreber's Säugthiere, Abth. ii. p. 439.
Lycaon tricolor, Brookes, Prod. Anim. p. 10 (1828).
Lycaon typicus, A. Smith, S. African Quarterly Journal, vol. ii. (1835) p. 91.
Lycaon venaticus, Hamilton Smith, Jardine's Naturalist's Library, vol. x. p. 266, plate 24 (1840); Gray, Proc. Zool. Soc. 1868, p. 497; id. Cat. Carnivorous Mammalia, p. 181.
Lycaon pictus, Pagenstecher, Zoologische Garten, 1870, pp. 197 and 238 (anatomy); Garrod, Proc. Zool. Soc. 1878, p. 373.

THIS animal, as its vernacular name implies, presents a certain resemblance to the Hyæna. That resemblance, however, is a merely superficial one, depending on its external markings and its general aspect alone. In its dentition it is quite dog-like, as is also the form of its cæcum, so that its generic separation from the other *Canidæ* depends mainly on the absence, externally, of the pollex as well as of the hallux.

The species ranges from the vicinity of the Cape through Eastern Africa to Kordofan. As to its habits, Burchell tells us that it hunts in regular packs, and that though habitually nocturnal, it nevertheless is often abroad by day, and is very fleet. Not only sheep but oxen are attacked by it, the latter being surprised in their sleep and often having the tail suddenly bitten off. Sir Andrew Smith says that it never barks, but

J. G Keulemans del. et lith.

THE HYÆNA DOG.
Lycaon pictus.

Mintern Bros. imp.

gives utterance to a shrill sound resembling *ho, ho, ho, ho, ho, ho,*—the sounds tending to run one into the other. This observer entertained the opinion that there were two distinct species. This we are convinced is an error; but the markings of the animal are in no small degree varied and inconstant.

The animal is said to hunt by scent as well as by sight, but not to possess the habit of burrowing, so common amongst the *Canidæ*. Attempts made to tame it in South Africa seem to have been attended with no success. The individual from which Temminck first described the species was purchased by him in London.

Several skins and five skulls of this species are preserved in our National Collection, and one of these skins has served our artist for his representation in our Plate XLIV.

This species attains the size of a tall greyhound, and its limbs are long compared with most species of the family. The head is broad and flat, with a rather short muzzle and large ears. The hairy coat is somewhat scanty.

The colour consists of black, yellowish ochre, grey and white variously disposed. The general ground-colour is an ochraceous grey, but with black markings, so that the body and outer sides of the extremities are blotched and brindled with black intermingled here and there with white spots edged with black, the markings being very irregular.

The muzzle is black, and a black stripe sometimes, but not always, passes backwards from between the eyes and ears and along the neck.

The root of the tail is ochraceous, then more or less black, with the terminal portion white or whitish; it is rather bushy. The lower parts and inner sides of the limbs are grey or whitish. The ears are said to be sometimes more or less naked; they are more or less black within, though with some white hairs, while externally they are of an ochre-colour at their root, above which they may or may not be black. In the specimen at the British Museum here figured the fore-limbs have numerous black marks.

Habitat. Africa, south and east of the Sahara.

THE HYÆNA DOG.

	Centimeters.
Length from end of snout to root of tail	112·0
„ of tail	45·0
„ from heel to end of longest digit	22·5
„ of ear	12·5

Cranial and Dental Characters.

The skull is short and thick compared with that of the great majority of the *Canidæ* and has a swollen appearance. It somewhat recalls the aspect of the skull in the genus *Cyon*, with which it agrees in having

Fig. 55.

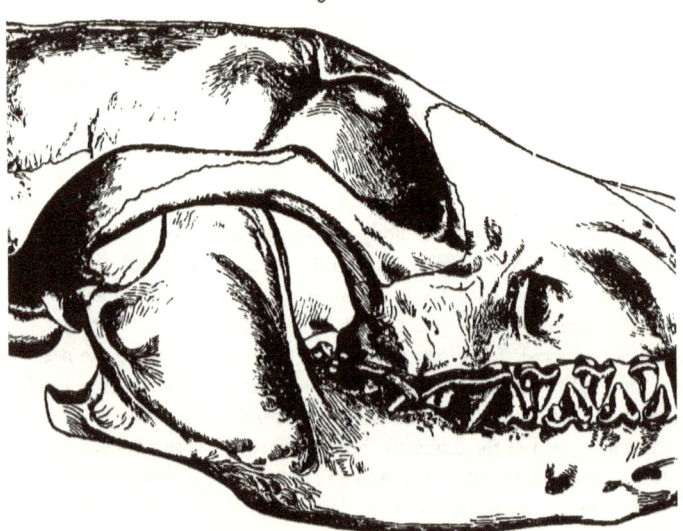

Side view of skull of LYCAON PICTUS.

large anterior palatine foramina and a strongly sigmoid external margin to the nasals, which extend backwards about as far as do the nasal processes of the maxillæ. The more strongly arched zygomata, however, give it a more tiger-like aspect than that presented by the skulls of the Dholes. The palate is relatively broad. There is no subangular process.

	Centimeters.
Length of cervical vertebræ	18·0
,, dorsal ,,	30·5
,, lumbar ,,	21·5
,, sacral ,,	4·0
,, caudal ,,	36·4
Length from atlas to end of sacrum	74·0
Length of pectoral limb	55·8
,, pelvic ,,	64·3
,, humerus	19·0
,, radius	19·1
,, femur	21·5
,, tibia	20·5
,, index metacarpal	6·6
,, third ,,	7·4
,, metacarpal of pollex	1·7
,, whole pollex*	1·7
,, last phalanx of third digit (manus)	1·4
,, index metatarsal	7·6
,, third ,,	9·0
,, metatarsal of hallux	1·4
,, whole hallux	2·3
,, last phalanx of third digit (pes)	1·5
Basion to ovalion	3·6
,, sphenoideum	5·5
Sphenoideum to gnathion	13·2
Length of palate	9·7
Breadth of ,,	6·8
Length of nasals	6·7
Breadth of ,,	2·7
,, brain-case	6·9
,, zygomata	13·3
Length of $\underline{P. 1}$	0·7
,, $\underline{P. 2}$	1·0
,, $\underline{P. 3}$	1·3
,, $\underline{P. 4}$	2·0

* There is no phalanx to the pollex.

	Centimeters.
Length of $\overline{M.1}$	1·5
,, $\overline{M.2}$	0·7
Breadth of $\overline{P.4}$	0·9
,, $\overline{M.1}$	1·8
,, $\overline{M.2}$	1·0
Length of $\underline{P.1}$	0·6
,, $\underline{P.2}$	1·0
,, $\underline{P.3}$	1·1
,, $\underline{P.4}$	1·3
,, $\underline{M.1}$	2·5
,, $\underline{M.2}$	1·1
,, $\underline{M.3}$	0·5
Breadth of $\underline{M.1}$	1·0
,, $\underline{M.2}$	0·8
,, $\underline{M.3}$	0·5

Genus OTOCYON, Lichtenstein (1838).

Otocyon, Lichtenstein, as referred to in Wiegmann's Archiv für Naturgeschichte, iv. Jahrgang, Bd. i. p. 290 (1838).
Agriodus, Hamilton Smith, Jardine's Naturalist's Library, vol. x. p. 258 (1840).

Generic Characters.

Digits 5—4. Pm. $\frac{4}{4}$, M. $\frac{3}{4}$.

Nasals extending backwards beyond the adjacent portions of the maxillæ; skull, viewed in profile, showing very little vertical elevation in the interorbital region; postorbital processes well developed; palate projecting backwards beyond last molars; mandible with a very large subangular process and slender horizontal rami; sectorial teeth relatively very small, and with small sectorial blades; ears very large; cæcum contorted.

THE LARGE-EARED CAPE DOG.

OTOCYON MEGALOTIS.

Canis megalotis, Desmarest, Mammalogie, Supplément, p. 538 (1822) ;
    A. Smith, South-African Quarterly Journal, vol. ii. p. 90
    (1835).
Canis lalandii, Desmoulins, Dict. Class. d'Hist. Nat. vol. iv. p. 18 (1823).
Megalotis lalandii, Gray, Griffith's An. King. vol. ii. p. 372; id. Proc. Zool.
    Soc. 1868, p. 523; id. Cat. Carnivorous Mammalia, p. 211.
Otocyon caffer, Lichtenstein, Archiv f. Naturgesch. iv. Jahrgang, Bd. i.
    p. 290 (1838) ; J. A. Wagner, Supplement to Schreber's
    Säugthiere, Abth. ii. p. 361.
Agriodus auritus, Hamilton Smith, Jardine's Naturalist's Library, vol. x.
    p. 260, plate 23 (1840).

This animal is by far the most aberrant of all the *Canidæ*, not only as regards the number of its teeth, but also as regards their relative proportions; and, indeed, the lateral aspect of the skull is very different from that of all the other *Canidæ*.

It comes from South Africa, that highly interesting region which has afforded so many exceptional forms of both animal and vegetal life. It was discovered there by M. de Lalande, who first sent its relics to Europe from the Cape of Good Hope.

We have not been able to ascertain any facts concerning its habits or life-history, except that it has lived in our Zoological Gardens, where it was shy yet gentle, was fed on raw meat, and slept during a great part of the day.

It is about the size of a large fox, but stands somewhat higher on the legs, and has a shorter but equally bushy tail. Its ears are very large, reminding us of those of *Canis zerda*, only that they are relatively broader.

THE LONG-EARED CAPE-DOG
Otocyon megalotis.

It is very interesting that, in spite of its singular divergence from the rest of the *Canidæ*, its cæcum is formed completely like that of the typical Dogs*.

The general colour is a brownish or iron-grey, variegated with yellow. The upper surface of the head and neck and the shoulders and outside of the thighs are more slate-colour with black and yellow intermixed. The throat and breast are occasionally very pale, sometimes whitish grey, sometimes buff-colour. The outsides of the limbs are more or less black. The tail is slaty grey, paler beneath, with a black tip and some other black marks on its dorsum, or at least many black hairs forming a longitudinal stripe. The muzzle is blackish, the cheeks grey. The ears are dark brown externally, bordered with black above, and the tips are black; they are bordered with white below, and have whitish hairs within.

There is, as usual in the *Canidæ*, merely individual variation. It may be almost uniformly grey, and it may be of a tint a good deal lighter than the specimen figured in our Plate XLV., which is one of those in the British Museum.

Habitat. Southern Africa.

	Centimeters.
Length from end of snout to root of tail	56·0
„ of tail	21·0
„ from heel to end of longest digit	12·5
„ of ear	10·0

Cranial and Dental Characters.

The skull of this animal seen dorsally has a considerable resemblance to that of *Canis virginianus* † in the shape of the temporal crests and raised sagittal area. The nasals extend backwards beyond the frontal processes of the maxillæ, and the postfrontal processes of both the frontals and malars are well developed. The palate extends backwards beyond the hindmost molars. The mandible has a very largely developed

---

* See Garrod, Proc. Zool. Soc. 1878, p. 376.
† See above, p. 89.

subangular process, and the horizontal rami of the mandible are very slender.

There are normally three molars in the upper jaw and four in the lower, but occasionally there are even four molars in the upper jaw.

Fig. 56.

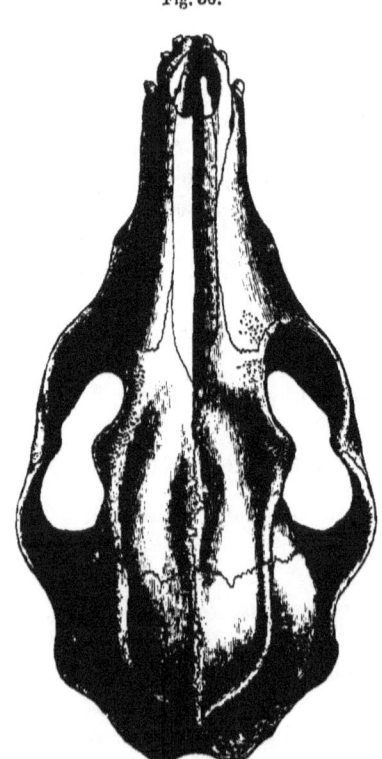

Dorsal aspect of skull of OTOCYON MEGALOTIS.

The fourth upper premolar is relatively very small, and each of the upper true molars has four cusps and an internal cingulum.

Fig. 57.

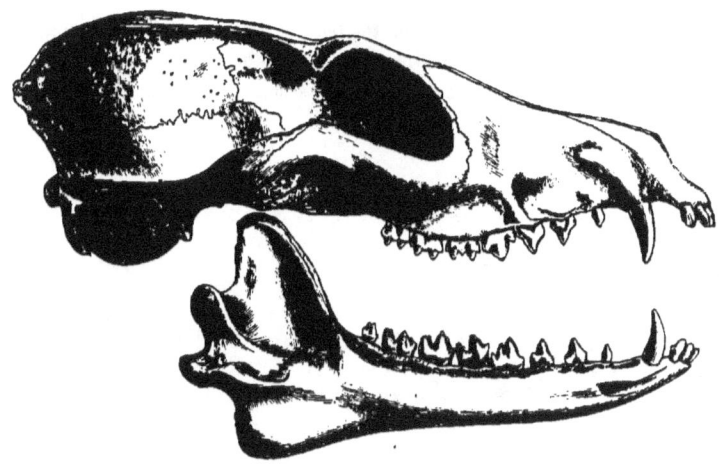

Side view of skull of OTOCYON MEGALOTIS.

Fig. 58. Fig. 59.

Upper molar teeth (right side). Lower molar teeth (right side).
(All of natural size.)

The proportion borne by the fourth upper premolar to the first two upper molars is as 100 to 220.

The less sectorial character of the teeth is very marked, and though the pattern they follow is the same as in the other *Canidæ*, the smaller development of the cutting-blades of the sectorial teeth is obvious on the most cursory examination.

	Centimeters.
Length of cervical vertebræ	8·0
„ dorsal „	12·7
„ lumbar „	11·1
„ sacral „	1·7
„ caudal „	23·5
Length from atlas to end of sacrum	32·5
Length of pectoral limb	26·0
„ pelvic „	34·3
„ humerus	9·0
„ radius	9·4
„ femur	10·9
„ tibia	11·0
„ index metacarpal	3·4
„ third „	3·9
„ metacarpal of pollex	0·9
„ whole pollex	2·4 (?)
„ third phalanx of third digit (manus)	(?)
„ index metatarsal	4·6
„ third „	5·4
„ metatarsal of hallux	0·8
„ whole hallux	1·3
„ last phalanx of third digit (pes)	1·2
Basion to ovalion	2·2
„ to sphenoideum	2·9
Sphenoideum to gnathion	7·3
Length of palate	5·2
Breadth of „	2·3
Length of nasals	3·7
Breadth of „	1·0
„ brain-case	4·2
„ zygomata	6·2
Length of $\underline{\text{P. 1}}$	0·2

		Centimeters.
Length of	$\overline{P.2}$	0·4
,,	$\overline{P.3}$	0·5
,,	$\overline{P.4}$	0·5
,,	$\overline{M.1}$	0·5
,,	$\overline{M.2}$	0·45
,,	$\overline{M.3}$	0·4
Breadth of	$\overline{P.4}$	0·5
,,	$\overline{M.1}$	0·7
,,	$\overline{M.2}$	0·7
,,	$\overline{M.3}$	0·5
Length of	$\underline{P.1}$	0·15
,,	$\underline{P.2}$	0·45
,,	$\underline{P.3}$	0·5
,,	$\underline{P.4}$	0·5
,,	$\underline{M.1}$	0·6
,,	$\underline{M.2}$	0·5
,,	$\underline{M.3}$	0·4
,,	$\underline{M.4}$	0·25
Breadth of	$\underline{M.1}$	0·4
,,	$\underline{M.2}$	0·4
,,	$\underline{M.3}$	0·35
,,	$\underline{M.4}$	0·26

INDEX.

Abyssinian Wolf, 18.
Adive, 117.
adusta (Vulpes), 49.
adustus (Canis), 49.
Agouarachay, 67.
Agouara gouazon, 21.
Agoura, 57.
Agriodus auritus, 202.
albus (Canis), 4.
—— (Lupus), 4.
alopex (Canis), 92.
—— (Vulpes), 92.
alpinus (Canis), 186.
—— (Cuon), 186.
—— (Cyon), 186.
Animal Anonyme, 147.
Anonyme (Animal), 147.
Antarctic Dog, 27.
—— Wolf, 27.
antarcticus (Canis), 26.
—— (Dasicyon), 26.
—— (Pseudalopex), 26.
anthus (Canis), 41.
—— (Dieba), 41.
—— (Lupus), 41.
Arctic Fox, 108.
argentatus (Canis), 92.
Asse Fox, 140.
ater (Lupus), 4.

aureus (Canis), 35.
—— (Lupus), 35.
—— (Sacalius), 35.
auritus (Agriodus), 202.
australasiæ (Canis dingo), 153.
australiæ (Chryseus), 153.
avus (Canis), xxxviii.
Azara's Dog, 66.
azaræ (Canis), 66.
—— (Cerdocyon), 67.
—— (Pseudalopex), 67.

barbarus (Sacalius), 41.
bengalensis (Canis), 127.
—— (Cynalopex), 127.
—— (Vulpes), 127.
Black-backed Jackal, 45.
borbonicus (Canis), xxxviii.
brachypus (Canis), xxxviii.
brasiliensis (Canis), 57.
brevirostris (Canis), xxxviii.
brucei (Fennecus), 147.
Bush-Dog, 190.

caama (Fennecus), 140.
cadurcensis (Canis), xxxviii.
caffer (Otocyon), 202.
campestris (Canis), 21.
cancrivora (Viverra), 57.

2 E

210 INDEX.

cancrivorus (Canis), 57.
—— (Thous), 57.
Canis adustus, 49.
—— albus, 4.
—— alopex, 92.
—— alpinus, 186.
—— antarcticus, 26.
—— anthus, 41.
—— argentatus, 92.
—— aureus, 35.
—— australasiæ, 153.
—— avus, xxxviii.
—— azaræ, 66.
—— bengalensis, 127.
—— borbonicus, xxxviii.
—— brachypus, xxxviii.
—— brasiliensis, 57.
—— brevirostris, xxxviii.
—— cadurcensis, xxxviii.
—— campestris, 21.
—— cancrivorus, 57.
—— canus, 132.
—— cautleyi, xxxviii.
—— cerdo, 147.
—— chama, 140.
—— chanco, 3.
—— chrysurus, 127.
—— cinereo-argentatus, 85, 104.
—— corsac, 117.
—— culpaeus, 52.
—— cultridens, xxxviii.
—— curvipalatus, xxxviii.
—— decussatus, 92.
—— dingo, 153.
—— dirus, xxxviii.
—— dukhunensis, 179.
—— eckloni, 121.
—— edwardsianus, xxxviii.
—— entrerianus, 66.
—— etruscus, xxxviii.
—— europæus, xxxviii.

Canis falconeri, xxxviii.
—— famelicus, 144.
—— familiaris, 161.
—— fennecus, 147.
—— ferrilatus, 121.
—— filholi, xxxviii.
—— fossilis, xxxviii.
—— frustror, 30.
—— fulvicaudus, 67, 76.
—— fulvipes, 66.
—— fulvus, 92.
—— gracilis, 66.
—— griseus, 3, 66, 85.
—— gypsorum, xxxviii.
—— haydenii, xxxviii.
—— hercynicus, xxxviii.
—— himalaicus, 92.
—— hodophylax, 3.
—— indianensis, xxxviii.
—— indicus, 127.
—— isatis, 108.
—— issiodorensis, xxxviii.
—— javanicus, 179.
—— jubatus, 21.
—— karagan, 117.
—— kokree, 127.
—— lagopus, 108.
—— lalandii, 202.
—— lateralis, 49.
—— latrans, 30.
—— leucopus, 123.
—— lupaster, 41.
—— lupus, 3.
—— lycaon, 4.
—— lycodes, xxxviii.
—— magellanicus, 52.
—— megalotis, 202.
—— melampus, 57.
—— melanotis, 57.
—— melanotus, 117.
—— mesomelas, 45.

Canis mexicanus, 3.
—— microtis, 62.
—— microtus, 104.
—— nemesianus, xxxviii.
—— noschersensis, xxxviii.
—— niger, 4.
—— niloticus, 92.
—— nubilus, 3.
—— occidentalis, 3.
—— ochropus, 31.
—— œningensis, xxxviii.
—— palæolycos, xxxviii.
—— pallidus, 142.
—— pallipes, 3.
—— palustris, xxxviii.
—— parisiensis, xxxviii.
—— parvidens, 76.
—— patagonicus, 66.
—— pictus, 196.
—— primævus, 179.
—— procyonoides, 134.
—— projubatus, xxxviii.
—— robustior, xxxviii.
—— robustus, xxxviii.
—— rudis, 57.
—— rufescens, 127.
—— rutilans, 179.
—— sævus, xxxviii.
—— simensis, 18.
—— sussii, xxxviii.
—— syriacus, 35.
—— temerarius, xxxviii.
—— troglodytes, xxxviii.
—— urostictus, 31.
—— validus, xxxviii.
—— variabilis, 3.
—— variegatus, 41.
—— velox, 104.
—— vetulus, 66, 76.
—— virginianus, 85.
—— viverroides, xxxviii.

Canis vulpes, 92.
—— vulpes montana, 92.
—— wheelerianus, xxxviii.
—— zerda, 147.
canus (Canis), 132.
—— (Vulpes), 132.
Cape Dog (The Large-eared), 202.
Carasissi, 57.
cautleyi (Canis), xxxviii.
cerdo (Canis), 147.
—— (Megalotis), 147.
Cerdocyon azaræ, 67.
—— magellanicus, 52.
Chacal, 35.
—— d'Alger, 41.
chama (Canis), 140.
chanco (Canis), 3.
Chien des bois, 57.
—— de la Nouvelle Hollande, 153.
Chryseus australiæ, 153.
Chrysocyon jubatus, 21.
—— latrans, 30.
chrysurus (Canis), 127.
cinereo-argentatus (Canis), 85, 104.
—— (Vulpes), 104.
Colishé, 85.
Colpeo, 52.
Common Fox, 92.
—— Wolf, 3.
corsac (Canis), 117.
—— (Cynalopex), 117.
—— (Vulpes), 117.
Corsac Fox, 117.
Coyoté, 30.
crucigera (Vulpes), 92.
culpaeus (Canis), 52.
cultridens (Canis), xxxviii.
Cuon alpinus, 186.
—— dukhunensis, 179.
—— primævus, 179.
—— rutilans, 179.

INDEX.

Cuon sumatrensis, 179.
curvipalatus (Canis), xxxviii.
Cynalicus melanogaster, 190.
Cynalopex bengalensis, 127.
—— corsac, 117.
—— ferrilatus, 121.
Cynogale venatica, 190.
Cyon alpinus, 186.
—— dukhunensis, 179.
—— javanicus, 179.
—— primævus, 179.
—— rutilans, 179.

Dasicyon antarcticus, 26.
decussatus (Canis), 92.
Desert Fox, 123.
Dhole (The Northern), 186.
—— (The Southern), 179.
Dieba anthus, 41.
dingo (Canis), 153.
Dingo (The), 153.
dirus (Canis), xxxviii.
Dog (Antarctic), 27.
—— (Azara's), 66.
—— (Bush), 190.
—— (Domestic), 161.
—— (Hyæna), 196.
—— (Magellanic), 52.
—— (Raccoon-like), 134.
—— (Small-toothed), 76.
—— (Striped-tailed), 81.
—— (The Small-eared), 62.
Domestic Dog, 161.
dukhunensis (Canis), 179.
—— (Cuon), 179.
—— (Cyon), 179.

eckloni (Canis), 121.
edwardsi (Vulpes), 142.
edwardsianus (Canis), xxxviii.
entrerianus (Canis), 66.

etruscus (Canis), xxxviii.
europæus (Canis), xxxviii.

falconeri (Canis), xxxviii.
famelicus (Canis), 144.
familiaris (Canis), 161.
—— Dingo (Canis), 153.
Fennec, 147.
—— (Rüppell's), 144.
—— (True), 147.
Fennecus brucei, 147.
—— caama, 140.
—— pallidus, 142.
—— zoarensis, 147.
fennecus (Canis), 147.
ferrilatus (Canis), 121.
—— (Cynalopex), 121.
—— (Vulpes), 121.
filholi (Canis), xxxviii.
flavescens (Vulpes), 93.
fossilis (Canis), xxxviii.
Fox (Arctic), 108.
—— (Asse), 149.
—— (Common), 92.
—— (Corsac), 117.
—— (Desert), 123.
—— (Grey), 85.
—— (Hoary), 132.
—— (Indian), 127.
—— (Pale), 142.
—— (The Kit), 104.
—— (Thibetan), 121.
frustror (Canis), 30.
fulvicaudus (Canis), 67, 76.
fulvipes (Canis), 66.
fulvus (Canis), 92.
—— (Vulpes), 93.

gracilis (Canis), 66.
Grey Fox, 85.
griffithii (Vulpes), 123.

griseus (Canis), 3, 66, 85.
—— (Lupus), 3.
—— (Vulpes), 66.
gypsorum (Canis), xxxviii.

haydenii (Canis), xxxviii.
hercynicus (Canis), xxxviii.
himalaicus (Canis), 92.
Hoary Fox, 132.
hodgsoni (Vulpes), 127.
hodophylax (Canis), 3.
hoole (Vulpes), 93.
Hyæna Dog, 196.
—— pictus, 196.
—— venatica, 196.

Icticyon venaticus, 190.
Indian Fox, 127.
—— Jackal, 35.
indianensis (Canis), xxxviii.
indicus (Canis), 127.
—— (Oxygöus), 35.
isatis (Canis), 108.
issiodorensis (Canis), xxxviii.

Jackal (Black-backed), 45.
—— (Indian), 35.
—— (North-African), 41.
—— (The Side-striped), 49.
japonica (Vulpes), 93.
javanicus (Cyon), 179.
jubatus (Canis), 21.
—— (Chrysocyon), 21.

karagan (Canis), 117.
Kit Fox, 104.
kokree (Canis), 127.

L'Adive, 117.
L'Agouarachay, 67.
L'Agoura, 57.

lagopus (Canis), 108.
—— (Leucocyon), 108.
—— (Vulpes), 108.
lalandii (Canis), 202.
—— (Megalotis), 202.
laniger (Lupus), 3.
Large-eared Cape Dog, 202.
lateralis (Canis), 49.
latrans (Canis), 30.
—— (Chrysocyon), 30.
—— (Lyciscus), 30.
Leucocyon lagopus, 108.
leucopus (Canis), 123.
—— (Vulpes), 123.
lineiventer (Vulpes), 93.
L'Isatis, 108.
littoralis (Urocyon), 85.
—— (Vulpes), 85.
Loup (le), 4.
Loup-renard, 27.
lupaster (Canis), 41.
Lupus albus, 4.
—— anthus, 41.
—— ater, 4.
—— aureus, 35.
—— griseus, 3.
—— laniger, 3.
—— sticte, 3.
—— vulgaris, 3.
lupus (Canis), 3.
Lycaon venaticus, 196.
—— pictus, 196.
—— tricolor, 196.
—— typicus, 196.
lycaon (Canis), 4.
Lyciscus latrans, 30.
lycodes (Canis), xxxviii.

macrurus (Vulpes), 93.
Magellanic Dog, 52.
magellanicus (Canis), 52.

INDEX.

magellanicus (Cerdocyon), 52.
—— (Pseudalopex), 52.
Maned Wolf, 21.
Megalotis cerdo, 147.
—— lalandii, 202.
—— zerda, 147.
megalotis (Canis), 202.
—— (Otocyon), 202.
melampus (Canis), 57.
melanogaster (Cynalicus), 190.
—— (Vulpes), 93.
melanotis (Canis), 57.
melanotus (Canis), 117.
mesomelas (Canis), 45.
—— (Thous), 45.
—— (Vulpes), 45.
mexicanus (Canis), 3.
microtis (Canis), 62.
microtus (Canis), 104.
minimus zoarensis (Vulpes), 147.
montana (Vulpes), 92.
montanus (Vulpes), 92.

nemesianus (Canis), xxxviii.
neschersensis (Canis), xxxviii.
niger (Canis), 4.
niloticus (Canis), 92.
nipalensis (Vulpes), 93.
North-African Jackal, 41.
Northern Dhole, 186.
nubilus (Canis), 3.
Nyctereutes procyonoides, 134.
—— viverrinus, 134.

occidentalis (Canis), 3.
ochropus (Canis), 31.
œningensis (Canis), xxxviii.
Otocyon caffer, 202.
—— megalotis, 202.
Oxygöus indicus, 35.
Oztuhua, 85.

palæolycos (Canis), xxxviii.
Pale Fox, 142.
pallidus (Canis), 142.
—— (Fennecus), 142.
pallipes (Canis), 3.
palustris (Canis), xxxviii.
parisiensis (Canis), xxxviii.
parvidens (Canis), 76.
pennsylvanica (Vulpes), 93.
persicus (Vulpes), 123.
pictus (Canis), 196.
—— (Hyæna), 196.
—— (Lycaon), 196.
Prairie-Wolf, 30.
primævus (Canis), 179.
—— (Cuon), 179.
—— (Cyon), 179.
procyonoides (Canis), 134.
—— (Nyctereutes), 134.
projubatus (Canis), xxxviii.
Pseudalopex antarcticus, 26.
—— azaræ, 67.
—— magellanicus, 52.
pusillus (Vulpes), 123.

Raccoon-like Dog, 134.
Renard, 93.
—— blanc, 108.
robustior (Canis), xxxviii.
robustus (Canis), xxxviii.
rudis (Canis), 57.
rufescens (Canis), 127.
Rüppell's Fennec, 144.
rutilans (Canis), 179.
—— (Cuon), 179.
—— (Cyon), 179.

Sacalius aureus, 35.
—— barbarus, 41.
sævus (Canis), xxxviii.
Side-striped Jackal, 49.

Simenia simensis, 18.
simensis (Canis), 18.
Small-eared Dog, 62.
Small-toothed Dog, 76.
Southern Dhole, 179.
sticte (Lupus), 3.
Striped-tailed Dog, 81.
sumatrensis (Cuon), 179.
sussii (Canis), xxxviii.
syriacus (Canis), 35.

temerarius (Canis), xxxviii.
Thibetan Fox, 121.
Thous cancrivorus, 57.
—— mesomelas, 45.
Tigrillo, 85.
tricolor (Lycaon), 196.
troglodytes (Canis), xxxviii.
True Fennec, 147.
typicus (Lycaon), 196.

Urocyon littoralis, 85.
—— virginianus, 85.
urostictus (Canis), 81.
Utah (Vulpes), 93.

validus (Canis), xxxviii.
variabilis (Canis), 3.
variegatus (Canis), 41.
velox (Canis), 104.
—— (Vulpes), 104.
venatica (Cynogale), 190.
—— (Hyæna), 196.
venaticus (Icticyon), 190.
—— (Lycaon), 196.
vetulus (Canis), 66, 76.
virginianus (Canis), 85.
—— (Urocyon), 85.
—— (Vulpes), 85.
Viverra cancrivora, 57.

viverrinus (Nyctereutes), 134.
viverroides (Canis), xxxviii.
vulgaris (Vulpes), 92.
Vulpes adusta, 49.
—— alopex, 92.
—— bengalensis, 127.
—— canus, 132.
—— cinereo-argentatus, 104.
—— corsac, 117.
—— crucigera, 92.
—— edwardsi, 142.
—— ferrilatus, 121.
—— flavescens, 93.
—— fulvus, 93.
—— griffithii, 123.
—— griseus, 66.
—— hodgsoni, 127.
—— hoole, 93.
—— japonica, 93.
—— lagopus, 108.
—— leucopus, 123.
—— lineiventer, 93.
—— littoralis, 85.
—— macrurus, 93.
—— melanogaster, 93.
—— mesomelas, 45.
—— minimus zoarensis, 147.
—— montanus, 92.
—— nipalensis, 93.
—— pennsylvanica, 93.
—— persicus, 123.
—— pusillus, 123.
—— velox, 104.
—— virginianus, 85.
—— vulgaris, 92.
—— Utah, 92.
—— xanthura, 127.
vulpes (Canis), 92.

wheelerianus (Canis), xxxviii.
Wolf (Abyssinian), 18.

Wolf (Antarctic), 26.
—— (Common), 3.
—— (Maned), 21.
—— (Prairie), 30.

xanthura (Vulpes), 127.

Zerda, 147.
zerda (Canis), 147.
—— (Megalotis), 147.
zoarensis (Vulpes minimus), 147.
—— (Fennecus), 147.
Zorro, 85.

THE END.

PRINTED BY TAYLOR AND FRANCIS, RED LION COURT, FLEET STREET.